HIS FATHER'S SON

HIS FATHER'S SON

EARL AND TIGER WOODS

TOM CALLAHAN

GOTHAM BOOKS

GOTHAM BOOKS
Published by Penguin Group (USA) Inc.
375 Hudson Street, New York, New York 10014, U.S.A.
Penguin Group (Canada), 90 Eglinton Avenue East, Suite 700, Toronto, Ontario M4P 2Y3, Canada
(a division of Pearson Penguin Canada Inc.) · Penguin Books Ltd, 80 Strand, London WC2R 0RL,
England · Penguin Ireland, 25 St Stephen's Green, Dublin 2, Ireland (a division of Penguin Books
Ltd) · Penguin Group (Australia), 250 Camberwell Road, Camberwell, Victoria 3124, Australia
(a division of Pearson Australia Group Pty Ltd) · Penguin Books India Pvt Ltd, 11 Community
Centre, Panchsheel Park, New Delhi – 110 017, India · Penguin Group (NZ), 67 Apollo Drive,
Rosedale, North Shore 0632, New Zealand (a division of Pearson New Zealand Ltd) · Penguin Books
(South Africa) (Pty) Ltd, 24 Sturdee Avenue, Rosebank, Johannesburg 2196, South Africa

Penguin Books Ltd, Registered Offices: 80 Strand, London WC2R 0RL, England

Published by Gotham Books, a member of Penguin Group (USA) Inc.

First printing, October 2010
10   9   8   7   6   5   4   3   2   1

Gotham Books and the skyscraper logo are trademarks of Penguin Group (USA) Inc.

LIBRARY OF CONGRESS CATALOGING-IN-PUBLICATION DATA
Callahan, Tom.
    His father's son : Earl and Tiger Woods / Tom Callahan.
        p.   cm.
    ISBN 978-1-592-40597-8 (hardcover)
    1. Woods, Tiger.   2. Woods, Earl, 1932–2006.   3. Golfers—United States—Biography.
4. Fathers and sons—United States.   I. Title.
    GV964.W66C35   2010
    796.352092—dc22
    [B]   2010028134

Printed in the United States of America
Set in Dante MT · Designed by Elke Sigal

For Sarah Jane, Ethan Thomas, and Tristan Lawrence,
and for Becky and Shray, Jen and Tom, and Angie

CONTENTS

Prologue   *ix*

PART I

EARL

Chapter One   *1*
Chapter Two   *10*
Chapter Three   *16*
Chapter Four   *22*
Chapter Five   *32*
Chapter Six   *37*
Chapter Seven   *41*
Chapter Eight   *52*
Chapter Nine   *63*
Chapter Ten   *70*

PART II

ELDRICK

Chapter Eleven   *85*
Chapter Twelve   *95*
Chapter Thirteen   *107*

Chapter Fourteen   117

Chapter Fifteen   126

Chapter Sixteen   136

Chapter Seventeen   143

Chapter Eighteen   150

Chapter Nineteen   160

Chapter Twenty   166

Chapter Twenty-one   171

Chapter Twenty-two   182

Chapter Twenty-three   187

Chapter Twenty-four   193

Chapter Twenty-five   199

Chapter Twenty-six   208

Chapter Twenty-seven   217

Chapter Twenty-eight   226

Chapter Twenty-nine   236

Chapter Thirty   241

Chapter Thirty-one   247

Epilogue   251

Acknowledgments   257

Tiger Woods's Record
  of Winning   259

Index   273

PROLOGUE

T iger Woods's little-boy room didn't fit him anymore.

"This is where I used to break things," he said, "when golf made me mad."

Just inside the door, tacked to the left wall, was a single football card, circa mid-1980s, of San Diego Chargers wide receiver Charlie Joiner.

"You've got the right guy," I said.

"What do you mean?"

Quarterback Dan Fouts and tight end Kellen Winslow were the stars of that team. But Joiner, one of Eddie Robinson's Grambling kids, was the player the other Chargers watched, especially downfield, away from the ball. He was the team's killer blocker, the hero of Tuesday film sessions. Shorter than six feet, lighter than 190 pounds, Charlie caught enough passes (750) and scored enough touchdowns (65) to make it to the Hall of Fame, but his toughness meant more to his teammates.

"I just always liked him," Tiger said.

On the opposite wall, above the headboard of his single bed, was the famous list of Jack Nicklaus's milestones. Judging from the typeface, the yellowed clipping may have come from the *Los Angeles Times*.

Tiger couldn't remember. "Age thirteen, shot a sixty-nine. Age fifteen, played in U.S. Amateur . . ."

"You know that top one," I told Tiger, "was actually a day-night doubleheader."

"How so?"

Jack and his father, Charlie, an Ohio pharmacist, went out late in the day and the summer to play the front nine at Scioto Country Club in Columbus, where Bobby Jones won the second of his four U.S. Opens. Jack shot 35 and begged his dad to play on. But Charlie said no. Dinner was waiting.

However, on the way home in the silent car, the pharmacist softened. "If we're mindful of your mother's feelings and still manage to eat quickly," he said, "we can be on the tenth tee in thirty-five minutes."

By the time they reached the 18th hole, a five-hundred-yard par 5, it was dusk. The sprinklers were out. Jack hit the green in two, and, with his father's help, moved the bulky hoses enough to clear a path for his eagle putt. It slipped into the cup for 69. That was the first time Nicklaus broke 70. He was thirteen.

"I did it when I was twelve," Tiger said. "He played in the U.S. Amateur when he was fifteen. So did I. He won the U.S. Amateur when he was nineteen. I was eighteen."

Though he had already won his first Masters, Woods hadn't changed yet. "He was such a great kid then," Ernie Els would say later. "I mean a really great kid."

The closet was papered over with a poster of Alec Guinness as Obi-Wan Kenobi. Somewhere in the Cypress, California, house, Tiger said there was a LEGO construction of a Star Cruiser. A few United States Golf Association and Stanford letterheads were taped to other walls, along with one "I'm With That's Incredible" bumper sticker. "I sat on Fran Tarkenton's lap," he said, "and at the end of the show hit Wiffle balls over the audience. I beaned the cameraman."

We could hear Earl and Kultida in the next room, entertaining several guests from Vietnam. "He's my inspiration," Tiger said of his father. "He's my conscience. I can honestly say he's the coolest guy I know. When I'd come back from a junior tournament feeling a little golfed out, he'd say, 'Forget golf for a while. Play some video games. Ride your bike. Get your mind off of it.'"

This memory may have flashed back to Tiger now because, shooting 70–76, he had recently missed his first pro cut in Canada. (He wouldn't miss another for 142 tournaments and eight years.) "My golf season this year has been ten months," he said. "That's three times as long as I've ever had to play golf. I'm tired. Getting used to playing so much has been the hardest adjustment really. Not overscheduling yourself, trying to maintain enough energy to always be at your best, I think that's the biggest challenge of professional golf."

A clutter of luxury cars overflowed the driveway. Almost the instant his big contracts were signed, Tiger bought a red Mercedes Benz, then threw it over for a white Porsche. Called to the Benz dealership, Earl found his son standing alongside a bright candidate. Earl checked out the front, checked out the back, looked everything up and down, took his time, while the salesman sweated.

"Why red, Tiger?" Earl asked finally. "Is it that you want to be stopped by every trooper on the highway?"

"I should pick a different color, shouldn't I?"

"No, Tiger," his father said. "It's you."

After driving the Vietnamese guests to his foundation, Tiger was on the phone with old Stanford classmate Jerry Chang when Tida summoned her son for a photograph. "I'll be right there," he said. A few minutes later, she called out again. "Just a second," he said.

"Tiger," Earl whispered.

"I got to go!" Click.

Sometime later, chuckling, Earl said, "That's still true today. All I have to do is change that voice. He may be the Masters champion, but he's still my son."

HIS FATHER'S SON

In the annals of unlikely events, one of the most unlikely occurred near Brooklyn in 1974 when a forty-two-year-old black soldier three months from retirement picked up a golf club for the first time and changed the game.

PART I

EARL

CHAPTER ONE

E arl Dennison Woods was born on March 5, 1932, in the college and military town of Manhattan, Kansas, the sixth child of Miles and Maude Woods, the ninth if you count Miles's first family (Earl would also have two families), the tenth if you include James Leonard.

James Leonard—never just James—died at two days old in the house at 1015 Yuma Street in a black section of Manhattan called The Stem. James Leonard wasn't Earl's imaginary friend. He was his real brother. He just wasn't there.

"If I didn't let him inside my life a little bit," Earl said, "he'd have had no life at all." So, during the Cookie League baseball games that the entire family attended, Earl would put his bat flush on the ball and say to himself as he rounded the bases, *We really got that one, James Leonard.*

Earl had a living brother, too, Miles Jr., but he was eleven years older and left for Chicago in his teens, never to return. "It was a house full of sheer forceful femininity," said his sister Mabel Lee—"Mae" to Earl, the one closest to him in age and in every other way. "There was Mama, Hattie, Freda, Lillian, and me. Earl was the youngest and the smallest"—the most doted on, lionized and spoiled—"and, I don't know how my mother did it, but she worked at keeping the masculine side of Earl apart from all of us strong women, and she worried about that, too. Let me tell you."

As a boy, Earl had an angelic singing voice. (As a man, he had a mellifluous speaking one.) "None of the rest of us could carry a tune to a graveyard," Mae said, "but at five years old, Earl would go around the house singing 'Pennies from Heaven' or 'A-Tisket, A-Tasket.' He had no fear." If he wasn't the youngest, he was one of the youngest, to make the robed choirs at church and school. "Mama encouraged Earl to play sports, too, and he played them all. Daddy only cared about baseball. Baseball and cussing. The other kids had younger fathers."

Maude's husband, twenty-two years her senior, was widowed in 1905, when Maude was twelve. According to a one-paragraph obituary in *The Manhattan Mercury*, his first wife, Viola Etta, died of peritonitis. Maude married Miles on the condition that he let her finish college. In fact, he put up every barrier in front of her that he could. But the archives of Kansas State University (nee Kansas State College of Agriculture and Applied Science) proved she made it. *Woods, Maude Carter, 1920, B.S., Home Economics.* She was twenty-seven, a black female college graduate in 1920. She spent her life as a domestic, cleaning other people's houses and doing their laundry, never allowed to use her degree. That was the source of Earl's lifelong grudge against Manhattan, and others.

Cultivating a little boy in a house full of strong women, Maude helped him assemble kites out of tissue paper and gold Good Conduct stars from the nearby Douglass grade school. All year long, they hoarded string from butcher shop wrappings and newspaper stacks. The two of them flew their beautiful sails expertly for hours.

They had private conferences in which Maude would talk gently and Earl would look up at the sky and listen to her. "She passed on a lot of wisdom and values," he said, "things unbeknownst to me at the time. I was too young to understand it all, but I absorbed it. Later in life, I realized what a powerful impact she had on me. She encouraged me to share and care. Those were her watchwords."

His mother was never entirely healthy; she had a permanent case of the sniffles. "I think she was allergic to life itself," he said, "but she never complained. She didn't blame anybody for anything, not even for being a maid. 'Don't judge people,' she told me. 'We already have a judge upstairs and He's pretty good at it. Remember, if you lose your temper, you haven't a chance. Find a method of adjusting, a way to keep your pride and dignity. Talk about it with your sisters, and laugh about it, and at it. Prejudice isn't only stupid, you know. It can also be pretty funny sometimes.' That really helped."

Finances were always precarious. Only after his sister Hattie found a teaching job did family life stabilize. Yet, in an economic mystery, Maude somehow kept Earl supplied with squadrons of model airplane kits and endless tubes of paint and glue.

Being the only boy in the house, he was the lone child with a room of his own. The girls shared an open space they dubbed The Dormitory. "You had to knock on Earl's door to get in," his sister Mae said, "and you wouldn't stay very long at that, because it was freezing in there. I mean, icy cold. You could see your breath!" To avoid being asphyxiated by fumes, Earl kept his windows open in all seasons.

"I had just finished gluing and painting a B-25 Mitchell," he said, "one of the planes Jimmy Doolittle's raiders flew off the USS *Hornet* to bomb Tokyo. I was waiting for it to dry, to put the decals on. I always did this just so. Here was going to be the prize of my collection. I spread out a newspaper and set it on the bed.

"One of my sisters—I'm not going to tell you which one—came in and sat on it, smashing it to smithereens. I don't know how she couldn't have seen it, but she didn't. I was about to explode in anger, the way I usually would—the way my father always would—but something stopped me, and it wasn't my mother's words about temper either. It was my sister's tears. Before I could react, she had started to cry. Don't ask me why, but from that day on, I've never blown up over anything. I can get angry at times, but I don't raise my voice, ever. When I'm mad, I get quieter. I get slower.

"'Don't worry, honey,' I told her. 'We'll just turn it into Captain Ted Lawson's Ruptured Duck and imagine that it's been shot up a little over China.' I even painted a Ruptured Duck with crossed crutches on the nose. It did become the prize of my collection."

As much as he enjoyed building things, he liked growing them even more. Earl raised roses almost everywhere he ever lived. Mae: "He just loved being outdoors. As a boy, he didn't mind feeding and watering the chickens, as long as he was out in the sun. He made it a game. I helped him pick the bugs off the potatoes. I was his assistant in all of the gardening duties"—cutting the lettuce, pulling the radishes, picking the green corn and the cucumbers—"but he'd never help me with the dishes. That was *women's work*. A farmer came into the neighborhood one time and rounded up all the little black boys and took them out to the potato fields. I remember, when Earl returned a week later, he was literally burned black. He had a lighter complexion than I. 'Earl!' I said. 'What happened to you!'" To his disappointment, Maude never let him go back.

The girls convinced Earl he was special, but that wasn't enough. He wanted to be great. He wanted to be stupendous. "He was the catcher on the Cookie League team," Mae said. "He told me the catcher was the most important one. The catcher was always the best player, the manager on the field. He gave me this afternoon lecture on why he was such a good catcher. He could throw to second base without leaving the squatting position. He provided me a demonstration, too. Now, the significance of that, I hadn't the slightest idea. But I certainly do remember how much it meant to Earl. I was supposed to be impressed, and I guess I was. Earl was always searching for something he could do or be that was better than anybody else. I don't know how to explain it. He was so desperate to make his mark."

Rosa Hickman, at 816 Yuma, and Don Slater, at 830, had crystal memories of those childhood days. Rosa, doyen of The Stem, eighty-seven in 2010, was a niece of Viola Etta, Miles's first wife, and the best friend of Earl's oldest sister, Hattie Belle. "I used to go up to their house after school to play," she said, "in the girls' room. We would congregate all afternoon while Earl stayed holed up in his inner sanctum. Sometimes then, Hattie Belle would open a can of tuna and make us all tuna fish sandwiches. Earl came out for that."

From her front porch, Rosa could still see the dusty, unpaved road and the milling chickens, horses and goats, and the tomato gardens and wildflowers, and the walnut and pear trees, and the grapevines. She could call back canning seasons and the delectable aromas of blue plums and cling peaches and string beans and rhubarb and pickled watermelon rinds.

"Yuma Street was like a big family," she said. "Everybody raised everybody's children. If you did something wrong, if they didn't whip you, they sure told your parents. You were going to get a whippin'. The older people, they would never let the kids listen in on their conversations, and they didn't tell you very much about the business of the family either. That was grown people talk. Not for children. Sometimes the teachers came to your house to visit. But when they walked in, you walked out. You never knew what was discussed."

There was a wood and coal stove in every kitchen, a wood and coal stove in every front room. Take the ashes out. Chop up kindling and bring it in. Clean the oil lamps. Trim the wicks. "I was in junior high before we had electricity," Rosa said. Coal oil was a nickel a gallon. They poured it from a tin can. "The bellies of the stoves got red-hot," she said, "and we'd sit as close to them as we could tolerate, and just sigh. We'd tell tales. We'd relive life. After the chores were done, my daddy treated us to licorice candy."

Slater, who was eight years younger than Earl, ran with the older boys. Don was the local rascal, famously fearless. When he was five, his mates put him up to asking twenty-two-year-old Lena Horne for a date. She was appearing at the Colored Soldiers USO nearby. The school, the church, the ballpark, the social centers—the whole grand world—seemed to be just a half a block off Yuma Street.

"Lena told me, 'You're a cute little kid all right.' 'Kid? I'm five!' I said. 'I'm almost a grown man!' Another time, when Joe Louis was in the neighborhood, I said, 'Hey, Big Joe, give me a nickel.' He told me to get a job. Well, he was lucky. If I'd have had a stepladder, I'd have punched him in the kneecap." Jackie Robinson came to Yuma Street, too. "But he looked a little mean to me," Slater said. "I left him alone."   .

Hickman and Slater had slightly different takes on Maude Woods.

Rosa: "Oh, she was such a lovely person. I just loved her. Everybody did. Friendly. Well, she never liked to stay home. About four o'clock, she'd be up and down the street visiting everybody, smiling and talking. Wonderful talker. Soft speaker. Smart. Relished a sentence put together well. You couldn't get a word in edgewise. Pleasant, nice, and just as kind as she could be."

Don: "Unfortunately, she was crazy. She was a good person, but she kind of lost her mind. She just walked up and down Yuma Street talking to herself. She was a super nice lady and raised those kids right. They all got an education. Four of them—Hattie Belle, Lillian, Mabel and Earl—earned Kansas State diplomas." Hattie Belle and Mabel became just the sort of teachers Maude had hoped to be. "Of course," Slater said, "Maude's husband was no help to her at all. He was abusive. Everybody on the street knew it. Miles had psychological problems. He might get up and start cussing in church. There were a lot of things Earl didn't want to admit about his father, I'll tell you that."

"Miles was a cussing man, yes he was," Rosa said. "I don't think

Maude had much love and respect for her husband. I don't believe the children respected him that much, either."

But Rosa did offer one sweet memory of Earl and his father, who was nearly sixty years old when Earl was born. "Miles was sitting on the concrete retaining wall out in front of their house," she said, "waiting for Earl to come home from school. After he arrived, the two of them sat there together for some considerable while, holding hands. Eventually, when it was almost time for the game, they got up and headed off, hand in hand, through the backyard, down the alley, across the railroad tracks, to Griffith Park."

Miles's nickname in the neighborhood was Frog or Froggy, a reference to his heavy-lidded eyes. Earl, who was rather sleepy-looking himself, had a moniker of his own. It wasn't a substitute for his given name, just a now-and-then endearment only his father ever used. Miles called Earl Tiger. "Let's go, Tiger," he'd say.

Earl thought of his father as a stonemason. Though, to put the most generous spin on it, he was a jack-of-all-trades. In later years, Earl rhapsodized about the buckles and latches on Miles's bib overalls, and the concrete powder on his hands. But that retaining wall out front may have been the only brick-and-mortar job of Miles's career. His steadiest employment was as a "door shaker" downtown, making sure businesses were locked. Also, and most magnificently, he was the keeper of the right-centerfield scoreboard for the baseball games at Griffith Park.

Thanks to his father's connection, Earl became a pregame fly shagger and sometime batboy for the home team in the Ban Johnson League, an all-white ball club from an all-black neighborhood. Earl also performed chores for a variety of barnstormers, including the Indianapolis Clowns, the Birmingham Black Barons and those pepper-playing proselytizers with their long hair and longer beards from the House of David. Happiest of all were the gala afternoons when Kansas City's stately Monarchs—the New York Yankees of the

Negro Leagues—went up against big league all-stars the likes of "Rapid Robert" Feller. Miles's loudest ambition was for his son to be a Monarch.

"Hot, sunshiny days on the baseball field," Earl said. "That was my childhood. In the summertime, we played almost dawn to dusk, on the dirt road when we couldn't get the real diamond. We got it quite a bit, though, because we'd help the groundskeeper get ready for the official games. There were only five or six of us boys. So we had to be content with infield drills, outfield drills, staging a few 'pickles' contests; you know, taking turns being caught in rundowns."

They invented game situations: runners on first and third, nobody out. A sizable imagination was required. "When you play a game almost entirely in your head," Earl said, "you learn to do the right things without thinking. It becomes natural. You just pick it up. Being around good players helped, too." He played catch with a lot of great ones.

"Before one game—I guess I was about eleven or twelve—Satchel Paige was pitching to Roy Campanella and I asked Roy if I could warm Satch up. So he gave me his glove. He said, 'Don't hurt yourself, boy.' I told him, 'Don't worry, I can handle it. And I have a major league arm. Nobody steals on me.' There was a Negro Leagues catcher who had 'Thou shalt not steal!' stenciled across his chest protector. I can still see him, but I can't remember his name. Well, that was my commandment as well. I told Roy, 'I can throw runners out from my knees and pick them off third base and first base, too.' He started laughing. 'And, by the way,' I said, 'tell Satch to duck after he throws the last pitch, number eight, because the ball's coming back full bore, straight through the box.' He laughed again.

"So, Satch began throwing the ball to me and I fired it back to him just as fast. He increased the speed. So did I. Always chest high, right around the letters, so he wouldn't have to strain himself reaching for it. As soon as Satch released that eighth pitch, he ducked right down, because by this time he knew. And my peg to second went exactly where his chest had been, took a little detour south and ended up ankle high to the first base side of the bag. I turned around and gave Roy back his glove. He said, 'Boy, you *do* have a major league arm!' Campy was a good catcher, but he was nothing compared to Josh Gibson."

Earl was probably eleven when *something* like that happened. Because eleven was how old he was the year his father died.

CHAPTER TWO

Earl wrote in his book, *Playing Through*, "The most painful thing for me was to watch my wonderful, dear mother literally grieve herself to death over the loss of my father. I remember her sitting there in her old oak rocking chair, humming to herself the hymn 'What are they doing in heaven today?' Over and over and over again. She was so devastated by her loss that she lived only two years after his death. She died of a stroke, just as my father had. I was 13 . . . To be 13 years old and have no parents."

His lifelong mantra—"From the age of thirteen on, I made every decision for myself"—would be so well known to his children that all four of them, independently, repeated it.

But, the truth was, Earl was almost sixteen when his mother died, nearly five years after his father, probably not of a broken heart. And, from the time Earl was thirteen, and for many years after, Hattie Belle made every decision in the family, including whether Earl would leave Kansas State following his freshman year to sign with the Monarchs.

Hattie Belle was the strictest and most beloved schoolteacher in Manhattan. "She had a belt that she called John Henry," said Don

Slater, who felt its sting a few times and still adored her. "Hattie Belle was an equal opportunity spanker," he said.

Earl's ambition was never to make the acquaintance of John Henry, and it was Mae's best guess that he succeeded. "Earl didn't even think of going against Hattie Belle," she said, "until he got married. He was afraid of Hattie. She was an absolute dictator."

Slater said, "The fact is, Hattie Belle was the one who raised Earl. She was raising him even when their mother was still alive, roaming around in her fog. I've heard, and I'll bet you've heard, him tell of the dream where his dead parents came to him in his sleep to argue back and forth the choice between playing for the Monarchs or getting an education. That was a dream, all right. Hattie Belle told Earl he wasn't going to be playing no ball. He was going to finish college. That was the end of it."

In 1951, '52 and '53, Earl played ball for the Kansas State Wildcats in what was then the Big Seven Conference. Over that span, his is the only black face in the team photographs in the Royal Purple yearbooks. Waiting his turn to catch, he was a starter at first base as a sophomore and had 108 putouts in 122 chances. K-State wasn't a top team. The Cats won only five of fifteen conference games, finishing in sixth place behind Oklahoma, Missouri, Nebraska, Colorado and Kansas, ahead of Iowa State.

The next year, they won just two of seventeen games in the conference (while handing Missouri its solitary loss, 5–4); the season after that, with Earl and only four others contributing home runs, they won one league game and settled into the cellar.

"I had received a scholarship to Kansas State," Earl wrote in *Playing Through*. "I was the only one in my family who received a scholarship to college, and that was to play baseball."

Coach Ray Wauthier had at his disposal exactly one baseball scholarship. It went to the team's most indispensable player, Perk Reitemeier, their best pitcher and hitter both. Earl may have felt like a scholarship athlete because, against the "Sanity Code" of the National Collegiate Athletic Association (enforced by new executive director Walter Byers in nearby Missouri), Wauthier helped Woods out once in a while with a little money under the table. He even let Earl move in with him from time to time, another violation. Sensitive to his catcher's position of isolation, the coach searched for hotels and restaurants—"dives," as the players called them—where the full roster could be accommodated. They weren't always findable.

On '50s sports teams that had just one black athlete, often a white player stepped forward. After the Boston Celtics made Chuck Cooper the NBA's first black draft choice in 1950, Bob Cousy walked the streets with Cooper if there was no room at the inn. "My Cousy," Earl said, "was an infielder named Jim Pollom. Good hitter. A shortstop. Really, a utility man. But we were all utility men. I played in the outfield some. I even pitched [with a record of one-and-one his senior year]. None of us was wed to a position. We all had to be versatile."

When Woods was permitted to stay in the same hotel with the others, Pollom was his roommate. "Otherwise," Earl said, "I roomed with James Leonard, like when we went to Oklahoma to play the Sooners. The rest of the team stayed in Norman while I stayed in Oklahoma City, an entirely different city." One of the first nights with Pollom, he confided to Jim how, as an American Legion player, he had so looked forward to making the all-star team, going to Kansas City, Missouri, and staying at the Muehlebach Hotel. Muehlebach just sounded like the big leagues.

Earl made the all-stars all right, but not the Muehlebach. "I had to stay with my aunt," he told Jim. "That's when I knew I was alone."

"Most of the time we just had fun playing baseball together," Pollom said. "But we all felt sad for him, because he didn't get to do everything we did. That bothered every one of us, but there wasn't a thing you could do about it. For all he had to take, you wondered how he could be so nice."

"If anything, he was quiet," said Gene Stauffer, who played on the '52 team. "There was something there. You couldn't see it on the outside. But I'm sure it was there. It was like 'I know what I can do, and I'm going to get to where I'm going one way or the other.'"

"I was playing right field once," Earl said, "when a spectator started picking at me from behind. There was no outfield wall, no bleachers at this particular field. Just a few people standing on a hill, students. When he finally got to the N-word, without even calling 'time,' I took off. But nothing happened. We just stared each other down for a while. Coach Wauthier got mad at *me*. I told him, 'You don't understand.' I shouldn't have said that."

For the shorter road trips, Earl drove himself in his own jalopy with Pollom riding shotgun. On the longer ones, Earl sometimes had to wait in the bus as the others stopped for dinner. They brought him out his food. But eventually, one or two, then five or seven, then nine or eleven, then all of them, took their meals to go. They sat together on the bus, ate their dinners and laughed. Prejudice wasn't just stupid, you know. It could also be pretty funny sometimes.

"My teammates treated me all right," Earl said. "It wasn't their fault."

At a nonconference stop in Mississippi, the Wildcats were taking pregame infield practice when the opposing coach spotted Woods beneath his catching gear and informed Wauthier that the game would go on only if Earl returned to the bus and remained there. "OK, he'll stay on the bus," Wauthier said.

"And I'll stay on the bus, and he'll stay on the bus, and he'll stay on the bus, and he'll stay on the bus . . ." One by one, as Wauthier counted them off, the whole team got on the bus and drove away.

The rest of Earl's life, he referred to himself alternately as "the first black athlete in the entire conference" or "the first black baseball player at Kansas State," neither of which was true. And Earl knew it wasn't true, because he was acquainted with both gentlemen. One,

Harold Robinson, grew up in The Stem; the other, Easter Elliott, came from Richmond, Missouri, but during the school year rented a room in a house at 812 Yuma, two doors from Rosa Hickman.

Robinson was a football player, a center primarily, a linebacker on defense. A year ahead of Earl at Manhattan High School, Harold actually *was* orphaned at thirteen. Maybe that's where Earl got the number. Without a Hattie Belle to lean on, Robinson raised himself and two younger brothers alone. He'd get up early and deliver newspapers, come home and feed his brothers, and then go to school. At night he washed dishes at the Scheu's Café on Poyntz Avenue for twelve dollars a week. After work, he mopped and waxed the floors of the bus station. Then he might go run laps at Griffith Field.

Former K-State great "Rammin' Ralph" Graham took over the Wildcats in 1949 (in the midst of a twenty-six-game losing streak), and one of his first recruiting trips was to the Scheu's Café, where he asked the proprietors to discharge Robinson. Once they did, Graham presented Harold the first scholarship ever handed out to a black athlete in what came to be the Big 12. A full ride. Robinson made first-team All-Conference center, twice.

Earl and Harold would die a few days apart and be buried a few feet apart. They must have had a lot to talk about.

Easter Ray Elliott, the black face in the back row the year before Earl arrived, was unrenowned. He was another utility man on the baseball team, an outfielder primarily. Though Woods was no less a pioneer than Robinson and Elliott, they were first.

Earl wanted to be first. As Mae had said, *He was always searching for something he could do or be that was better than anybody else . . . he was so desperate to make his mark.*

He wasn't an irredeemable liar, but you had to know him awhile to know that, and maybe he had to know you, too. The first seven or eight times baseball came up, he'd mention again his major league arm and re-invite the inference that his skin color overruled a potential career. But the eighth or tenth time ("or twelfth or fourteenth," said the writer Pete McDaniel, his friend), red cabooses would follow along at the end of Earl's trains of thought, stocked with saving graces. Again and again, this happened.

"I was just an average hitter," he'd confess finally, "maybe a two-sixty hitter. I didn't hit for enough power, either. Do you know what all the home run hitters in the Negro Leagues had in common? Big, fat derrieres. I tried to grow mine, too, with various exercises but with no success. [*How does one grow a derriere?*] Looking back, I was a better teammate than anything else. That was my best skill. High school, American Legion baseball, town ball, college ball, service ball. I made all of the teams. Basketball, football. In track, I ran the eight-eighty, hating it every step of the way. I ran like a catcher. But I was always a positive influence on my teammates. I was always a leader."

It's possible Earl invented the Monarchs offer, but unlikely. Because Earl wasn't a whole-cloth prevaricator. He was a grain-of-truth guy.

"I'm glad I didn't sign with the Monarchs," he said. "That would have been a one-way ticket to nowhere. A bus ride. One-night stands. A few bucks, but nothing to hang your hat on. Let's face it, I wasn't good enough."

When any man votes against himself in the end, it's becoming. When a vainglorious man does it, a world-class braggart like Earl Woods, it can be touching. But no one who encountered him just once or twice ever knew that.

CHAPTER THREE

Hattie Belle married a GI Bill–financed medical student, Jesse Spearman, who became an obstetrician, a gynecologist and a sounding board for his young brother-in-law. Earl would come to believe his entire life was a series of serendipities leading inevitably to Tiger Woods. If this was so, the first fated moment was a two or three a.m. conversation with Spearman, when the former World War II Army officer talked Earl into applying for Advanced ROTC at Kansas State. Without a thought to how he might eventually make a living, Earl had majored in sociology and minored in philosophy and psychology. A whiz at metaphysics, epistemology and especially logic, he could pursue a syllogism from Manhattan all the way to Wichita without dropping so much as a minor premise. In between was Abilene and Barbara Ann Hart.

The sisters called her "Horse Face," though she wasn't a bit horse-faced. She just wasn't good enough for their Earl. No girl was.

Because her mother was Barbara, too, she was called Ann. (In Earl's book, she is referred to as Barbara. "Only in print," she said, "did he ever call me that. Strange.") "I had known Earl since I was about ten," Ann said. "My brother Dale and he were baseball friends. Dale eventually made it to Double-A ball. Even though the Woods family lived forty miles from us, our church and theirs would do things together, choir contests and things. They were Methodist; we were Baptist. I don't know if Earl had other motives for being in the choir, but I do know one thing. There were girls in the choir. He was always very taken with the girls, and very popular with them, too. My girlfriends loved him. I had one little friend who vowed, 'I'm going to marry that Earl Woods and our first baby's name is going to be Eileen.' Nowadays, you would say he was 'a chick magnet,' I guess. In retrospect, I think he may have liked me because I didn't throw myself at him, like all the other girls did, like his sisters did."

At a high school popcorn and Kool-Aid party, they danced a slow dance. "How would you like to go out with me?" he asked. "What's such a big deal about going out with you?" she replied. They kept dancing.

After they started to date, Ann's grandmother sounded a warning. "He's a nice, intelligent young man," she told Ann, "but awfully full of himself, wouldn't you say? We know he loves himself. But is there room in there for him to love you, too?"

They called Earl's old car "the jitney." It seemed to burn as much oil as gas and sounded a little like a cracker grinder. On Sundays he would make the smoky trip to Abilene, and they would picnic in the park. "There was a Black and White Ball coming up," Ann said, "and I just knew he was going to ask me. But, when the time came, he said he had promised another young lady's parents." That stalled their relationship for two or three years. As Earl pressed on in school, Ann went off to San Francisco, seeking a career. "I ended up running a little employment office," she said proudly. "After about a year, Earl stopped calling and writing."

Returning home for two weeks in 1954, just to flaunt her clothes and progress, Ann reconnected with Earl. She called him. "He came down every night, eighty miles roundtrip, to take me to a movie. We had to sit in the balcony, but we didn't mind. This was late March. He was due to go on active duty in early April. That final night, he said, 'Let's get married. Let's not wait.'" Thirteen days earlier, Earl had turned twenty-two. Barbara Ann was twenty.

They were married twice. Once at the Abilene Courthouse, and then again by a minister at Ann's grandmother's house during a terrific thunderstorm.

Speaking of thunderstorms, from there they went straight to 1015 Yuma to spring the news on Hattie Belle, who was washing dishes in the kitchen. "We did it, Hattie," Earl said.

"Did what?" she asked.

"Ann and I got married."

There was a stony silence.

"Well, if it's already done," she said without looking up from the soapsuds, "then I guess there's nothing to say but congratulations."

"They gave me Earl's room that night," Ann said. "He slept in the living room. Our wedding night. The next morning, we packed for Georgia, and Fort Benning."

Earl was a second lieutenant. His clerk, a white man, was a private first class. "After he 'yes-sirred' and 'no-sirred' me all day long," Earl said, "we'd climb on the same public bus to go home, and I was the one who had to walk to the back."

Four young officers in civvies, two blacks and two whites, went to Columbus, Georgia, on a Sunday afternoon, to scope out the town. "Just to window shop," Earl said. "All of a sudden, a patrol car pulled up alongside. Cops jumped out and threw us against the wall, patted us down, handcuffed us, put us in a van and took us to the judge, who said, 'Two white guys walking with two black guys on a Sunday. That's what we call disturbing the peace. Guilty. That'll be thirty-seven dollars and fifty cents. Each.' Welcome to the South in the nineteen-fifties."

Ann received her own greeting at a Kervin's department store in Columbus. "It had white and colored drinking fountains," she said. "I took a sip from the white fountain and all the salespeople gasped. Then I took a sip from the colored fountain, turned to them and said, 'Isn't it funny? The water doesn't taste all that much different.'"

Even on the base, Earl's beginning was rocky. A trivial exchange with his commanding officer almost ended his career.

"Lieutenant Woods," the man asked pleasantly, "how do you get your shoes to shine like that?"

"A little bit of shoe polish, sir, and a whole lot of elbow grease."

The smile left the commander's face.

"You're one of those smart niggers, aren't you?" he said.

Earl's efficiency ratings plummeted. The straight sevens he had been earning (7-7-7) fell to straight ones (1-1-1) and then to straight zeroes (0-0-0). The company typist, a black sergeant, leaked to Earl the evaluations that were being sent to the Pentagon. "You better get out, lieutenant," he said.

"I fell behind everybody," Earl said. "They all made captain before I did. But, going to new places, racking up perfect sevens again, I pretty much regained my place by the time I was promoted to major, and I made lieutenant colonel just about on schedule. I never caught up completely, but I didn't let the bastard run me off, either. I'm proud of that."

For the first few months in Georgia, Earl and Ann rented a room in the home of a black schoolteacher, who employed her own black maid. "Named Suzy," Ann said. "Suzy boiled the clothes in a big steel pot out back and tutored me on life in the American South. 'You're a damn Yankee, aren't you?' she asked. 'I sure am,' I said. She was so very sweet to me. Almost everybody was, eventually—black and white." Ann decided the South and North were no more different than those drinking fountains.

This point was impressed on both Earl and Ann when, during one leave, they drove to St. Louis to visit Hattie Belle and Spearman, who was interning at a city hospital. Jesse, whose sense of humor was indomitable and dry, had Earl choking with laughter as he made a comedian's sketch out of his and Hattie's introduction to the town. The very first week, their apartment was burgled; the following week, when Jesse went to get a haircut, he felt right at home in the barbershop. "Seeing," as he said, "it was furnished with all of our stuff." Earl's and Ann's St. Louis experience wasn't so funny.

"Earl wanted to take in a Cardinals game," Ann said. "It was a breathless, muggy, Missouri summer day. We went to the stadium to buy tickets and, on the ride back, at a four-way stop, we were broadsided." She was knocked out of the car onto the pavement. "They picked up the white woman who hit us and put her in an ambulance to the hospital. But Earl and me, they put us in a paddy wagon and took us to the police station."

"I love you," Earl said in the wagon. She said, "I love you, too."

"At the station, Earl was shouting, 'My wife's hurt! You've got to get her to a hospital!' The desk sergeant just ignored him. But a black sergeant came along and saved us. It turned out that he knew Spearman—or knew of him, I think. Within three hours or so, my body became so swollen all over, I looked like a monster."

When Ann was well enough to make the trip home, in their battered car with the doors tied shut, Earl kept muttering at the wheel, "A paddy wagon. They put us in a paddy wagon." Ann said, "That was the most disheartening thing. It disappointed him so terribly. I don't think he ever let go of that. 'Baby,' he told me, 'there are paddy wagons everywhere.'" They drove silently for many miles until Earl added,

"In life you live with blinders on, because it doesn't happen in your area of the country or it doesn't happen to you. But then something like this opens your eyes, or reopens them, and one thing's for damn sure. You'll never be able to kid yourself again."

Many years later, Ann still hated two things: four-way stops and St. Louis.

CHAPTER FOUR

Their first foreign posting was to Germany, where Earl Dennison
Woods Jr., who would be called "Den," was born in the Army hospital
at Landstuhl. In quick order, a year or so apart, a second son, Kevin,
was delivered in Abilene and a daughter, Royce, in New York. "Other
than war zones," Ann said, "I pretty much went everywhere with
Earl. Except Thailand later on." With a rueful sigh, she added, "I guess
you know how that turned out."

Actually she followed Earl to Germany, three months behind him
by slow boat. "There was a mob scene of soldiers at the dock," she
said, "and I'm looking for him, and looking for him, and looking for
him. There he was, standing outside the fence. He didn't have the
right deutschmarks for the turnstile. But I didn't care. I was overjoyed
to see him."

While waiting for housing to come open on the base, Ann again
mixed with the locals. At a private residence where they boarded, the
man of the house was a whittler. In the yard, as she pinned laundry to
a line, he whittled away. And like Suzy, he schooled her on German
idiosyncrasies and brushed her up on her *guten Tag*s and *wie geht*s.

The morning Ann and Earl shifted to the base, the whittler placed a small knapsack in her hand. "I opened it up later, and do you know what was inside? He had whittled me twelve clothespins. Twelve perfect clothespins. They worked! I cherished those clothespins until, on one of our many moves, they were lost. I cried."

Earl said, in his understated way, "We caused traffic jams all over Germany. Jammed solid, like gridlock. People pointing and telling each other something or other. 'What are they saying?' I asked a German acquaintance. 'They're looking for your tails,' he said. 'When the white American soldiers came through at the end of World War II, they told us that black people in America have tails.' The sad thing is, the soldiers were the ones who perpetuated it."

In New York, Ann's favorite station, she and Earl attended concerts and Broadway plays, including *West Side Story* with Carol Lawrence and Larry Kert, and *Toys in the Attic* with Jason Robards and Maureen Stapleton. From cavernous Carnegie Hall to the most claustrophobic jazz clubs, they mined Manhattan for music. At the famed Village Vanguard, they took in the great trumpeter Miles Davis. "We got all gussied up for that," Ann said. "We thought we were hot stuff, sitting ringside at one of those little postage stamp tables brought in especially for us. When Miles came on, the first thing he did was turn his back on the audience. Without acknowledging a soul, he started right into playing. From beginning to end, he ignored everybody in the room. 'What's with this guy?' I whispered to Earl. 'That's Miles, baby,' he said. 'That's just Miles.' 'It's rude,' I told him. 'No, no,' he said, 'it's jazz.'"

Den said, "To understand my dad at all, the first thing you have to know is how much music mattered to him. I was in a band as a kid. I sang, too. That came from him and I didn't even know it. Music was my old man's salvation, his escape. It could take him wherever he wanted to go. Jazz especially, but all kinds of music really. 'I don't just like jazz,' I told him once. 'I like everything. The way I look at music, there's nothing wrong with any of it.' 'I'm glad you think so,' he said, 'because that's what I taught you to think. That's what I hoped you'd think.'"

Many years later, Earl said, "I don't know this to be true. Never heard it. Never read it. But I believe Miles Davis considered it unmanly to blow a horn in front of people. What could he do, though? That's how he got paid. So he blocked everybody out and did it as if he were alone.

"Here's another theory that didn't occur to me at the time: with his head bent down and his chin on his chest and his knees slightly cracked and his feet in an open stance, Miles was set up sort of like a golfer playing a fade. No, I'm serious. And instead of pointing his horn to the sky, like Dizzy Gillespie or Louis Armstrong, he pointed it at the ground. As a matter of fact, it was perfectly on plane. Even between sets, when he sat down, he could have been a golfer on a bench under an umbrella waiting out a rain delay, leaning forward with his legs spread wide apart, his head up now, tilted back. He had that look. You know, Miles was the blackest black man you ever saw. He was nearly purple.

"So after the fact—as I said, it didn't register at the time—I have come to believe that, if a golfer is good enough, he can make music. And that music is jazz. If he's really, really good, he might even become like Miles Davis, entitled to turn his back on everything and everybody if he wants to—'Go to hell, world'—and just play. Today, young people like rap. And certainly they're allowed to have their own sound, though I hate it. I don't understand it. It's not music. It's talking. It's not melodic. For me, it doesn't qualify as song. Give me Miles Davis every time, and Nancy Wilson."

"Miles was his boy," daughter Royce said, "and Nancy was his girl."

"Those two," Ann said, "played the background music, the sound track, to Earl's and my eighteen years of marriage."

Sad songs.

If it occurred to Earl that his father and older brother had the same given name as Davis, he didn't mention it.

During extended separations from their father, the Woods children mustered weekly at the dining room table to record messages for Earl on tape. In that slow, rich timbre, he answered them in kind. "It was like listening," Royce said, "to the voice of God."

"To a kid," Den said, "a father is an imposing figure anyway. Now put him in a military uniform with a Green Beret on top, and have him go missing for long periods of time, on classified tours, secret missions, where your mother doesn't even know where he is. Well, he's going to be larger than life, isn't he?"

When "The Ballad of the Green Berets" was a number one song, by Sergeant Barry Sadler, Den, Kevin and Royce bought the little 45 record and played it endlessly.

"The day he'd return from Vietnam or someplace else," Den said, "felt like Christmas and New Year's to us, the absolute best thing that ever happened. I think my mom kind of resented that. After doing all the hard work at home by herself, suddenly she's chopped liver. Don't get me wrong, Mom could take care of herself. She was no slouch. She was a very strong and intelligent woman. But her voice was just a little too high, if you know what I mean. We missed that male influence. And those times when Dad was gone, I'd have to say, were the times we needed him the most."

During Earl's first Vietnam tour, in the early '60s, he was an administrator, a personnel man. He hired, trained and paid hundreds of Vietnamese to assist the Americans, starting with interpreters. He found the work numbingly dull. A decade later, he returned as a combat specialist, one who had taught psychological warfare (and practiced some of it at home). But he wasn't a warmonger or sadist. He was a pro. As a matter of fact, over his entire Army career, Earl personally knew only one certifiably crazy soldier. "And not in Vietnam," he said. "At Fort Bragg. A demolitions guy. Scary son of a bitch."

Romance, melodrama or John Wayne weren't what drew Woods to apply for the Green Berets, though the Wayne movie was actually being filmed at Fort Bragg when Earl was there. "I met Duke; I shook his hand," he said, "but I wasn't looking for glory in the Green Berets. I was just so desperate for a level playing field, and they were the only ones in the whole Army who took you totally at face value. What you got there, you earned. I was thirty-five, about seven years from retirement, when I was accepted. At jump school, I was a monumental curiosity to all of the eighteen-, nineteen- and twenty-year-old kids in my class. *What the hell is this old man doing here?* At first, they thought I was some kind of plant. But I could have answered them in one word. *What am I doing here? Competing.*"

The children's best memory of Fort Bragg was a military jamboree, where that ghost who parachuted in and out of their lives showed them exactly how he did it. "Before Dad jumped out of the plane," Den said, "he tied a colored scarf around one ankle so we could pick him out. But you couldn't miss him. The sky was full of paratroopers, but Dad seemed to be the main one."

Royce had the same feeling. "My brothers screamed, 'There he is! There he is!' And that scarf flapped in the wind." Later in the day, he taught them about rip cords and counting one thousand, two thousand, three thousand . . . and waiting until ten thousand to even consider popping the emergency chute. "It's not a good idea to have both chutes open at the same time," Earl told the kids. "Never mind why."

"The whole pageant excited us so," Royce said, "just finally to be able to see Dad at work. Outside our home, there was always a little name plaque: CAPTAIN WOODS, MAJOR WOODS. I'd run my hand over the letters. We'd go to the PX or something, and all of the other soldiers would salute him. Den, Kev and I were dazzled by everything. He paid us to spit-shine his boots; Kevin was the champion spit-shiner. Both of my brothers were spit-shining little fools. I polished Dad's medals. When he was decked out in his dress blues, it was really something to see. It definitely had an impact on us kids."

Out of uniform, Earl was more approachable. Den said, "My earliest memories of my father, the real person, are of his teaching us, Kevin and me especially, grammar, whatever—baseball!" Like the boys of Yuma Street, they played pepper games. "We absolutely devoured it," Den said. "In Brooklyn, he signed us up with a baseball league. A guy named Duffy was the coach. Duffy wasn't much of an athlete, and he wasn't much of a coach. After coming out and watching us for a couple of practices, Dad said, 'Hell, this is helter-skelter.'"

Soon, Earl took command and Duffy stopped coming. "It was a hilarious team," Den said, "kind of like the Bad News Bears. One kid's dream was to be a movie stuntman, and not surprisingly he was always hurt. I swear to God, he threw himself downstairs every day. Another boy was set on being a major league catcher—he owned all the equipment—everything you could think of. You can imagine how that delighted Dad, the old catcher. Taking over the reins, he just taught and taught in every direction, a mile a minute. Of course, Kevin and I excelled. Our dad was the coach. I'd have to say this was the most normal time in our lives. It gave Kevin and I a taste—just a little taste—of what it would be like to have Earl Woods dedicate every ounce of his being to zooming you all the way to the top."

Realizing how that must have sounded, Den quickly said, "It wasn't his fault that he was away so much. I don't blame him for it. You know, my brother started out to be a lefty hitter, but peer pressure switched him to right. When Dad returned from one of his missions to find Kevin had been turned around, it more than just hurt him. It sort of crushed him. Whenever he came home, Dad always said it was to three completely different children every time."

At the beginning and for years, Earl and Ann were working partners. "At officers' cocktail parties," she said, "I was his eyes and ears. Back home, we'd critique each other's performances, not judgmentally, constructively. *You shouldn't have said this. I shouldn't have said that.* The military is a political profession, you know. And, during the good times, we were a team."

When Earl was off in exotic places, Ann slept with a hammer under her pillow. But she filled her days by chairing wives' committees, and, with the help of Fort Bragg commander General William Westmoreland, integrated the First Citizens Bank & Trust of North Carolina. Ann was known across the installation for driving whole gangs of rednecks into the sea.

"Are you mad at me?" she asked Earl, who came home to the news of how much drama he missed.

"No, justice is worth fighting for," he said. "Do what you think is right and I'll back you. But try not to get us shot."

In 1967, orders arrived for Thailand, stamped UNACCOMPANIED TOUR. Ann and the children, now twelve, ten and nine, fell back to their in-between billet, San Jose, to record the tapes and wait twelve months for Earl's return.

Ann said, "Throughout our marriage, I won't say I never heard things or saw things, suspicious things. But I never went looking for trouble. Maybe I should have."

Following Earl's year in Thailand, he was assigned to Fort Totten in New York. "Almost immediately," Ann said, "he started finding fault with everything I did.

"'What did you do that for?'

"'Do what?'

"'You don't know what you did?'

"'I don't know what you're talking about.'

"'Girl, you're losing it.'"

Playing Charles Boyer to her Ingrid Bergman, Earl was *Gaslight-ing* her.

"I started to second-guess everything I was doing and feeling," she said. "There was no shouting or anything like that. It was worse than shouting. Constant, subtle reminders of my defects, my shortcomings. Psychological warfare. He was an expert at that. The take-charge person I had been my whole life slowly died. I called my sister, weeping, saying, 'I know I'm not losing my mind, but Earl says I need help, that there's something wrong with me. Is it possible I *am* crazy?'"

At Totten, they befriended one couple in particular, a reserve officer named Larry and his wife, Sylvia. Larry was an attorney.

"He dropped by one day," Ann said, "attaché case in hand. Earl was in his easy chair. Larry said, 'Sit down, Ann.' He took my hand. 'This is undoubtedly the hardest thing I've ever had to do.' He opened his case and unraveled this long legal sheet of paper. 'Woody wants me to read this to you, OK?' The only word I heard was 'separation.' I signed the documents in a daze. As I walked down the hall, I heard the clinking of glasses, and Earl whispering, 'We did it! We did it!'"

Zigzagging across the country, the family drove back to San Jose. Bizarrely, the trip turned into a sightseeing marathon. They dropped by the Liberty Bell in Philadelphia, the Lincoln Memorial and JFK's eternal flame in Washington and Virginia. They paused in Kansas to visit relatives, and told nobody what was brewing. In Denver, they toured the mint and took in the mountains. They sampled the Las Vegas neon. "It was like a second honeymoon," Ann said. "The kids swam. He and I slept together. We made love. 'I don't get it,' I said. He put his arm around my shoulder gently as we walked. 'What are we doing separating?' 'Because we have to,' he said. When we got home to San Jose, my uncle Joe Hart took Earl to the airport and that was that."

Before too long, Ann became sick. Eventually she would undergo a hysterectomy, paid for by the Army. She and Earl were still married. Joe Hart returned to the airport to pick up Earl.

"Uncle Joe didn't tell me this until later," Ann said, "but a strange Oriental woman got off the plane with Earl." He told Uncle Joe he had just met the woman on the flight and was going to see about finding her a job in New York. But Joe wasn't fooled.

Her name was Kultida Punsawad.

In Thailand, Earl had been a special services officer. "I ran the bowling alleys," he said, "movie theaters, softball diamonds, libraries, resorts, everything. I did a lot of hiring and firing. One day, I was interviewing potential interpreters, and a young American girl walked in, an exchange student from Boston.

"She looked at me and said, 'What nationality are you?'

"I said, 'I'm an American.'

"'You don't look like an American,' she said.

"'What does an American look like?' I asked.

"'I take it I'm not getting the job.'

"'Don't worry about it, you're hired.'"

Needing five hundred laborers, Earl and his assistant had an appointment at an employment office, where the Thai receptionist took the white man for the boss and the black man for the subordinate. "'May I help you, sir?' she addressed my aide, not even looking at me. Once we were admitted, and I put my feet up on a coffee table, she could see through a plate glass window that I was doing all of the talking, and I must be the one in charge. I could read the embarrassment in her eyes. 'You take over here,' I said to my assistant. 'I'm going to go out and talk to this fine little thing.' She apologized over and over. 'Oh, I'm so sorry. I didn't know. I didn't mean any disrespect.' 'That's OK,' I said. 'You've just seen too many American movies.' That was Kultida."

She was twenty-three years old, twelve years younger than Earl.

"Walking away," Earl said, "I was smiling like hell. I had me a date."

In a confusion of cultures, they stood each other up. He arrived at the appointed restaurant before 9 P.M. She was there at 9 A.M., with a chaperone in tow.

"When we finally got it together," Earl said, "we ended up going to several Buddhist temples, and then to dinner. That was our first date."

On the lengthening list of happenstances that led to Tiger Woods, obviously Kultida was the most necessary link. In 1969, Earl divorced Ann in Mexico and married Tida in New York. Some six years passed, punctuated by the typical Army separations, before Earl and Tida achieved the pregnancy that, according to Earl, her religion mandated.

"If I hadn't been sent to Thailand," he said, "and I almost wasn't— they needed someone with the rank of major. And if I hadn't met Tida, and if she hadn't mistaken me for the subordinate, and if we hadn't cleared up the nine o'clock misunderstanding, and, most of all, if her Buddhism didn't demand a pregnancy, there never would have been a Tiger Woods.

"And, don't forget, I had to survive Vietnam again."

This time, the real Vietnam.

CHAPTER FIVE

For Vietnam Part Two, beginning in August of 1970, Earl was an advisor assigned to the province chief of Binh Thuan province, an oily politician he instantly despised and with whom, happily, he had very few direct dealings. "If you want to know what went wrong in Vietnam," Earl said, "it started with this guy and all the other guys like him. Was the war winnable? Hell yes, it was. The men on the ground were fine. Some of them were admirable. Their leaders sucked."

The assistant province chief, a light lieutenant named Phong, quickly became Earl's closest friend, and not just in Southeast Asia—in life. Using the name his dad had called him, Earl nicknamed Colonel Phong "Tiger." "He sure fought like a tiger," Earl said.

"To describe Tiger Phong, the first thing I'll say is just that he was a really, really nice guy. At the most, he stood maybe five feet five inches tall. He looked pretty much like the schoolteacher he dreamed of becoming some day. A history teacher. Going back to the French occupation—Dien Bien Phu—Tiger taught me all about his beautiful green country. He loved Vietnam as much as I loved America. We were tennis friends at first, believe it or not, in the down times of the fighting."

For their inaugural tennis match, Tiger showed up in gleaming whites—little short pants and a crocodile shirt, whiter than white, like for Wimbledon. Earl almost fell down laughing. "'Oh, Tiger,' I said."

They labeled Earl's quarters in Phan Thiet "the Blue Room." When public information officers had requested a darkroom for the photographers, a room painted entirely black, including the ceiling and floor, was delivered. So Earl asked for infantry blue, hoping for the same absurd result, and got it. "You should have seen it," he said. After battles, Earl and Phong sat back in decrepit Naugahyde chairs in the Blue Room, flicking their ashes at old-fashioned ashtray stands like the ones from smoking cars on turn-of-the-century trains, and listening to Aretha Franklin or Nancy Wilson on Earl's phonograph.

"We might have a drink, too," Earl said. "More than one."

Some rule of protocol prevented Earl from entering Phong's home in Saigon, but he came to the back of the house once to deliver a gift, a giant-headed painting of a tiger. Two or three of Phong's sons bantered with him in the courtyard. Earl showed the oldest one, Trung, who was fourteen, a snapshot of Royce. "She's expensive to feed," Earl said, "but if someday you can afford to feed her, you may marry her."

The children were excited to meet Earl Woods because his name came up so often at family debriefings, where, going around the room, all of them were expected to list the positives and negatives of their week. It amused the children when their father included among his negatives a lost tennis match to Colonel Woods.

"How are you, big tiger?" Phong would say when he looked up at the painting on the wall. It was burned in 1975. Everything American was.

Woods's and Phong's two-jeep caravan was well known through-out the province. The Viet Cong had placed a bounty on each man and offered double the total for both. "Our drivers were instructed never to leave the vehicles," Earl said. "Never. Because the Viet Cong recruited a battalion of sweet-looking little kids, four-, five- and six-year-olds, to slip bombs under the jeeps. 'I know you want to kill me,' I'd say to these little heroin salesmen who were always hanging around. 'You're not fooling me one damn bit.' Oh God, it was so sick. You'd be riding along on a mountain trail, weapon cocked and ready, hair standing up on your neck, when all hell would break loose in the valley below. Tracers zinged in the dark. Have you ever seen a laser show? 'Sort of pretty, isn't it Woody?' Tiger would say."

Once, when U.S. forces were changing positions, and South Vietnamese relievers were overdue, Colonel Phong told Earl, "That's all right, we can defend the fire base ourselves until my boys get here."

"Huh?" Earl said.

"You take this cover, I'll take that. My driver can man the third flank, your driver the fourth."

"Tiger, this is ridiculous."

"Don't worry, Woody," Phong said. "I've never lost an advisor yet."

"I'm glad to hear it, Tiger, but I damn sure don't want to be the first one."

Before pretending to be a quarter of a company, Earl retrieved an M-79 grenade launcher from his jeep and set it down in a row with his M-16 rifle and a .45-caliber pistol. For three hours, he waited and perspired.

"I was never one of those 'Why are we fighting?' kind of guys," Earl said. "We were there and that was that. To a professional soldier, war is just part of the job. God help us, it's the most interesting part of the job. I wasn't one of those 'Give yourself up for dead, you're not going home' guys, either. That's faulty thinking. My only concern was the battles. We won all the battles. There was no point in arguing politics. Tiger and I rarely discussed combat at all, not even tactics or strategy. Most of what we did was obvious, automatic. On our own time, we talked about philosophy and jazz."

Finally the Army of the Republic of Vietnam (ARVN) troops arrived. Abandoning their jeeps, Earl and Tiger hopped on a helicopter. It hadn't spun fifty yards from the field before they were under attack. That's how close the Viet Cong had been all along. The rounds sparked the floor of the helicopter between the two colonels and their drivers.

"Tiger," Earl said casually, "is it my imagination or are you a crazy son of a bitch?"

They lost track of how many times each saved the other's life. "I was standing on the dike of a rice paddy," Earl said, "calling in air support. 'Where do you want the explosives dropped?' I asked Tiger, who was in a nearby ditch.

"'Fifty yards in front of my troops,' he said.

"'No, that's too close.'

"'Seventy-five then.'

"'Let's say a hundred.'

"'OK.' He went off to mark the perimeters with smoke. I'm on the radio to the gunships when I was vaguely aware of Tiger hollering something. You could hardly hear yourself think over the sound of the propellers. He wanted me to move this way. I did. I'm still talking to the helicopters, coming around for another pass. Now Tiger wanted me to move that way. I did again. We went through this dance a third time. Then, after I sent the copters back to the base, I jumped down into the ditch beside him, and asked, 'What the hell's going on?' He said, 'A sniper had bracketed you. The first shot kicked up the dirt to your left. The second shot kicked up the dirt to your right. I was worried the third one might go right through your chest.' A few minutes later, he said, 'Don't move. There's a bamboo viper about two inches from your right eye.'

"Keeping my head still," Earl said, "I rolled my pupils right. The snake's fangs were bared. Its tongue was flitting in and out. I shut my eyes and thought of the World Series. Paul Blair was playing a shallow centerfield for the Orioles. 'He's gone,' Tiger said. 'Yeah,' I said, 'so am I.'"

With tennis, music and tutorials about Miles Davis, they were desperate to carve out patches of normalcy. Appalled by Vietnamese watermelons, no bigger than American cantaloupes, Earl wrote to his sister Freda and, against regulations if not laws, she sent him an envelope full of seeds. "Tiger and I planted them," Earl said, "and nurtured them between fire fights. They were growing up huge until a gopher came tunneling along and ate everything, roots and all. We wanted to cry but instead we laughed. There was a little yellow dog running around camp. That gave me a certain feeling of home, too. I've always had dogs. One day at dinner, the officers were passing around a platter of ribs, and I said, 'Great, I love ribs.' But Tiger took the plate out of my hand. 'Remember that little yellow dog, Woody?' he said. 'Aw, Tiger.'"

Falling asleep in their chairs in the Blue Room, Earl said to Phong, "We're going to know each other when this shit is over, right?"

Tiger didn't answer. He just hummed along to a Billy Strayhorn tune called "Lush Life."

"What do you wish for more than anything?" Earl asked his friend.

"A world without helicopters," he said.

CHAPTER SIX

T hree months before Earl's twenty years in the Army were up, a
fellow black staff officer at Fort Hamilton in Brooklyn invited him to
play golf. "He had grown up caddying," Earl said. "I think his father
may have been a pro." The man probably never knew the part he had
in advancing the sport.

Actually, what he said to Earl was, "Have you ever played golf?"
They had been talking about life after retirement. The other man's
long hitch was expiring even sooner.

"I've never even been on a golf course," Woods answered.

"Would you like to give it a try?"

"Not really."

"What are you doing tomorrow?"

"Nothing."

"OK, I have a tee time, and we're playing golf."

Earl disliked the fellow too much to turn him down. "I couldn't
pass up the opportunity," he said, "to beat this guy at anything."

The morning of his first round of golf, Earl bought a pair of golf
shoes. They had flaps over the laces. He didn't know whether you

wore those inside the shoes or out. "I had golf balls but no glove or clubs. I played out of his bag, which was against the rules, so I had to wait until we were out of sight of the starter to begin my round on the second tee. I shot ninety-one that day for seventeen holes. I've never shot a hundred in my life. I don't know why, but I didn't have any trouble hitting my woods. As for the irons, I couldn't tell the six from the nine. He advised me to hit straight down on them, and I did. The first iron I swung, I never got through the grass. I stuck it straight in the ground. I just stood there and vibrated. I've never recovered from that shot, either. My body shies away still. I'm physically unable to take a divot. I have to pick the ball off cleanly. Meanwhile, this guy's rolling in the fairway laughing. When we finished, he said, 'I've never had a more hilarious experience on the golf course in all my life.'

"I got mad. 'When exactly are you retiring?' I asked.

"'Two and a half weeks before you.'

"'I'm going to beat your ass before then,' I said."

Earl went directly to special services to requisition clubs, balls and a glove. Then he dropped by the library and checked out Jack Nicklaus's *Golf My Way* and Ben Hogan's *Five Lessons: The Modern Fundamentals of Golf*. "I can't remember if they were the only instructional books available," he said, "or if I just happened to pick the right two. Because they were absolutely the right books."

He read Nicklaus's first, paying particular attention to the asides of Scioto teaching pro Jack Grout, a courtly Oklahoman who believed in golf's eternal verities, sometimes grabbing a fistful of boy Nicklaus's stubbly hair to hold his head still. "Grout was as soft-spoken and mild-mannered a personality as I ever met," Jack said in his office. "He had a very, very pretty golf swing. He wasn't a talker; he was a listener. We'd go to the practice range and I'd hit balls for an hour and he wouldn't say a word. Then he'd say, 'Looks good, Jackie Buck. Maybe we ought to take that left hand and just slip it over a little bit.

What do you think? It might help you get left of the ball a little easier. There, how's that feel?'"

Earl said, "Both Grout and Nicklaus were opposed to tips and in favor of fundamentals. That stayed with me for years, forever. The way they described golf, it was a game of emotional control and logical reasoning, or I might have stopped reading. They were talking about me. Golf was talking *to* me."

If he had opened Hogan's book first, he might have stopped reading, too. "Nicklaus taught me enough to understand Hogan," Earl said. "I didn't read *Five Lessons* so much as I studied the pictures, the drawings. Looking down at the book, I stood up at lunch to spread my feet the width of my shoulders, and a young corporal strolling by set down his tray and, without saying anything, bent my knees and straightened me up a little bit, then picked up his tray and walked away. I never saw him again."

On the practice range, Earl ruined his only glove. The heels of the clubs twisted so violently in his hands that a hole was quickly worn at the base of the palm. He patched it with adhesive tape and, thinking "strong left arm," went off to the big match at Fort Dix in New Jersey.

"The first hole had an elevated tee box over a lake," he said. "I hit my drive dead in the middle of the lake. Two skips and over, onto the fairway. It wasn't a manicured golf course. The fairways were like rough. Having driven his ball way past mine, my opponent said, 'This is going to be a long day for you.' I hit a fairway wood and an iron to the green. He took a six. I had a five.

"He teed up at two. I said, 'What do you think you're doing? It's my honor.' I took a four. He took a five. The next hole was a par three, only ninety-some yards. 'What are you going to use, a seven-iron?' he asked. 'Don't you worry about that,' I said, and hit a pitching wedge right next to the flag. This is the truth. I got a two. He got a five.

"I shot thirty-nine on the front, three over par. On the back, I hit the same dad-gum lake again and this time the ball didn't skip over. But I beat him by two on the back. At the finishing hole, I said, 'Look at your tee.' 'What's wrong with my tee?' 'It looks to me like it's an inch or two in front of the marker.' 'What?' 'We're playing by the rules of golf, aren't we?'

"When we were done, he said, 'I don't believe what I just saw. I'm glad I'm leaving. I won't have to hear you talk.'

"After I retired, I went to California and my first established handicap was at the Navy Golf Course. A twelve. That year, I dropped from twelve to seven. By the next summer, I was a four. Eventually I would shoot a sixty-two at the Navy course."

Until the cigarettes caught up to Earl—he would undergo heart bypass surgeries in both the mid-1980s and the mid-1990s—golf possessed him.

"I wasn't just captured by golf," he said. "I was shanghaied."

CHAPTER SEVEN

A son was born to Tida and Earl on December 30, 1975: Eldrick Tont Woods. Starting with *E* for Earl and ending with *K* for Kultida, Eldrick was a one-of-a-kind name invented by Tida. After his Vietnamese comrade, Earl called the boy "Tiger." The nickname was so prevalent that while filling out forms or titling drawings, little Tiger sometimes had to stop and ask himself, *How do you spell Eldrick?*

"I never talked to Tiger like he was a kid," Earl said. "I never treated him as a kid. When he was six months old, I invited him into the garage, where I had set up a mat and a net, so he could watch me hit golf balls. I told him exactly what I was trying to accomplish. I practiced and he looked on, strapped in his high chair. His mother had to feed him off to the side because he wouldn't turn away from me. I'd monitor him out of the corner of my eye, and he'd be staring at the club, his eyes like marbles, waiting for my next swing. When I hit a particularly loud one, oh, boy, did he get excited."

Tiger was ten months old when Earl unhooked him from the chair. "Right away he picked up his little putter, the one he dragged all around the house, put a ball down, waggled once, waggled twice, and then hit it into the net. First time. 'Get in here!' I yelled to Tida. 'Quick! Check this out!' For a while, I thought I had a little lefty there. But then I realized he was swinging in a mirror image of me. The thing is, when I turned him around, he instantly changed his grip from a left-hander's to a right-hander's. Now, how would you ever explain a golf grip to a ten-month-old child? But I didn't have to. He figured it out for himself. I thought, *Oh my Lord*."

Some five years earlier, some ninety miles away, Phil Mickelson also learned to swing in a mirror image of his dad. But Phil, a right-hander in every other activity, wouldn't let anybody flip him around. He'd hit a few balls right-handed just to please his audience, but as soon as he was alone, he always reverted to lefty. Phil had one wooden club cut down in the shaft and sawed off at the back that was eventually worn into nothingness.

Tida was the one who telephoned Jim Hill, a Los Angeles sports anchor, former defensive back for the Chargers and Packers. "How much do you practice?" Hill asked Tiger in the first local interview. "About a whole bunch," he answered. Afternoon host Mike Douglas happened to see that piece and asked his staff to book the child. So, three months short of his third birthday, Tiger made his national TV debut with Bob Hope and James Stewart on *The Mike Douglas Show*. After Tiger smashed a few drives, Hope said, "I don't know what kind of drugs they got this kid on, but I want some." Douglas proposed, "How about a putting contest with Mr. Hope?" Out of the corner of his mouth, Hope said, "You got any money?" As part of the shtick, Tiger picked up his ball, set it right next to the cup and tapped it in. The studio erupted. Earl, the old Army PR guy, played it perfectly.

On *That's Incredible!*, cohosted by Fran Tarkenton and Cathy Lee Crosby, Tiger looked directly into the camera and proclaimed, "When I get big I'm going to beat Jack Nicklaus and Tom Watson."

Speaking in May of 2006, Douglas recalled, "Hope and I were totally charmed by Tiger, but he made Stewart sad. After the show,

Jimmy and Earl got to talking about Vietnam. You know, Jimmy's stepson, a marine, was killed there about ten years before. 'In the picture business,' Jimmy told me, 'I've seen too many precocious kids like this sweet little boy, and too many starry-eyed parents.' He was seventy then and lived long enough to see Tiger win the Masters, though I don't know if he did see it. He died that summer. When I heard that Jimmy had passed away, I remember thinking of our day together and wondering if he realized that there had been a happy ending."

Hughes Norton, an agent of the International Management Group, kept clip files on everything going on in sports. Tiger didn't escape his attention. Reading about the five-year-old in *Golf Digest*, Norton resolved to stop by the Woods home the next time he was in Los Angeles. When he did, Tiger was riding his tricycle out front as Earl came to the door.

That day, Earl told Norton, "I believe that the first black man who's a really good golfer is going to make a hell of a lot of money."

"Yes, sir, Mr. Woods," Norton said. "That's why I'm here."

From ages eighteen to twenty-one, Den, Kevin and Royce moved in with their father at Cypress for what he called "finishing school." It turned out they were there for the birth of the legend—literally. "I took Tida to the hospital," Den said. In their time, all three changed Tiger's diapers.

"At the beginning," Royce said, "he called everyone 'La-La.' Then Dad became 'Daddy,' Kevin 'Kebbin,' Den 'Den-Den,' and I stayed 'La-La.' When I was in college, he was a little toddler. Very seldom would Dad and Tida go out, but the times they did, I babysat. Tiger had a little putter he walked around with all the time and I was constantly afraid that he was going to break something in the house. I'm like, 'Tiger, putt easy, putt easy.'"

He came to La-La's room every morning to wake her. "Tiger was a schedule guy," she said. "He put himself on a daily routine. No one made him come shake me at the exact same time every day, but he did. Half asleep, I'd tell him, 'Go ask Daddy for a dollar.' Off he'd go, in his Spider-Man pajamas. 'Daddy, La-La dollar, La-La dollar.' Dad would say, 'Tell her no,' and Tiger would throw himself on the floor and start shrieking. He'd toss a perfect fit. 'OK, OK,' Dad would say, and Tiger would run back to me, flashing a knowing smile, waving a dollar bill."

"La-La," he asked her one time, "are you my half sister?"

"'I guess so, legally,' I told him, 'but I just say you're my brother.' Thrilled, he ran off to double-check with Den."

"Den-Den, are we half brothers?"

"You know what, Tiger?" Den said. "In this family we aren't half-assed about anything. We're brothers. With us it's all or nothing."

Many years later Den would say, "It turned out it was nothing." By 2010, Tiger had no relationship with any of them. "To Tiger, family got to be less and less important as time went on," Den said. "My dad was more his best friend than his father, I believe. They were each other's best friends. You see, the three of us were raised as a family. But he was raised as an individual. Tiger's whole world revolved around Tiger. I'm sorry he didn't learn to value family. I honestly am. Sorry for him."

"I have to say," Royce said, speaking at a handsome home in San Jose, complete with swimming pool, "all three of us benefited in different ways. Tiger bought this house for me. When he was still Daddy-La-La-Dollar, he promised me after he grew up and became famous and beat Jack Nicklaus and Tom Watson that he would build me a house. It became a family joke. As he got older, he tried to change it to a condo. Tiger's a little tight, as I'm sure you know, and not a bit ashamed of it. 'Oh, no,' I said, 'though I might settle for a town house.' So, time went by. Prior to attending Stanford, he called me up and said, 'Do you want to earn your house?' 'Sure, what do you want me to do?' 'My laundry,' he said, 'for four years.' 'No problem.' Of course it turned out to be only two years. As soon as he went pro, he said, 'Go find your house.' I had this one built from the ground up, with everything I wanted. My son went to boarding school in Boston. Tiger paid for that, too. I appreciate what he's done. However, I would live in a shack, literally a shack, if I could have my relationship with my brother back."

Tiger kept a special fondness for everybody who was there at the beginning, like Jim Hill. "Everybody," Royce said, "except his family. Oh, you know, it's a shame. He's not aware of it, or he refuses to believe it, but we love him more than all of the people around him."

Den said, "Tiger knows he has two brothers and a sister. What he chooses to do about it is up to him, even if what he chooses is nothing. He and I have no relationship at all anymore. I just got tired of trying to reach him. He's a solo flier. That's the way he is. You know, during those early 'Let the Legend Grow' days, I never laughed at it. To tell you the truth, I believed it. I knew how good Tiger was compared to the other little kids, and I knew my dad would carry him forward. Dad never said Tiger was the second coming of Jesus. He just said he was going to change the world. Well, didn't he? He put a whole new face on one small piece of it, anyway. I still remember the little boy who used to say 'sand twap' and 'wa-wa,' meaning 'water hazard.' I remember the Spider-Man games he and I played in the backyard by the tree. Long, long ago."

Before Tiger could count to five, he knew the difference between par 4 and par 5 holes. As Tiger stood on one of his first real tees, Earl asked him, "What are you thinking?"

"Where I want my ball to go, Daddy."

"That's when I really knew what I had on my hands," Earl said.

"At his first bad miss, I said, 'Who's responsible for you missing that shot, Tiger? Was it the club?' 'No.' 'Was it the noise?' 'No.' 'Was it the curvature of the earth?' 'What's curvature, Daddy?' 'Take my word for it, Tiger. It wasn't the curvature of the earth. *You're* the one who's responsible for that miss. It's you.' And, do you know something? He got that right away.

"Then I started teaching him how to look at a golf hole, how to recognize its design. Again, he grasped the concept intuitively. He started to plan his attack based on the design of the hole. Afterward I'd quiz him: 'Why didn't you go down the right side, Tiger?' 'Because there's a sand twap,' he'd say with a little twang to it. 'OK, why did you hit your second shot over here?' 'Because of the wa-wa.' 'Well, why did you hit your third shot over there?' With a look of impatience, he'd say, 'Daddy, the green opens up over there.' So, he was learning course management. Two years later, three years later, he could tell me, shot by shot, every club he used on every hole. You know, a child's personality and how he will react to the world around him is established by the age of five. Up to then, you can develop him, mold him, through experience, guidance, companionship, love, respect and trust. I told him that love was a given, but respect and trust had to be earned. And that went two ways. Because, when you have to earn respect from your child, rather than thinking it's owed to you as a parent, miracles can happen. That was our personal services contract, Tiger and me. That's what this whole thing has been based on from the start."

Only once did Earl take Tiger back to Manhattan, Kansas. Eldrick was four. Hattie Belle stood in the yard tossing a football to Tiger while Earl and Tida headed out to do some shopping. Once Tiger's parents were out of sight, Hattie put the football down and picked him up. She worried about him. Earl spoke to him as a miniature adult. Tida mostly corrected him. Hattie didn't think he was touched enough.

"As Tiger grew up," Earl said, "I never once asked him to play or practice golf. He always asked me. I was working at McDonnell Douglas, buying and managing materials for the Delta rocket program, and he had my work number memorized. He could tell you that number if you asked him today."

Tida saw to the schoolwork and the homework and parceled out the punishments and permissions. "She set the rules," Earl said into a microphone at a clinic in Long Beach, "and Tiger and I followed them."

One time, when Tiger was a first- or second-grader, they packed up for a Saturday tournament. "He and Tida were in the front seat of the car," Earl said, "and I saw Tiger's little bag of clubs on the living room floor. I slipped them into the backseat and covered them up. When we got to the course, Tiger said, 'Dad, quick, open the trunk! Where are my clubs?' 'I don't know,' I said, 'they're *your* clubs.' 'Dad, I left them in the living room.' 'Well, Tiger, I guess you won't be playing golf today.' I milked that for about five minutes. He was just about to cry when I brought the clubs out. He never left anything behind ever again."

Most of Earl's allegories ended with something never happening ever again.

"My childhood wasn't that different from anyone else's," Tiger said. "I did what the other kids did. I studied and went to the mall. I was addicted to wrestling on TV, rap music, heavy metal and *The Simpsons*. I got into trouble and got out of it. I loved my parents and within reason obeyed them both. The only difference is, I chipped golf balls around the living room. 'You better not break anything,' Mom would say. I called that 'practicing pressure.'"

Earl said, "I never hit him, never had to chew him out. I take it back, I have chewed him out. But he was self-motivated from the beginning. Individual responsibility. Self-responsibility. Love of self. I had taken est training, you know. It helped me with his instruction. It provided me some of the language. Taught correctly, the lessons of golf can stick to you even without you knowing it, and they stuck to Tiger. Golf being a microcosm of life is an awful cliché, but it's true when everything is taught right. How to win. How to lose. Listen to Tiger when he loses. He always says the other man was the better golfer that day. But he never says he was the better golfer. Because he knows differently."

Neither Earl nor Tida had to stretch to see what was over the horizon. Cosmetic investments, from contact lenses to orthodontia, were indicated even before recruiting letters began arriving from colleges when Tiger was thirteen. "That million-dollar smile of his," Earl said, "cost me four thousand bucks."

Dear Coach [Wally] Goodwin,

Thank you for your recent letter expressing Stanford's interest in me as a future student and golfer. At first it was hard for me to understand why a university like Stanford was interested in a thirteen-year-old seventh grader. But after talking with my father I have come to better understand and appreciate the honor you have given me. I further appreciate Mr. Sargent's [local pro Tom Sargent] interest in my future development by recommending me to you.

I became interested in Stanford's academics while watching the Olympics and Debi Thomas. My goal is to obtain a quality business education. Your guidelines will be most helpful in preparing me for college life. My GPA this year is 3.86 and I plan to keep it there or higher when I enter high school.

I am working on an exercise program to increase my strength. My April USGA handicap is 1 and I plan to play in SCPGA and AJGA tournaments this summer. My goal is to win the Junior World in July for the fourth time and to become the first player to win each age bracket. Ultimately I would like to be a PGA professional. Next February I plan to go to Thailand and play in the Thai Open as an amateur.

I've heard a lot about your golf course and I would like to play it with my dad some time in the future.

Hope to hear from you soon.

Sincerely,
Tiger Woods 5-5/100

Five feet five. One hundred pounds.

Earl said later, "Tiger went to Stanford University for an education. He narrowed his choices down to Stanford and the University of Nevada at Las Vegas, and if his priority had been golf development, he would have gone to UNLV. But he came back from the visitations, looked me squarely in the eye and said, 'I have chosen Stanford.' I asked him why, and he told me, 'I'm completely at home there.' 'In what way?' 'Dad, everybody is extraordinary at Stanford. I'm not anything special there.'"

Looking back from Stanford, Tiger would tell Larry King, "It was hard, really hard. Let me tell you, I had a couple of amazing friends, one who had a photographic memory. My roommate my freshman year was unbelievable. He never studied and just kept getting A's. I am like 'How do you do this?' He's obviously brilliant. It was really neat to see all the different people there. I mean you have people who are brilliant in whatever they do. It's just amazing. You've got Olympians there. You've got people who build their own computers from scratch. I mean, all different things like that. When everybody's special, nobody is. And all that celebrity stuff can be forgotten."

He was enough of an everyman at Stanford to be mugged at knifepoint outside Stern Hall, slugged in the face by the handle of the knife. He called his father to say, "Dad, remember how I used to have a slight overbite? Well, my teeth are lined up perfectly now."

Royce raced to Tiger's hospital room straight from the dentist's chair, her jaw puffed out with Novocain.

"What happened to *you*?" she asked.

"What happened to *you*?" he answered.

On the golf course, father and son were relentless rivals. "I was never overly long off the tee," Earl said at a practice range, proving it with a basket of balls. (He had no swing speed. He had no pop.) "But I was pretty accurate," he said, dropping a 7-iron on the 150-yard sign. "At one point it took Tiger a little more than two shots to reach my drive. But when it got so that he could drive with me, we'd play longest drive in the fairway. Later, when he was forty or fifty yards ahead of me, we were still doing it. 'You're six inches into the first cut of the rough,' I'd tell him. 'I win.' That used to infuriate him so much that he'd grind his teeth."

They competed off the course, too. "Tiger'll compete with you on drinking a glass of water," Earl said. Watching baseball on television, they played a game of their own invention dubbed "call pitch." Not just fastballs and curves. Circle changeups. Backdoor sliders. Cutters and splitters, high and inside, low and away. "What do you say we play for ABC gum?" Tiger suggested.

"ABC gum?"

"Already been chewed."

Notoriously, Earl applied what he called "prisoner of war interrogation techniques" on the course.

"Have you noticed how Tiger can stop his club in the middle of the downswing? Have you ever seen anyone else who could do that? It's because he'd be just starting his downswing when I'd clear my throat or say, 'Don't forget there's out of bounds on the right.' He'd stop and start again. This time I'd drop my bag or sneeze. I'd jingle coins and keys in my pocket. I'd sing a little ditty. He'd set up a third time, and just know something was coming—something had to be coming—but then I wouldn't do a thing. I'd harass, he'd react. I'd harass, he'd react. It was part of our regimen. There was a 'safe' word, but he never used it. He'd just smile that confident smile of his, until finally I stopped. 'Son, the training's over. You'll never play anyone who's mentally stronger than you are.'"

At one of the U.S. Amateurs, Tiger drew an opponent who fiddled around, and took his time, and teed up the ball, and re-teed it, and then said, "Wait a minute, it's still not lined up right," and started all over again. "Tiger looked all around frantically," Earl said, "until he found me in the crowd." When he did, he flashed that old smile.

Earl liked following all of the young players, not just Tiger. During his son's great junior years, Earl would drift away from the gallery for long periods. "Tiger knew I was gone because he didn't hear anyone speaking to 'Sam.' That was one of our codes, too: Sam, so he'd know it was me talking."

("Pop called me Sam as much as he called me Tiger," Eldrick said, "sometimes more. When I was little, I'd say, 'Why aren't you calling me Tiger today? 'I don't know,' he'd reply, 'you just look more like a Sam today.'" Tiger would name his first child, a daughter, after himself, Sam.)

"Tiger would be playing the ninth hole," Earl said, "but I'd be over at twelve checking out some other youngster. I just loved seeing young talent that was learning and developing. To me, that was a beautiful sight. When I'd eventually wander back to Tiger's group, he'd see me and nod, because he knew exactly where I had been."

CHAPTER EIGHT

"On road trips to junior tournaments," Earl said, "Tiger would sign us in and I would sign us out. Then, after a while, he would do the whole thing. As soon as he was well grounded enough to handle everything at a tournament, he became the father and I became the follower, just for the duration of the event. He'd tell me what time we'd get up in the morning. He'd decide whether we'd go out for dinner or eat in. Then, as soon as the last shot was hit, without either of us saying a word, we switched back."

They did a lot of talking on those trips. "He was a great one," Earl said, "for questions out of the blue." In Houston for a junior tournament, they were about to fall asleep in the motel when eleven-year-old Tiger suddenly asked his father, "What's male menopause?" Earl said, "We talked about that for about an hour. Then he wanted to know about the convicts who homesteaded Australia. So, we talked about immigration policies for another hour. Then Tiger said, 'Dad, what is . . . ?' I didn't even let him finish the sentence this time. 'God damn it,' I yelled, 'go to sleep!'"

Their tensest moment on the road came in Miami at an Orange

Bowl Junior Classic, when Tiger held a lead but lost it, fell behind and quit. "I could see it in his body language," Earl said. "He threw away a few strokes, got down on himself and blew the tournament in a funk. I unloaded on him off to the side when everybody stopped afterward at a restaurant. I pulled him into an empty room and really let him have it. 'Who do you think you are? How dare you not try your best? You embarrassed yourself and you shamed me.' I went on and on and on. I can honestly say that's the only time in Tiger's life that he ever feared me. He wouldn't sit with me then on the bus and he didn't say a word on the flight back to L.A. We sat in the same row on the plane, but he moved as far over to his side as he could get. However, the next morning, it was all over. And Tiger never quit on a golf course again."

Did he cry?

"Oh no," Earl said. "You have to understand, I do almost all of the crying in our family."

Jaime Diaz of *Golf Digest* said, "I telephoned Earl in nineteen-ninety, around September, October, telling him I'd like to do something on Tiger. 'Find a place where we can play,' he said, 'and we'll do it.' We met at Coto de Caza near Cypress, in the parking lot. Tiger was quiet, extremely wary. 'Just ask anything as we go,' Earl said, so I bounced back and forth between their two carts. Missing short putts on the first couple of holes, Tiger seemed nervous. 'Hey, Tiger,' Earl said. 'It's just a normal day.' But by the third hole, he was fine. I started to see the joy the two of them took in golf and in each other. Tremendous joy."

He took special note of how much Tiger loved to rag his father, whose forte wasn't chipping. "I can smell a chili dip coming," Tiger said. Rolling putts was Earl's strength, and pretty soon he was coaching Diaz. "Lock your right shoulder," he said, "like this," and Jaime started making everything. "Look at this guy," Tiger said. By dinner time at a Sizzler, they were comfortable enough in each other's company for Tiger to turn to Jaime and ask plaintively, "Why does the media have to know everything?"

The following day, when Diaz went over to Teakwood Street, Tida served refreshments, not speaking unless spoken to. She seemed to Jaime to be "kind of subservient in the house." Then she pulled out the scrapbook and plunged into a practiced routine that the local writers had already suffered.

Diaz said, "Earl told me his life story, and it was fun listening to him. He was candid. He saw himself as the buffer between us and Tiger, freely admitting he taught Tiger to answer only the question as it was asked. Never expand on it or give anything extra. Tell the truth but not necessarily the whole truth. 'Tiger! Come on out!' he called, and Tiger emerged from his room looking less than excited."

Jaime's main read didn't change much through the years. "Tiger had never been any good at other sports, no matter what Earl tried to tell you. Golf was Tiger's fun. Achievement was his fun. Everything else was biding time between achievements."

In 1990, at the age of fourteen, Tiger lost the last USGA Junior Amateur match he would ever lose, 3 and 2 to Dennis Hillman in the semifinals at Lake Merced in northern California. Mark Soltau of the *San Francisco Examiner* had arranged with Earl to interview his son behind the green at the finish. But Tiger bulled by him in a fury, heading to the car. "Don't worry," Earl told Soltau.

When they caught up to Tiger, who was slamming things, Earl told him to get a hold of himself. "We've given this man our word," he said. At first with a sigh, but eventually with a smile, Tiger told Soltau the old story. "All I did was sit in a high chair and watch my dad hit balls into a net in the garage," he said. "Every time my mom took me out, I threw a fit."

What did it feel like to be the only black in the 156-player field?

"I've learned to live with it. I'll have to face it my whole life. It'll make me tougher. I think I'm more mature than the normal fourteen-year-old. Not physically, emotionally."

Would he be going to college?

"I have to go," he said. "I don't want to be dumb."

The next year began a six-summer runaway that Tiger never stopped rating as his greatest accomplishment in golf, far above all the majors to come. At fifteen, sixteen and seventeen, he won three straight Junior Amateurs. "I really haven't had a chance to think about what it means now or what's up ahead," he said after that first national triumph at fifteen. "I was so tired afterward, I couldn't talk. The pressure was so intense. At the thirteenth hole, I could barely hold on to the golf club. That's why I hit a ball out of bounds there. Rigor mortis had set in. But, the best part is, I recovered at fourteen. School, golf, sleep is my life, and I'm no good at sleeping. But it's all worth it. There's nothing in life that is more fun than beating everyone in the field."

At eighteen, nineteen and twenty, he won three straight U.S. Amateurs. Over six years, that made thirty matches in all and a half-dozen consecutive United States Golf Association trophies. In the middle of that blitz, he filled out a USGA questionnaire. Earl made copies and, as part of the orientation process, passed them out to visiting writers:

Golf Background Information

Please tell me something about yourself that others would find interesting or unusual. For example, maybe you are related to a famous athlete, or didn't begin playing golf until last year, or have overcome a handicap of some sort, or did unusual work for some time, or have run for a political office.

"Began playing golf at 6 months old. Was on numerous TV programs. *That's Incredible, Mike Douglas, Two on the*

Town, Good Morning America, CBS, NBC, ABC, *Primetime Live*, ESPN."

Please tell me about any honors, awards, and achievements in golf or outside golf that you would like to share.
"Winner of the Dial Award as the top senior high school scholar/athlete in the United States."

Any lucky charms or superstitions?
"None."

My favorite athlete is?
"None."

My favorite movie is?
"None."

My favorite food is?
"Junk/fast food."

List your hometown/local newspaper and the golf writer on staff.
"*L.A. Times* (Martin Beck), *Orange County Register* (John Strege)."

Other locally oriented sports radio and TV stations in your hometown area.
"Too many to list in the Los Angeles area."

My most memorable golf experience or moment is?
"Comeback in 1993 U.S. Jr. when I was two down with two holes to play—winning on the 19th hole."

That match against Ryan Armour at the Waverly Country Club in Portland, Oregon, was Phil Knight's most memorable, too, though the founder of the Nike company wasn't there. "If you lived in a house with my father," Knight said in his Oregon office, "you had to live through every round of golf he ever played." Waverly was their home club.

"It was August and I was away somewhere, but I knew the course so well and followed the reports closely. In the final round, Tiger is one down with three to play and hits his tee shot over the green, a par three, up against a wooden backstop. He has no play. Two down, two to go. Nobody had ever won three of these things, you know. That was the pressure.

"Seventeen is a par five that they turned into a four. He makes three. Eighteen is a real par five. He's in a trap with his second shot, maybe fifty yards from the green. Knocks it to about eight feet and sinks it. Birdie-birdie. Or, the way I looked at it, eagle-birdie. All even. Of course, the next hole, the other guy almost hits it out into the street."

Actually, Armour three-putted the extra hole, barely missing a seven-footer for par. Woods holed his second putt, from four feet, to win.

"That was the most amazing comeback of my career," Tiger was still saying many years and many comebacks later. "What people don't realize is, I was coming off a case of mononucleosis three weeks before. I had to play the best two holes of my life under the toughest circumstances, and I did it."

"When we embraced on the green," Earl said, "all Tiger could say was, 'I did it! I did it!' and I kept saying, 'I'm so proud of you,' over and over. Time stops in moments like that."

Three years later, practically to the day, Nike signed Tiger for $37 million. "At the time we signed him," Knight said, "we had no thought of getting into equipment or golf balls. I was skeptical. I knew how superstitious these guys are." (Not Tiger. *Any lucky charms or superstitions?* None.) Anyway, as Knight said, Nike farmed out its manufacturing to contractors. He and his company didn't really make the shoes, the clothes, the clubs or the balls.

They made the heroes.

In the second round of the 1993 U.S. Amateur, seventeen-year-old Tiger lost the last U.S. Amateur match he would ever lose at Champions Golf Club in Houston. Earl telephoned Butch Harmon at nearby Lochinvar to see if Greg Norman's teacher wouldn't mind having a look at Tiger's swing.

"I gave Tiger all of his fundamentals," Earl said, "but I can't take credit for the swing. It was his own swing; it was natural. I knew enough to know what I didn't know, to turn him over for expert instruction first to Rudy Duran, then to John Anselmo, and finally to Butch Harmon. But each time I told them the same thing: 'Let's make damn sure we coordinate, so he isn't getting mixed signals; and, whatever we do, let's promise each other that we'll never screw up the part of him that is natural.'"

Duran, who had a cup of coffee on tour, was an assistant pro at a par-3 course in Long Beach, Heartwell Golf Park. Tiger was four and a half years old and playing with a three-club set when Rudy watched him hit balls for the first time. "He had a little seven-iron," Duran said, "and on command he could hit it high, low or medium. He was a shrunken pro with a perfect address position and a perfect swing plane. He was Mozart."

Concocting what he called "Tiger par" at Heartwell, consisting of the number of full shots Tiger required to reach the green, plus two putts, Duran saw him shoot 8-under-par at age five. Nearly thirty years later, Rudy continued to consider this the finest round of golf Tiger ever played.

When Woods was ten, Anselmo took over. "Earl had instilled in him a great first rule," John said. "'You may swing as hard as you want, as long as you stay in balance.' Balance, rhythm. Those were the things that stood out. Plus curiosity, ingenuity, hunger to learn." Anselmo was older; he also had a brush with the tour. Mostly he provided Tiger seasoning, perspective. When as a pro Tiger would get around to conducting his own junior clinics, he often brought back the octogenarian Anselmo to assist. As a lengthening line of teenage boys kept hitting deeper and deeper drives into the clouds, the old pro continued to dispense perspective. "They're coming, Tiger," he whispered.

At Lochinvar in 1993, wearing tennis shoes on the range, seventeen-year-old Tiger hit a bucket of balls for Harmon. "Hit them out of sight," Butch remembered, "you wouldn't believe how far. He was way longer then than he is now and didn't have a clue where the ball was going."

"I've always been naturally long," Tiger said, "always long for my age, whatever age it was. Enormous hip speed and shoulder rotation. Never had to be taught that. Ask a power hitter how he hits those five-hundred-foot home runs. Ask a fastball pitcher how he reaches ninety-eight on the radar gun. They won't be able to tell you because they don't really know. They just do it. A golfer can work on mechanics, control, consistency, a lot of things. But what he starts with is a mystery."

"How do you hit a high fade?" Harmon asked him.

"I dunno. Just kinda aim over there and it just kinda goes over there."

"Tiger, what do you do when you're on a really tight hole and you absolutely have to drive it in the fairway?"

"I just aim down the middle and swing as hard as I can. No matter where it goes, I know I'm not going to be too far from the green. Then I figure out how to get there."

"The funny thing is," Butch said, "he was serious."

"Can I come back tomorrow?" Tiger asked when they were through.

"Sure," Harmon said.

According to Earl, it was expressly written in their agreement that Butch was never to talk to Tiger about putting. That was Earl's baili-wick. An even more emphatic clause wasn't recorded anywhere, but was clearly enunciated by Earl. "You're his teacher," he told Harmon, "but you're not his father. I'm his father."

Butch's father, Claude Sr., won the Masters in 1948 and all but won the U.S. Open in 1959 at Winged Foot, where he was a forty-three-year-old club pro. In 2010, Claude's twin 61s remained the records at both the West and East courses there. At Seminole in Florida, Ben Hogan's favorite golf course, Claude once shot 60. He was a good player.

He was a tough man. When Butch was a struggling tour pro, he called home one Saturday to report a third-straight missed cut. Claude said, "But, according to the newspaper, you're leading the tournament."

"No, Dad," Butch said. "I finished dead last."

"Oh, wait a minute. I'm holding the paper upside down."

All of Claude's four sons tried to be tournament players. All of them ended up teachers. "Here's my green jacket, boys," Claude would say. "Where's yours?"

The youngest boy, Bill, was competing in a junior event at sixteen when, landing in a greenside bunker on the first hole, he wiggled his spikes into the sand (a patented Harmon technique) and looked up to see his father standing beside the green. "I kind of lost my focus," he said, "skulled the ball out of the bunker, over the green, across a road, out of bounds, right through the stained-glass window of a Catholic church."

Bill froze in place for a second or two. "Then," he said, "I heard my father say, 'Light a couple of candles for me.'"

On the range, when the Harmon boys asked Claude's opinion, he might respond, "Oh, very pretty."

"No, what do you really think, Dad?"

"Beautiful, like you're posing for the cover of a magazine."

Disgustedly, Claude shook his head. "What I can't figure about you boys is that you're practicing to impress the fifteen handicappers out here on the tee. But you're going to get on the first hole and that flag-stick's going to be in the back left and there's going to be a little left-to-right breeze and it's going to be into you slightly and you're not going to have a shot because you practice 'pretty.' You don't practice golf."

Butch said, "Dad was physical in his teaching to us. He'd lean over with his golf club and go *whap!* 'I mean *that* knee.' He would never, ever tell you when you did anything right. He would always beat you down, try to make you angry, so you would do better just to show him. Maybe that was the way his dad treated him. I don't know. It didn't work on me, and that's why I left home when I was eighteen. His house, his rules. I just wasn't going to live by them."

Butch was a tough guy, too. Like Earl, he had fought in Vietnam. But Butch's experience there was darker, more unspeakable. Harmon had been in the back room behind the back room. "Earl and I understood each other about a lot of things," Butch said. "As far as the swing went, he totally turned Tiger over to me, and never disputed anything I said. I admired Earl for that. It can be hard to let go."

For a while, Harmon was an ideal teacher for Tiger. "He'd sit for hours on end," Tiger said, "analyzing, criticizing, trying to boil the smallest thing down even smaller. Just his hard work gave me confidence."

Sampling a half-dozen major tournaments as an amateur, without ever contending, Tiger once found himself wedged on the range between Greg Norman and Nick Price. He pretended to be concentrating on his own ball flight but was really watching theirs.

"How far away am I, Butchie?" he whispered. "When will I be that good?"

CHAPTER NINE

"Tiger grew up pretty fast," Earl said, "but I don't think he hurried. I didn't throw him into any deep ends."

As a junior player, he never did much against the good amateurs. As a good amateur, he never did much against the pros. But when he arrived at every new level, he wasn't just quickly successful; he was immediately the best.

Before the 1995 U.S. Open at Shinnecock, when Tiger was eighteen, he introduced himself to the media in writing, pointing to a stack of papers on a table in the pressroom. "These are for you guys," he said. His one-page introduction read:

The purpose of this statement is to explain my heritage for the benefit of members of the media who may be seeing me play for the first time. It is the final and only comment I will make regarding the issue.

My parents have taught me always to be proud of my ethnic background. Please rest assured that is, and will be, the case. Past, present and future.

The various media have portrayed me as African-American, sometimes Asian. In fact, I am both.

Yes, I am the product of two great cultures, one African-American and the other Asian.

On my father's side I am African-American. On my mother's side I am Thai. Truthfully, I feel very fortunate, and *equally proud* to be both African-American and Asian!

The critical and fundamental point is that ethnic background and/or composition should *not* make a difference. It does *not* make a difference to me. The bottom line is that I am an American. . . . and proud of it!

That is who I am and what I am. Now, with your cooperation, I hope that I can just be a golfer and a human being.

Tiger Woods

Den said, "When Tiger went on *Oprah* and described himself as a 'Cablanasian' [Caucasian, black and Asian], I laughed out loud. [One-eighth Caucasian, one-eighth American Indian, one-quarter black, one-quarter Thai, one-quarter Chinese.] I didn't take it at all seriously. I knew he was proud of his African-American heritage. I knew him that well."

"To call Tiger just black is to deny *my* existence," Tida said. "You know what my grandfather on mother's side is? *Dutch!* White! Hah! Tiger is universal child."

How quickly he would go pro after the third amateur championship was a matter of mock debate, but the other amateurs didn't miss an obvious signal. On 100-degree days at Pumpkin Ridge in Oregon, Tiger was the only player in the field wearing long pants.

In the finals he met University of Florida sophomore Steve Scott and Scott's girlfriend/caddie, a tandem Johnny Miller referred to throughout the NBC telecast as "Young Love." Every putt Tiger absolutely had to have, he made. All the ones that would have just been nice to make, he missed. And the match went thirty-eight holes. On the 28th, Scott dropped a greenside flop shot to go two up. But, on the 29th, a 553-yard par-5, Woods hit a 350-yard drive, a 230-yard 5-iron and holed a forty-five-foot eagle putt to trump Scott's birdie. Missing a six-footer he needed to halve the next, Tiger was two down with three to play. But he knocked in first an eight-footer and then a thirty-five-footer to reach overtime. After Young Love was bunkered on the second extra hole, Woods won with a par. He was ready to be a pro.

The next PGA event on the schedule, the Greater Milwaukee Open, was elected. IMG's plan in the closing days of August 1996, was for Tiger to compete as an amateur in the pro-am and then debut as a professional the following day. But he was tired of all the intrigue around decisions that had long since been made.

Monday morning, Hughes Norton (the agent who found Tiger on his tricycle at five) telephoned colleague Bev Norwood at the home office in Cleveland. "I'm here at the hotel with Tiger," Norton said, "and he doesn't want to go out to the golf course in civilian clothes. He wants to wear Nike. He doesn't want to put on that charade."

"Let me speak to him," Norwood said.

"Tiger, what time are you planning to go out to the golf course today?"

"I'll be there around ten o'clock."

"Well, you'll be a pro when you get there."

As Norwood recalled, "I telephoned the PGA Tour and dictated a two- or three-sentence statement that Tiger was turning pro immediately, and that was that. He played in the pro-am as a professional golfer."

"I guess, hello world," Tiger said to begin his Wednesday press conference. This was taken for a charming ad-lib, but it turned out to be the catchphrase of a Nike newspaper and television campaign.

Hello world.

I shot in the '70s when I was 8.

I shot in the '60s when I was 12.

Hello world.

I won the U.S. Junior Amateur when I was 14.

I played in the Nissan Los Angeles Open when I was 16.

Hello world.

I won the U.S. Amateur when I was 18.

I played in the Masters when I was 19.

Hello world.

I am the only man to win three consecutive Junior Amateur titles.

I am the only man to win three consecutive U.S. Amateur titles.

There are still golf courses in the United States that I cannot play because of the color of my skin.

I'm told I'm not ready for you.

Are you ready for me?

"We've never shied away from the hard edge," said Phil Knight of Nike. "The ad was put together very quickly by Jim Riswold, who did the 'Bo Knows' series [Bo Jackson] and other campaigns. In his conversations with Tiger, that's really kind of what he heard Tiger saying. And Tiger, if you noticed, didn't back away. When Tiger stepped up to the microphone, he said that's what he'd been exposed to as he came up through the ranks, so the people who don't like it be damned. We think it defines who he is. We're quite proud of it."

Other notes in Tiger's overture included the wonder he felt at being the pro in the pro-am and how amazed he was that the range balls in this rarefied new world were all brand-new Titleists. To the tune of close to $20 million, Titleist was his other big company.

Earl sat behind Tiger on the stage, close enough for them to touch, which, at the midpoint of the speech, they did. "I was the one who set up Tiger's financial empire," Earl said later, "but I wasn't even there when he signed the contract with Nike. Tiger came down to my room afterward and said, 'I need three hundred dollars, Dad.' 'What for?' 'For my entry fee into the tournament.' 'Will it never end?' We both laughed. 'Thanks, Pop,' he said."

Few of the stars had room on their schedules for Milwaukee. To fill out the field, limbo had to be emptied: Rik Massengale, Mike Donald, Bill Kratzert, Jack Renner, Robert Wrenn, Andy Bean, Bob Gilder, Leonard Thompson, Bruce Fleisher, Gary Hallberg, Mac O'Grady. The Tiger Woods Open was a convention of lost boys with faintly familiar names who grew up after all.

O'Grady's real name was Phillip McGleno. He rechristened himself "Mac O'Grady" because it sounded so archetypically like a golfer and Mac Divot was already taken by a comic strip. O'Grady flunked the PGA Tour qualifying school a resounding sixteen times, but persevered to win a Greater Hartford Open and a Tournament of Champions. Among golf's journeymen, Mac's knowledge of the swing was legendary.

What did he know that the others didn't?

"They don't know that if your chin goes up or your chin goes down," he said, "it affects the endolymphatic fluid in the inner ear.

The eyes, through the vestibular-ocular reflex, work with the neuro-systems of the hands, and the antigravity proprioceptors of the neck respond to movements of the endolymphatic fluids. The direction, right or left, in which you tilt your ear toward your shoulder at address affects both the vestibular-ocular reflex and the optic-kinetic reflex. They don't know that."

For ABC Television, Curtis Strange asked the newest pro, "What would be a successful week here in Milwaukee?"

"If I can play four solid rounds," Tiger said, "and a victory would be awfully nice, too."

"A victory?" Strange said, taken aback. "Do you think, uh, to me that comes off as, uh, a little cocky or brash. Especially talking to, you know, the other guys who have been out here years and years and years. And, you know, certainly an incredible amateur record—but what do you say to those guys when you come out here? You know what I'm saying—you come out here, your first pro tournament, and you say, 'I can win'?"

"I understand," Tiger said calmly. "But I've always figured, why go to a tournament if you're not going there to try to win? There's really no point even going. That's the attitude I've had my entire life. That's the attitude I'll always have. As I would explain to my dad, second sucks, and third is worse. That's just a belief I have."

"But on tour that's not too bad. . . ."

"That's not too bad, but I want to win. That's my nature."

Giggling, Strange said, "You'll learn."

In the company of somebody named John Elliott and somebody else named Jeff Hart, Tiger hummed his first pro drive a measured 336 yards straight down the fairway. He birdied the third and fourth holes, eagled the fifth, and went on to shoot a 4-under-par 67. He was already five strokes behind. His Friday score was 69. Now he trailed by eight. After 73 and 68 on the weekend, including a Sunday hole-in-one, Tiger finished in a tie for sixtieth place and was cut a check for $2,544. Nike be damned, "This is the real money," he said.

In answer to a question, Tiger declared, "My long-term goals are private," but he did share one. "To hit the perfect shot," he said.

Was he the new Nicklaus?

"That's what you guys are saying," he said. "What matters is what I say. Inside."

CHAPTER TEN

After the "hello world" press conference, I met Earl for the first time. In a small scrum off to the side of a large hall, his knack for exaggeration was on showy display. The kickoff question was: If basketball or chess had been his father's passion, would Tiger now be a point guard jumping from Stanford to the NBA? Would he be Bobby Fischer? "No," Earl said with surety, "he would be a world-class four-hundred-meter runner and he'd be kicking [Olympic gold medal winner] Michael Johnson's ass. If you think Tiger's swing is pretty, you should see him run." Just as believably, he said, "And I'm not your typical optimistic parent. I'm very objective." He also said, "I've been working for this day for twenty years."

By rule on the PGA Tour, newly declared pros with no playing status could accept up to seven tournament invitations, providing them an outside shot at climbing the money list high enough to avoid qualifying school. "Giving Tiger seven chances to win a tournament," Earl said blithely, "he's going to win *one* of them, isn't he?" He won two of them: the Las Vegas Invitational in a playoff against Davis Love III, and the Disney World/Oldsmobile Classic by a stroke over Payne

Stewart. Still, sports had seldom come across a bigger blowhard than Earl Woods.

"His mother named him Eldrick," Earl said. "Mothers stick kids with names. Fathers have to suffer along."

Mentioning the three "practice" children from his previous marriage, Earl allowed that, in 1975, when he was forty-three, he would not have been inclined to father another child if Kultida's Buddhism hadn't required a pregnancy to consummate their union. "And I don't shoot blanks," he said, the definitive Earl pronouncement.

On the second day of Tiger's life, his father gazed through the maternity glass like it was a crystal ball and saw both the future and the past. "I knew—instinctively knew," he said, "that Tiger was going to have worldwide fame. That's why I named him 'Tiger.' Someday, my old South Vietnamese comrade, Tiger Phong—Colonel Nguyen Phong, a bitch in combat—would see him on television, or in a magazine or newspaper, and say, 'This must be Woody's kid,' and we'd find each other again. That would make my year."

Not just his son, *everything* about Woods sounded far-fetched. More than a retired Army colonel, he was a former Green Beret, who had taken some of his extreme training in the Arctic, where he estimated the temperature at forty below zero and said the wind was screeching at forty to fifty knots and the tires of the two-and-a-half-ton trucks were exploding and when he blew his nose icicles came out.

"When were you in Vietnam?" I asked a little meanly.

"I'm not sure," he said.

"You're not sure when you were in Vietnam?"

"I was there twice."

"Before or after Tet?"

"After, I would guess. When was Tet?"

When was Tet?

I was a marine of no note, but I can tell you the day and hour I arrived at Quantico, Virginia.

My next question wasn't particularly nice. "I live in Washington, D.C.," I said. "Can you give me the name of anybody who died around you? I'll go to The Wall [the Vietnam War Memorial] and tell you exactly when you were there."

"Only Vietnamese soldiers died around me," he said. "I was an advisor."

I wondered if this guy had even been in the Army.

Golf Digest suggested I go to Vietnam to try to find out what happened to Tiger Phong, but I wanted to make sure he existed before I left. Traveling that far to expose a lie wouldn't be any fun. First, I made a Freedom of Information Act request to the National Personnel Records Center in St. Louis, hoping to obtain Woods's military records. Everyone who ever fought in an American war, including the Revolutionary War, was on file there. While awaiting a reply, I telephoned a marine who knew Vietnam, Oliver North.

"It sounds to me like he was there," North said.

"Really?"

"Sure, it's only the guys who were there who have vague recollections. The phonies can tell you what company, what battalion, all the places, all the numbers. And, of the ones who really went, there are almost always two kinds of Vietnam vets: the guys who hang around The Wall in camouflage jackets welcoming each other home; you know, the pothead marauders, the rear-area heroes, the Oliver Stone version. Then there are the guys who go on with their lives, who don't try to remember things, who don't think about it all that much, who never go to The Wall."

"Woods says he's never been there and would never go there."

"That almost proves it," North said. "You can't go to that wall without crying."

When Earl's records arrived from St. Louis, they showed he had served in the Republic of Vietnam from February 12, 1962, to February

24, 1963, and from August 15, 1970, to August 13, 1971. Before I left
for Hong Kong, I went to Cypress, for the first of what would be several visits to the little house on Teakwood Street where, rummaging
around in that famous garage, Earl had come across a mahogany
campaign stick, a gift from his men. Its tarnished metal plaque read:
BANGKOK, 1968.

"I was in Bangkok," he said, "in nineteen-sixty-eight."

The year of the Tet Offensive.

For the journey, Earl offered two pieces of advice: Don't be afraid
of drinking the coffee boiled, iced and sold on the street, but be very
afraid of eating anything with *nuoc mam* fish sauce poured over it. "As
for drinking wine from a bottle that has a snake in it," he said, "use
your own judgment."

Ostensibly, according to the visa, my business in Vietnam was to
scout the country's sixth golf course, a new Nick Faldo design in Phan
Thiet (Earl's main theater of war) called Ocean Dunes. "If you accept
their 'keepers,'" North warned, "you'll only see what they want you to
see." So, I ignored the instruction to check in at the Ministry of Foreign
Affairs ("where you will be assigned a guide/interpreter to help you
realize your program"). North said that if the magazine would spring
for it, bribery could be a great help.

Flocks of motorbikes sailed through Ho Chi Minh City, the former Saigon, banking and honking on a Sunday morning. Some hauled
cargo, chickens in cages, but most carried extra passengers, limber
girlfriends primly sitting sidesaddle. On a country road to the seaside
village of Phan Thiet, the scooters thinned out in favor of oxcarts.
The sea of baseball caps made way for straw conical hats. I went to
work.

"That's him!" Earl had shouted when an LAPD artist finished

sketching Tiger Phong from Woods's twenty-six-year-old memories. After a police computer aged the drawing thirty years, I had my calling card.

"Stop showing the picture on the street," came a message from the ministry to my hotel. "We are really disappointed that you tried to ignore our advice." To the list of the rules I had broken was added the somewhat disquieting "and, furthermore, we could show you additional evidence." But then the tone softened.

"However, taking into consideration of the fact that this is your first visit, to show our goodwill, we let you continue to work in Phan Thiet. But it is time to concentrate on the golf. . . . It is not easy to get information on Mr. Phong. There are three hundred thousand Vietnamese MIAs. Very difficult problem. We have contacted authorities in Phan Thiet. He was in reeducation camp maybe ten years—I think, less than ten years. Many people believe he is in some other country now. America, Australia, Canada, or someplace else. Most of them are in America now. It is time for the golf."

At a tiny television station, the program director had me hold up the drawing for the camera like the newsworthy mute that I was, and the next thing I knew I was seated at a table with doilies and teapots and being interrogated by two Communist bureaucrats whose business cards read "Bachelor of English—Expert in External Relations" and "Foreign Relations Expert of Binh Thuan Province."

"Mr. Phong is dead," one of them said. "He deserted the service in nineteen-seventy-four and died in nineteen-eighty-six." Taking my elbow, the second man steered me out the gate and around the corner to an idling car, where a grandmother behind the wheel was shaking. "She's a witness," he told me. "But she doesn't want to speak to you. They had one son. That's it. That's everything."

"That's bullshit," Earl said from Cypress. "I know of three kids anyway, and I think there were a lot more. Deserted? Tiger Phong? Not hardly."

Later that day, I was flashing the picture in a fragrant fishing village, Mui Ne (and getting the usual nods of recognition; Asian politeness, the inclination to say yes, was working against me), when a moonfaced woman in a conical hat and yellow pajamas became the first person to say his name before I did.

"Colonel Phong!"

Tracing the charcoal lines with her tobacco-y fingers, she looked grief stricken. "Vinh Phu," she murmured. "Vinh Phu."

At Faldo's course, Ocean Dunes, I played twenty-seven holes in a hot wind just to torture a furtive character in a ridiculous overcoat who was following me from tree to tree. For the third nine, I had the company of a thirty-five-year-old North Vietnamese businesswoman named Lan Luu. She and I went to dinner afterward. At the table, Lan told me her story. I sat up straight when she mentioned her home in the north, Vinh Phu. By the end of the meal, I had been demoted to Doctor Watson, and Lan had taken charge of the case.

In 1975, when the war ended, she was thirteen. Everyone in her village was aware that tucked into the jungle nearby was a rice farm and a reeducation camp. Lan's aunt was employed at the farm. A cousin on her father's side was imprisoned in the camp. Lan visited him once. "He was incredibly thin," she said. "I told him I was the granddaughter of his grandmother's sister, and though he never met my father or our family, we loved him."

On the tablecloth, Lan began composing a newspaper advertisement, not for the papers in Vietnam ("That's too dangerous," she said) but for the Vietnamese press in America. "We have to think of the softest possible memories," she said, "and make the most straightforward request. If there is one false or worrisome word, no one will answer."

The softest memories Earl had conveyed to me were the tennis whites and the blue room. The ad under my phone number read: *Quy vi biet duoc tin tuc hay so phan cua Cuu Trung Ta Nguyen (Tiger) Phong, Pho Tinh Truong Binh Thuan nam 1971, xin vui long lien lac voi Tom Callahan. Trung Ta Phong co biet danh la "Tiger" do ban cua anh, vi co van Hoa Ky Earl Dennison Woods (chup chung trong hinh) dat cho. Ho da tung danh nhau, choi tennis va nhau chung trong "blue room."*

A few weeks later, a Vietnamese garment worker in Stanton, California, was listening to "Little Saigon" radio when Lan's advertisement came under discussion and one word in it cracked the code. The word was "Nguyen" (pronounced Win).

He telephoned the station, saying, "Not Nguyen, not Nguyen." "Yes," they told him, "Nguyen." "No! No!" They hung up on him. He called his daughter in Phan Thiet and asked her to run an errand to Ho Chi Minh City. Being a dutiful daughter, she dropped everything and went. Then he called me.

After we talked in circles for a while, I asked what I thought was an idle question and the vault sprang open.

Did he know Phong's middle name?

"Tiger."

"No," I laughed, "that's a nickname. I mean his real middle name."

"Dang."

"Nguyen Dang Phong?"

"Name not Nguyen! Name not Nguyen!"

His name *wasn't* Nguyen?

"Vuong," he said. "V-U-O-N-G."

Vuong Dang (Tiger) Phong.

All the years Earl had been searching, he had the wrong surname. He was looking for a Smith in a country where over 60 percent of the population was named Smith. But his man was named Jones.

The garment worker, formerly a captain in the ARVN, said his daughter had come upon what might be a pertinent phone number in Ho Chi Minh City. But he was reluctant to pass it along. He said a call from the States was risky. After the war, there wasn't much left for the losers to lose. But they still had their fear.

If I promised to have someone in Ho Chi Minh City place the call, would he trust me with the number? I held my breath for an eternal moment. When the answer came back yes, I sent the number to Lan. In the middle of the next night, the phone woke me. Alarm bells were ringing.

"Oh Tom, oh Tom," she said. "His picture is everywhere. I've been to the house."

Saigon fell on April 30, 1975. For more than a month, Tiger Phong hid out in the village of his birth. But as the Communists were closing in, he slipped back into Saigon to be with his family for one week before surrendering on June 15.

One by one, he kissed his nine children good-bye: seven sons and two daughters, the younger daughter adopted after her father was killed in battle. "I was six," said the youngest son. "Every time my dad came home from work, I'm the person who took off his shoes. He gave me a cookie or candy. I remember the day he say good-bye to us. Before he left, he cry and he hold us. He touched my head and said, 'I'll be back.'"

For the first year, letters arrived written in longhand on incongruously cheerful stationery, pink-tinted envelopes engraved with a map of Vietnam and the full figure of Ho Chi Minh. All were addressed to Colonel Phong's wife, Ly Thi Bich Van. Phong wrote lovingly of his family but increasingly, heart-wrenchingly, of his favorite foods. The children read them together and wept.

"How are Xiu and Be?" he wrote. "Do they grow up? How are all our children? Please don't let them go too far into the countryside. Because, after a war, munitions are everywhere. Do they go to their grandmother's home? Please don't let them swim, either. To the children—All of you must try to study hard at school. Trung, Phu, Chuong, Quang, Minh, and Duc. Tu [the adopted daughter], please help your mother and family. I miss you all very much. I always dream, and in the dream I saw you, honey, and our children. I also saw my father two times, and maybe it's a good sign. Remember, I belong to you."

For ten years then, they heard nothing. The death certificate that arrived eleven years later indicated that the "criminal Phong," the "lieutenant colonel of the puppet government," died of a heart attack on September 9, 1976, when Tiger Woods was eight months old. Tiger Phong was forty-seven.

He was buried in high grass on the edge of the Chinese border by his fellow prisoners. Phong was so venerated in the camp that he was the only one in the graveyard whose headstone was made of concrete, a crude and makeshift job, but a lasting monument. Otherwise, his sons never would have found him. The wooden markers for all the others had broken down and faded. Time and monsoons erased everyone else.

Phong's sons dug up the bones and brought them home. Ly Thi Bich Van recognized the shirt the skeleton wore and the blanket cuddling it. As she cooked all of her husband's favorite foods, the children washed the bones on the living room floor and prayed that their father would come home and eat all of the things he loved. Then they buried him in his home province.

Where was Phong's widow now? That was another surprise.

At an apartment complex in Tacoma, Washington, Ly Thi Bich Van came to the door wearing blue woolen pajamas and brilliant red house slippers. She had round, blurry eyeglasses, a bright, gummy smile, and almost no English.

I brought Phong's wife and two of his children (the ones he called

Xiu and Be) to Cypress, where Earl, Tida and Tiger were all waiting. Tiger had flown in from Orlando. He didn't care about this—not really. On a practice tee before I left, Tiger had hooted and said, "You're crazy to go. You're wasting your time." But his father cared deeply, and Tiger cared for his father. I expected Tiger to be dutifully polite to these people. But he wasn't. He was amazingly sweet to them.

He gave them a tour of his old room, showed them everything, let them in.

"I always knew there was another Tiger," he told me aside. "I didn't know him as Tiger Phong. I just knew him as Tiger One. He saved my father's life. So if it wasn't for him, I wouldn't be here."

"Tiger Woods's psyche is full of Tiger Phong lore," Earl said. "The concept evolved within him. It's been a subtle assumption of responsibility. I imagine he will understand it even better when I go."

Did Tiger Two feel a connection to Tiger One?

"A stronger one than I can explain to you," he said. "From all I hear, I'm exactly like him. It's like, all those years ago, Pop lost a brother [another brother, James Leonard] and is just finding out how. He *starved.* It's hard. The three of us [Earl, Phong and Tiger] are the same. I have a worse temper than my father. I wear my emotions on my sleeve. But Pop used to have his moments, too. I can remember when, if things weren't done the right way, he could be pretty unhappy."

Tida told me, "In our New York days, Earl went to one of those agencies that locate people. Years later, he try again in Los Angeles. He talk about Tiger Phong all the time. 'He a bitch in combat!' he say. But I think in his heart Earl knew Tiger Phong was dead."

Intermittently, throughout the reunion, Earl shed tears. "It's hard to keep from crying," Xiu told me later, "hearing how much he loved our dad." Earl said, "Tiger was taught at a very early age that it was all right for a male to cry, to have feelings and to let them out. Life isn't a blissful ride to glory. It's a painful process from start to finish. Endure. Survive. Move on. After you telephoned, I cried like a baby for two days. It just kills me that he starved. I called Tiger. 'I know, I know,' he kept saying over the phone. 'It's OK, I know.'"

They had changed places.

Before the 1996 Masters, Tiger's second and last as an amateur, he played a Wednesday practice round with Jack Nicklaus and Arnold Palmer, his first round ever with either man.

At Augusta National's par-5 13th hole, where a slithering creek fronts the green, Tiger popped up his tee ball and for once was away.

Facing Nicklaus, whose back was turned to Woods, Palmer peeked over Jack's shoulder and saw the kid pull out an iron for his second shot.

"He's laying up," Arnold whispered.

"Oh, Arnie," Jack said affectionately. "He's not."

PART II
ELDRICK

CHAPTER ELEVEN

❧

Major No. 1, the 1997 Masters

For his two amateur tries at the Masters, first making the cut (ultimately sharing forty-first place) and then missing it, Tiger stayed at the course in Augusta National's freshman dormitory, a clubhouse garret under a sun-streaked cupola known as the Crow's Nest. In 1959, Jack Nicklaus roomed there with Californian Phil Rodgers, who was just as blond, just as plump, and—many believed—just as promising as Jack. Both missed the cut, Nicklaus by a solitary stroke. A couple of years later, Phil won the first tournament Jack entered as a pro, the L.A. Open. Nicklaus tied for last place, earning $33.33.

Tiger couldn't sleep very well in the Crow's Nest: too many ghosts. That first April, he came straight from exams at Stanford—fried. The second year was even worse. Finals were ahead this time, and he was obliged to cram for them in the midst of the tournament. In addition he had to write a paper. "The shadows there roll all around the walls," he complained. "That attic is haunted."

"He's not kidding," Earl said. "Tiger has always believed in ghosts.

He gets that from his mother. Last year, coming downstairs from the Crow's Nest, Tiger became hopelessly lost in the dark. It was around ten o'clock at night. He was looking for the front desk, but somehow ended up in the Champions' Locker Room, where all the real ghosts are. Not knowing whether he was allowed to be there, he didn't turn on the light. He just sat down in front of Jackie Burke's locker and communed with the boys."

Tiger and Earl were squeezed onto a couch with plates of beans and barbecue balanced on their knees in a crowded party at the *Golf Digest* house. In two days, the 1996 Masters would begin. Tiger was full of blasé it's-just-another-tournament talk. And, nope, driving down Magnolia Lane hadn't thrilled him any more this year than last. "Pretty short drive," he said. Tiger's practice partners were recommending he press the issue, go for everything, take maximum advantage of his stupendous length, especially on the backside par 5s. It was poor advice.

"Of course you want to be hitting your approach shots with the smallest clubs possible," he said, "because your only chance around here is to be below the hole. And the greens are so firm that even the highest shot that doesn't fly the perfect distance will spin back to the front or off the green entirely. Or else it will skip past the pin to an impossibly quick two-putt. The wrong spin, the wrong flight—an up-shooter, say—forget it. I've been trying everything I can think of to get close to these pin placements. I've been hitting a lot of balls just above the green, trying to suck them back on. I've even tried spin-kicking a few of them straight-right off the shelves. I'm basically going crazy."

In 1997, less than four months after turning twenty-one, Tiger returned to Georgia for his first professional major with clearer eyes and a saner plan. "I'm not going to force it this time," he assured his father. "You can't take on every pin here, I've learned that much anyway—the painful way. I'm going to position my irons as best I can to take a run at the putts that you should take a run at and then just try to two-putt the others. Two-putt and move on. I'm striking the ball well enough to be selective in the chances I take."

Mark O'Meara could vouch for that. During the friends' final tune-up at home in Florida (the natural habitat for wealthy golfers; no state income tax), Woods neglected to birdie two of the Isleworth Golf & Country Club's par-5 holes or to make any putts of unusual length, and still shot 59 for the only time in his life. News reports had O'Meara shooting 66, but as a matter of fact, he didn't break 70. "Geez, Mark," Tiger said as they settled their bet of $65, "what did you shoot, around eighty-seven?"

But there was no trash talk on the plane as Woods and O'Meara flew together to Augusta, each buried in his own reverie. When Tiger was three years old, Mark was the United States Amateur champion. He was going to be the next important player on the PGA Tour. And, while he had banked a significant amount of cash in the years since, he had made no history. He was 0-for-56 in major championships without even a close call, and was about to turn forty.

Finally, Tiger broke the silence, asking in a low voice, "Do you think it's possible to win the Grand Slam?" Meaning, the Masters, the U.S. Open, the British Open and the PGA, all in the same year.

O'Meara thought, *You're the first guy since Nicklaus even to ask the question*, but didn't say that out loud. After a few seconds, he replied in a word, "Unrealistic."

To Earl later, Tiger said, "Whether it's realistic or not, I don't know. But I think it's possible. I think it could be done."

Tuesday, two days before the first round, Woods threw in with Severiano Ballesteros and Jose Maria Olazabal for nine holes of practice. The American media never *got* Ballesteros, so the American public never got to know him. Europeans loved Seve not for how much he won (though he won quite a bit, including three Open Championships and a couple of Masters) but for how much he cared, how hard he tried. No other golfer ever bounced in place with the ineffable joy of Ballesteros. All champions hug their trophies, but Seve caressed the Claret Jug like an awed father protecting a newborn's head.

The American players understood. Sometimes it seemed that the best shot any of them ever saw was a blow struck by the Spaniard. Nicklaus nominated a full 3-wood Seve somehow hoisted out of a high-faced fairway bunker at a Ryder Cup. At a Masters once, Raymond Floyd was asked if he could describe a towering flop shot Seve pulled off from the tightest lie on the 4th hole, a long par 3. "Yes," he said, "but it's going to take me a while." To Tiger, Ballesteros represented something of a last stop in his Masters and majors preparations.

"Seve is amazing around the greens," Woods said, holding court under a spreading oak beside the clubhouse (held up like backstage scenery with nuts and bolts and hidden wires). "He showed me a few little things today. There are some things you can only learn from another player." Breaking away from Ballesteros and Olazabal, Tiger played his second nine holes alone, to work on some of those little things in private.

Living off-campus now, in a rented house crowded with parents, agents, sponsors, Stanford friends, video games and a Ping-Pong table for marathon matches into the night, Tiger pulled out his putter early Thursday morning and started to practice on the living room carpet. His father was stretched out half awake on a couch. Two months earlier, Earl had undergone a second heart-bypass operation, and the Masters was his first tournament back.

"I wasn't going to say anything," Earl said, "unless he asked me. Not on Thursday. Game day. Uh-uh."

Eventually, Tiger did ask him.

"How do you like my stroke, Pop?"

"I don't," Earl replied in that deadpan, singsong voice that sometimes made Tiger laugh, but not this time.

"What's wrong with it?"

"Your right hand is breaking down just slightly on the takeaway," Earl said.

With just his right hand on the grip, Tiger rehearsed a few strokes back and forth. Then he put both hands on the club, back and forth. He swore gently and smiled.

How did Earl, a handicap golfer, know so much about putting?

"Let me give you the theory," he said. "Putting is an exercise in hand-eye coordination and technique. I taught Tiger to putt when he was so young that he didn't know the difference between thirty feet and a hundred feet and one foot. So he would putt to the picture. I'd tell him to rotate his head—go ahead, rotate *your* head. *Do* it, right now. Rotate it and look, and come back. Now rotate it again and look at the picture. Do it again, once more. Do you see the picture? Putt to the picture.

"I started Tiger off by placing a ball in his right hand and having him stand sideways, like you do at address. I had him swivel his head back and forth until he saw the picture, until it was ingrained in his mind. 'OK, toss the ball across your body to the hole in the picture. Put the ball in the picture at that spot.' He tossed it about six inches from the cup. He was one year old.

"By doing that, no thought of distance was involved. No thought of direction was involved. And those are the two main elements of putting. Of course, there are other variables. Uphill. Downhill. With the grain. Against the grain. But they can be programmed into your computer. You make a conscious checklist. You say, 'Uphill. With the grain. Greens are fast.' Now, you have to trust it. Tiger had to trust me. He did. Then, more importantly, he had to trust himself. He does."

Charlie Sifford saw Tiger play for the first time at a junior tournament in Houston. "The two of us were following Tiger in the gallery," Earl recalled. "Tiger was on the green lining up about a twenty-five-footer for birdie. 'He's going to make this putt, Charlie,' I said. He looked at me as if to say, 'Harrumph.' Then I told him, 'Let me show you something. After I see Tiger set up, I'll turn away and let you know exactly when the impact occurs. OK, he's set up.' I turned my back on Tiger [and Earl continued narrating for Sifford]. 'He looks at his ball and turns away. He looks at the target. He looks at the ball. He looks at the target. He looks at the ball. He forward-presses slightly. Contact.' Charlie said, 'Goddamn.' When I said contact, Tiger hit it. It went right in the hole.

"Then I told Charlie why. I explained to him what Tiger was doing. He was looking at the picture. And I said, 'Charlie, he has *no idea* how long those putts are.' In fact, that's where Tiger got in trouble with you guys in the media when he first came up. You guys thought he was blowing you off when you asked, 'How long was that putt at sixteen?' and Tiger said, 'I don't know.' He really didn't."

Sifford, of course, was the sorrowful symbol of the PGA Tour's evil "professional golfers of the Caucasian race" clause that ruled off Charlie from 1948, the year he turned pro, until 1960. There, basically, went his prime. He won the 1967 Greater Hartford Open at the age of forty-five and the L.A. Open two years later. But the constantly shifting rules for acceptance at the Masters never favored him. Augusta National's position was conveniently convoluted, but two facts were beyond dispute. There was a time when the club was desperate to keep blacks out of the tournament. And there came a time when it was desperate to let them in. "There were Opens and there were Invitationals," Tiger said with ice in his voice. "Invitationals were the ways around the Opens."

Earl made sure Tiger knew about excluded pioneers Bill Spiller, Teddy Rhodes, Zeke Hartsfield and especially Sifford, who became an honorary grandfather to Tiger. "Charlie reminds me of my baseball days," Earl said, "starting with the loneliness. The cigar. That fixed grimace on his face makes me think of a batter who's just been hit by a pitch and doesn't want to rub the spot. Doesn't want to show how much it hurts. Doesn't want to give anybody the satisfaction. He didn't come to Augusta. He wasn't about to step on that property. Lee Elder [the first black player at the Masters, 1975] came. Tiger put his arms around Lee and whispered, 'Thanks for making this possible.' But Charlie sent Tiger a fax. It said: 'Don't fire at all the pins. Be cautious. Be smart. Play the golf course.' Tiger was already thinking the same way. Finally, it said: 'But when the time comes, let it go. Turn it loose. Be strong. Be yourself.'"

As the reigning amateur champion, Woods drew the Masters defender, Nick Faldo, in that traditional opening-round pairing. The prior spring, Faldo won his third green jacket at Greg Norman's excruciating expense. "Nick and I talk more than you'd think on the golf course," Tiger said, "or more than he does with most people, I hear. I don't know if it's just me, but he has things to say. You know, just briefly. Just comfortably. He's a good guy to play with."

The wind Thursday morning whirled and whistled and blew the first thirty players over par by the turn. Flying pine needles punctured the air. Both Faldo and Woods went out in 4-over-par 40s, but Tiger came home with a 6-under-par 30, five better than Nick. Earl watched on television as his son plundered the back nine. "Tiger can play with or without me," he said, "but I can see better on TV. Before and after the round, we went over what he planned to do and what he did; you know, ran through it together, just like we always have."

Tiger said, "He and I both enjoy that."

Woods birdied the 10th, 12th and 13th, eagled the par-5 15th with a mere pitching wedge to just six feet and birdied the 17th for the 2-under-par 70, worth fourth place behind John Huston (67), Paul Stankowski (68) and Paul Azinger (69). Earl assumed Tiger's chip-in for a two from behind the green at 12 was the crucial shot. Being a sentimentalist, he went so far as to wonder if that dainty play in the face of a pond wasn't one of the little things Ballesteros had passed along. Tiger laughed and said, "Come on, Pop, don't get carried away." It was just a greasy little chunk-and-runner that happened to go in.

"That hurt my feelings a little," Earl said. "No, I take it back. It didn't hurt my feelings. It just let me know that I was really outside the ropes now. We were getting farther apart. But this had been the plan all along. One day, just after Tiger turned pro, he was a little down in the dumps and I told him, 'I know exactly how you feel.' He looked straight at me and said, 'No, Dad, you don't.'"

Earl was stunned, slapped. "But, you know something?" he said. "He couldn't have been more right. I realize nobody believes me when I say this, but I've never been one of those parents who lived through his child. Never have. Never will. Go ahead and laugh—everybody else does—but Tiger'll verify my story. He's completely in charge of his own life, and I'll tell you something else you won't believe. He always has been. But I've enjoyed following him, figuratively. And thinking along with him, step by step. I still can, most of the time."

On Friday, Woods shot 66 to take a three-stroke lead over the Scot Colin Montgomerie, a prolific winner on his side of the Atlantic Ocean, eight-time holder of the European Order of Merit, whose record in the majors was dotted with disappointments. Losing two playoffs, he finished second in three of the four, including the U.S. Open twice. In the pressroom before his Saturday date with Woods, Monty talked up his superior experience and tried to downplay his resemblance to the movie character Mrs. Doubtfire. But after Tiger overwhelmed him by nine strokes with the purest 65, Colin surrendered for everybody. "He's nine shots clear [of Costantino Rocca]," he said. "I'm sure that will be higher tomorrow."

Both Montgomerie and Faldo followed up their Tiger appointments with identical 81s and were never factors at Augusta again.

Despite his enormous lead, Woods believed his father when he said Sunday morning (about one a.m., while splitting a bowl of ice cream), "This is going to be the hardest round of golf you'll ever play, and the most rewarding." To himself on the course, Tiger kept urging, *Finish the race.* Constructing a careful 69, exhaling only after he was clear of the water hazards at 11, 12, 13, 15 and 16, Tiger broke by one stroke the 17-under-par 271 record that had prompted Bobby Jones in 1965 to say Nicklaus played a game with which he was not familiar. Woods's margin of victory over runner-up Tom Kite was a full dozen shots, another Masters mark. Only Young Tom Morris at the Open Championship in Prestwick, Scotland, (1862) ever won a major title by as many as 13. (His father, Old Tom, won one by 12.) A single major into his professional career, Tiger was already reaching back to shepherds and crooks, and the Morris standard had just three more years to stand.

First in driving distance (323.1 yards), first in greens-in-regulation (55 of 72), only ninth in putting but with no three-putts, Woods seemed to be challenging the basic geometry of the sport. "It wasn't all that complicated," he said. "The majority of my putts were uphill because I was able to control my irons into the greens. Why was I able to do that? Because I had short irons into the greens. Why did I have those short iron shots? Because I drove the ball great. Putting was just a reflection of everything working, from the tee box to the green. Or from the green to the tee box, if you think about it. My dad always taught me to *think* every golf course backwards."

Sunday's television audience in the United States scored a rating average of 20.3 million viewers, the most ever counted for a golf tournament. Golf, of all Republican, pot-bellied things, was about to be reclassified as cool. Ticket brokers who normally dealt in $3,000 badges saw the price vault that week to $7,000. As a result, suppliers who promised small local businessman Allen F. Caldwell III seventy tickets for big-shot corporate clients didn't come through at the last minute and returned his deposit. Caldwell killed himself with a twelve-gauge shotgun.

That was the major tragedy of the 1997 Masters. A minor one

involved former Masters and U.S. Open champion Fuzzy Zoeller, who, trying to be funny for a television crew, warned Tiger off serving fried chicken at the next Champions Dinner. Or collard greens. Or "whatever the hell they serve." That cost Zoeller a contract with Kmart and a legacy of laughter.

"My Tiger have no idea what collard greens are!" Tida exclaimed. "I never cook collard greens!"

"Fuzzy's a jokester," Earl said. "Everybody knows that. The mistake wasn't fried chicken. It wasn't collard greens. Who the hell could eat a collard green? It was the word 'they.' Whatever 'they' serve. That was something inside Fuzzy, or around him—or around all of us—that just slipped out. It's always slipping out, isn't it? That's what Tiger meant when he said, 'I forgive but I don't forget.' He had gone off on vacation to Cancun and really had no idea this whole controversy was raging. But he forgave Fuzzy. He knows Fuzzy's a jokester."

When Tiger walked off the 18th green into his father's arms ("My favorite shot of the day," President Clinton said on the telephone, "was that last shot with your dad"), old Charlie Horse at home in Kingston, Texas, could hold his fixed grimace no more. "I cried," Sifford said. "As far as I'm concerned, it put the Masters to rest for me. You know, it's fifty years [practically to the day] since Jackie Robinson broke baseball's color line. Whenever Tiger tips his cap on the golf course, I consider that recognition to the unrecognized."

Back at the rented house, everyone was standing around in the kitchen Sunday night, drinking, talking and laughing, when Earl suddenly realized Tiger was missing. He led a search party to his son's bedroom, where they looked in and found him in bed asleep, fully clothed, with his arms wrapped around the green jacket.

CHAPTER TWELVE

Major No. 2, the 1999 PGA

Earl and Tida were living in separate houses, but Earl resisted the word "separated." In *Playing Through*:

> From the time we discovered that the little guy had an affinity for golf, Tida and I made a personal commitment to each other that we would devote all of our energies and finances to assure that he had the best that we could give him. Total commitment! Well, something had to give, and it was our relationship.
>
> The priority became Tiger, and not each other, and in retrospect I see that our relationship began to decline from that day on. Not the trust, not the respect, just the unbridled love . . . Tiger was aware of the situation between his parents. Even when he was young, during our trips around the nation to golf tournaments, we had in-depth conversations about relationships, my specific relationship with his mother, his future relationships, etc. From these discussions came his pledge

that "when I become a professional golfer, Dad, I will take care of Mom" . . . And so, when he did in fact become a pro, his first order of business was to buy his mother her dream house in Tustin, California. Tida had always wanted a large showy home, while I preferred our small intimate home in nearby Cypress. I chose to remain in the family home where Tiger was raised, so I could be in touch with the childhood memories of him . . . Who knows, maybe one day Tiger's childhood home will become a national monument!

What happened to our marriage? Not much really. I have a belief that relationships never end; they just change their form . . . Today, we're best friends, have a beautiful amicable relationship and ardently follow Tiger's development and progress every step of the way, still fully supportive. She has her home, I have mine. Some people would call that separated. I call it affluence.

"When Dad had his second bypass," Royce said, "he stayed at the big house, I don't know how many months. I call it the big house [Earl called it "the big-ass house"]. And Tida nursed him back and took care of him. I've put it together even more lately, but I always knew the truth. There were women in Dad's life."

Den said, "He didn't have that many vices. Cigarettes. An occasional Jack [Daniels]."

And women.

"And women," he repeated.

I broached the subject gently to Earl's sister Mae. "You must know," I said, "he was something of a womanizer."

"Oh Lord," she said. "If he had been my husband, I'd have shot him." And she loved him.

Earl wouldn't have said "womanizer"; he'd have said "player." He thought of himself as a player. From all signs, he wasn't ashamed of it. In fact, he was proud enough of his playing equipment (justifiably) that, if he knew who was at the front door, he didn't mind coming straight from the shower naked.

When he was just a few days out of the hospital, where he told me he surreptitiously blew cigarette smoke out of the cracked window beside his bed, we went to lunch. "Where do you want to go?" I asked. "Chili's," he said.

"Earl, we're on scholarship. Let's go someplace nice."

"I like Chili's."

He ordered a jalapeño cheese soup that looked like a dip, along with a supersized portion of baby-back ribs, not a week after a heart procedure. Then he smoked a chain of cigarettes, about half a pack. On the way out, he tried to pick up the waitress.

It became my habit, at British Opens, to drop by the Woods's rented house one day of the tournament, to watch Tiger on television with Earl. "Squeamish" (Earl's word) at the specter of his parents back under the same roof, Tiger seldom stayed in any of these homes he paid for at a dear premium. He crashed with Mark O'Meara, usually.

At one of the earliest UK stops—Lytham & St. Annes in England—IMG's Bev Norwood and I visited Earl, who was in the courtyard smoking. "I couldn't find any ashtrays in the whole house," he said, "so the people who live here must not smoke. That's pretty rare in Europe." Every twenty minutes or so, he went back outside to have another cigarette. "I don't want to be inconsiderate," he said, "and smell up these people's home."

Earl introduced us to his cook, a comely young woman from Cape Town, South Africa, who lived in London.

"Didn't I meet her at the Masters?" I asked after she moved into the next room.

"Yes, she's always with us at the Masters and the British," he said.

"She must be a hell of a cook," I said.

"She sure knows how to keep that potato chip bowl filled up."

"Earl, is that some kind of sexual metaphor I'm too unsophisti-cated to understand?"

"No, Stud. Literally. See? It's full."

Lounging on a sofa in front of the TV, Earl regularly dozed be-tween shots, but he had the uncanny ability to jerk himself awake the instant Tiger came on-screen. Earl offered mysterious commentary like "meow" or straightforward advice like "Tiger, you're standing too close to the ball. All right, that's a little better."

"Tiger told me later," Earl would tell *me* later, "'Thanks, Pop. I heard you.'"

"Come on, Earl," I said. "Stop it."

He laughed for about twenty seconds.

"You don't mind if *I* believe it," he said, "do you?"

As Earl told it, he had a part in recruiting Tiger's closest friends on tour—O'Meara and John Cook—while Payne Stewart volun-teered. For dying young, Stewart would be canonized and have his name attached to a good guy award. But, at least among the players, he was not synonymous with selflessness or sportsmanship. As his teaching pro and friend, Chuck Cook, said, "Payne was ungracious in victory at the PGA Championship and ungracious in defeat at the Tour Championship—he wouldn't shake Tom Kite's hand." So, it was a little surprising that he walked up to Earl on a clubhouse balcony and said, "Don't worry about your boy, Mr. Woods. I'll look after him."

Tiger's tightest bond was forged with O'Meara, and the main catalyst may have been Alicia O'Meara, who told her husband, "That poor kid is sitting over there in his house alone. Let's get him over here for dinner." Tiger said, "Mark became a big brother to me. He taught me a lot of off-the-golf-course things, or tried to. Some of those things, like how to deal with the media, didn't completely take. But I wouldn't have ever had the success I had early on without his help."

At the start, Woods wasn't fastidious about either clothes or cars. "Tiger had a nice car he hadn't washed in about a year," O'Meara said. "I told him, 'Bring that filthy thing over here, will you? I'm doing my cars. I'll wash it. I'll wax it.'" But, before long, they were competing at everything ("like at fly fishing," Tiger said, "five bucks a cast, ten bucks a catch"). And even at sartorial neatness. "Mark-O finally got himself an iron," Woods said, not referring to a golf club. "I have never ironed a shirt in my life," said O'Meara. "I always iron," Tiger said. "Every morning I've got to iron all my stuff. Got to do it. Even if it's dry-cleaned, I'll iron it just a little bit, all of the little creases."

As Tiger's seven a.m. practice partner most days, Mark was the first to know exactly what was coming. And, in a way, he would be the primary beneficiary, only starting with the 1997 AT&T Pro-Am at Pebble Beach, historically O'Meara's happiest hunting ground.

Earl's heart was at issue again, and for the first two days of the tournament, Tiger didn't care much about golf. At the midway point, he stood 60th in the field. But as soon as the emergency passed, Woods lifted off. Finishing 63-64, he barely missed an eagle putt on the 72nd hole that would have caught his friend. Any other leader might have gagged at the sight of something approaching that fast in the rearview mirror. But Mark just shook his head and smiled. Professionally topping off a fourth straight 67, he lifted another Pebble Beach loving cup, his fifth.

A week or two after the '97 Masters, Tiger sat down to watch the tape for the first time and was rattled by what he saw. "I was by myself," he said, "so I was able to concentrate on critiquing my swing, to see if there was some flaw I might be able to work on. I didn't see one flaw. I saw about ten. I got on the phone and called Butch."

Hanging an Under Reconstruction sign on his game, Tiger traded the four tour victories he collected in 1997 for just one in 1998, the nondescript BellSouth Classic. "Wouldn't you make that trade," he asked, "for the chance to almost always be there at the end? I would."

(Tiger also won a tournament in Thailand, the Johnny Walker Classic, that was significant for whom he beat and how he beat him. South African Ernie Els held an eight-stroke lead after the third round. The reporters asked Tiger, "Can anybody catch him?" He replied, "I can." When apprised of this later, Els wondered, "What's he on?" But Woods did catch him, and on the second extra hole, beat him. Tiger's principal victim had been identified. Earl said, "I think his rival both in the short term and in the long term is going to be Ernie Els.")

During the renovations, Tiger loaned his number one ranking to David Duval and left the majors department to O'Meara. Without taking one step in the lead all day or all week, Mark made the final putt at the Masters to break through as a major winner at 41. It was his fourteenth Masters, the most of any first-time champion. Before O'Meara, only Arnold Palmer and Art Wall could say they birdied the last two holes to win. Performing the defending champion's traditional task, Tiger helped his friend into a green jacket.

Three months later, O'Meara added the British Open, taking a four-hole aggregate playoff from Brian Watts at Royal Birkdale, 17 to 19. Mark was the oldest winner of two majors in a year ever. They would be his only two.

"I'm not sure I'd have ever won a major without Tiger's influence," he admitted. "His youth and enthusiasm, his competitiveness, got inside me a little. It lit something."

Tiger finished third at that British and was secretly pleased. Tom Seaver used to talk about especially valuing the victories that came when he was missing his best stuff, when he won just by pitching. "I had nothing—flat nothing—at Birkdale," Tiger said, "and I finished third. Nobody else will remember that, but I will."

A tour de force awaited in 1999, followed by a bigger one in 2000. But before the rebuilding year ended, Tiger and Earl had an appointment to keep in South Africa. At Sun City, Woods rallied from four strokes down in the final round of the Nedbank Million Dollar Challenge before losing a playoff to Nick Price. But that was an afterthought next to his audience—Earl might say summit—with Nelson Mandela.

"It was the first time Tiger met a human being who was equal to him, who was as powerful as Tiger was," Earl said with his usual restraint, lighting another brushfire. "We went to Mandela's summer home, where the instructions were, 'No flash photography.' All the years in prison had sensitized him to brightness. When we walked in, Tiger and Nelson locked eyes, and they knew each other immediately. They began to talk, to communicate. I just watched, amazed. I couldn't believe the ease they both felt in each other's presence. It was a beautiful thing to see. It was like a teacher talking to a pupil but acknowledging that the student was clearly superior to my other students, so I have to pay special attention to him because he's going to do great things. And Nelson counseled him, telling him that he did have this ability and that he had to go out and do a lot of good in the world."

That was the public rendition. Sometime later, with no microphones around, Earl fell back in his living room easy chair and said, "I don't know whether it meant as much to Tiger as it did to me. I think so. I hope so. I'm a reasonably intelligent person. I wasn't the one who brought up the names Gandhi and Mandela in comparison to Tiger. They were brought up to *me*. I just said yes. Yes, in the sense that he'd have that kind of world recognition. Bigger, really, because today's megaphones are so much bigger. Before he's done, Tiger could have the biggest international forum of anybody who ever lived. I meant Tiger is like Gandhi in that he's interested in kids like that, and probably never will be a political individual. Political power isn't the only power, you know. There's social power, too. Fame and popularity can give you the most basic power of all, the power to do good. Tiger will be an ambassador without portfolio, of kids. Why is that so ridiculous? And is it outrageous to say God picked me and God picked Tiger? Who else would have ever picked us?"

Some players and caddies took a less-inspiring memory home from Sun City: the steady procession of professional ladies on their way up to Earl's room.

In 1999, Tiger became the first golfer in twenty-five years (Johnny Miller) to win eight PGA Tour events, the first in forty-six years (Ben Hogan) to win four tournaments in a row. The highlight came at the Medinah Country Club outside Chicago, in the PGA.

Three months into the season, Tiger cashiered snowy-lipped caddie Mike (Fluff) Cowan, replacing him with New Zealand auto racer Steve Williams, former aide to Greg Norman, Raymond Floyd and others. "I promised Tiger when he was a little kid," Earl said, "that I'd have no input in two areas of his life—his selection of a caddie and his selection of a mate."

Regarding that second pick, Earl did voice a generic preference (or the lack of one, actually) to everyone who brought up the subject, including *The New York Times*. "I've told Tiger that marriage is unnecessary," Earl told the *Times*, "in a mobile society like ours."

Not only Fluff, "Everybody Tiger has fired [caddie, lawyer, agent, et al.]," according to Earl, "was let go for one reason, always the same reason: betrayal. Loyalty is number one to Tiger. If you're not loyal, you're history." By the way, enough of the dirty work fell to Earl for him to acquire the nickname "The Terminator."

But Cowan's betrayal was slight. Mike had a young girlfriend. Tiger asked him to stop bringing her around. He didn't. The few people Tiger admitted to his inner circle were not entitled to bring guests.

During their final loop together, neither Tiger nor Fluff uttered a word, not even about yardages. In the parking lot afterward, they said good-bye.

Butch Harmon's demise a couple of years later would be more complicated, but Earl pinpointed a moment when he and Tiger were watching a television interview in which Butch, like a boxing corner man or a caddie, kept saying "we" did this and "we" did that, until Tiger turned to his father and inquired in an edgy voice, "We?" Bye-bye, Butchie.

"There's only one guy I can't fire," Tiger said with a wan smile. "I think you know who I'm talking about."

"Are there times when you'd like to fire him?"

"No comment," he answered at first. But then he said, laughing, "Isn't he a beaut?"

The center of attention at Medinah wasn't Tiger, but an obstreperous nineteen-year-old Spanish terrier yipping at the heels of golf, Sergio Garcia. Sergio was just fourteen when, with a toothy grin on his face and a tube of acne cream in his golf bag, he made the cut in his initial thrust at a European tour event. He finished first at the Catalonia Open on the Spanish tour, second in the Argentina Open on the South American tour, and third in North Carolina on the American Nike Tour.

On the phone from Malaga early in 1999, still an amateur but on the brink of the profession, Sergio Garcia Fernandez sounded like the happiest-go-luckiest golfer in history. With his father and coach, Victor, Sergio was glowing from a trip to Augusta National, where nothing about the experience affected him more than meeting Charlie Yates. "Bobby Jones's old friend, Charlie Yates," he said. "Do you know him? I met him. He won the British Amateur in nineteen-thirty-eight, *sixty* years before I did. [Sergio was the reigning title-holder.] All the way around the course, I watched my father play and we talked about meeting Charlie Yates. *Nineteen-thirty-eight!* That's the thing about Augusta, isn't it? It's like stepping into the past."

In one sentence, had anyone ever described the place better?

He wouldn't declare for the business until April, but Sergio said, "This round with my father felt like the first day of my pro life. We're coming to the seventh hole, which they sometimes showed on TV, so everything started getting familiar. Then, the ninth hole, I recognized completely. Don't be short or you'll spin off the front of the green like Greg Norman. And the back nine. Oh, the back nine. Amen Corner! How can you not know that? Once you've arrived at the twelfth hole, you feel like you've been there before. Freddie Couples on the bank. It's the home of all your dreams, isn't it? Then you go to thirteen—the great par five—and you keep climbing and climbing. How we say in Spain, it breaks your legs, the whole course is so much uphill. You can't see that on TV. You're looking up all the time. You're hitting into the clouds. You never seem to come down.

"When I left there, I told myself, 'Now you're ready to be a pro golfer.' When you are five, six, seven, eight and nine, you don't realize how much you love the game you're playing, whether it's football, tennis or golf. When you realize the love, now you're ready to go. But, I asked myself, 'Are you ready to come down to the end of a major championship with a chance to win?' We'll see."

Four years younger than Woods, Sergio met Tiger on the telephone. "At Mark O'Meara's house," he said. "Mark invited me to have a game at Isleworth. At one point he handed me the telephone. It was Tiger! Everyone was so beautiful to me."

"All I know about Sergio," Tiger said at Medinah, "is that he brings it. You can see it just in the way he walks. It's good to see."

Coming down to the end of that major championship with a chance to win, the two clinked swords on Sunday's back nine. Reacting to the sparks, the Chicago-area crowd actually preferred Sergio. He won them with a single shot executed from between the toes of a great oak on 16. Two strokes behind with three holes to play (one group ahead of Woods), Garcia was desperate enough to open a 6-iron, close his eyes and let fly. He looked like a blind man trying to kill a snake. Somehow, his club hit the ball instead of the root. Somehow, the ball missed the tree and didn't ricochet in his face. As the golf ball curled overland, left to right, Garcia stampeded after it, freezing in mid-gallop like a steeplechaser clearing Beecher's Brook. It landed as soft as a leaf on the green. Four of the five strokes in Tiger's lead were gone.

"After I made double-bogey and he made birdie," Tiger said, "everything changed. The crowd went completely over to his side. They really started revving it up."

"A thousand dollars you knock it in the water!" slurred one spectator, prompting Steve Williams to whisper to his boss, "Man, golf has changed a lot over the last twenty years." He meant twenty months, but it was just the right thing to say. Woods-Williams was going to be a workable partnership.

The issue came down to Tiger's eight-footer for par on the 17th hole. "Inside left," was all Williams said. "Perfect," was all Tiger replied. "I ran it inside left," Woods said later, "and made sure it stayed steady. I emphasized the release of the blade through the ball, because a lot of times the left-to-right putt is the one you block."

When the ball tumbled in, Tiger consciously dispensed with his trademark ride across the green on the back of Silver while throwing uppercuts at the sky. "People were all over me for that," he said. "I've tried to cool it a little, and I was especially concerned with keeping my emotions in check today. Too many beverages had been consumed in that gallery. I definitely didn't want to stir these people up any more than they already were. You know, Sergio wears his emotions on his sleeve, too. I wonder if people will start getting on *him* now."

They would. Sergio's wide-eyed charm wouldn't last. After Woods and Garcia finished a stroke apart, everyone said young Sergio would win a major championship any minute now. More than a decade later, they would still be saying it.

CHAPTER THIRTEEN

Major No. 3, the 2000 U.S. Open

Anybody walking around with a black face in America knows more than a little about racism, but Tiger didn't know as much as his father. Eldrick grew up in Ozzie and Harriet's old house just around the corner from Disneyland and Knott's Berry Farm, about as far away as can be imagined from a typical black environment or the average black experience. A large share of Tiger's racial sensitivities and grievances was borrowed from Earl.

"But don't forget," Royce said, "Tiger has been getting hate mail and death threats since, as Dad would say, Christ made corporal." Henry Aaron, present in Milwaukee at Woods's pro debut, advised him to read every one, and keep them, for his children. "One time," Royce said, "Tiger tossed me a letter that read, 'You can take the monkey out of the jungle, but you can't take the jungle out of the monkey.'"

Earl said, "I taught Tiger about 'The Look,' that expression on people's faces that says, *What the hell are you doing here?* 'We have an extrasensory perception,' I told him. 'All blacks have it. It lets us know when racists are nearby, trying to hide behind their smiles, as if their eyes didn't give them away.' Tiger and I would be on a practice putting green somewhere, and he'd whisper to me, 'Do you feel it, Dad?'"

"Sometimes at country clubs," Tiger said, "I could feel people staring at me. If they stared long enough, I stared right back at them. Racism was their problem, not mine."

He told and retold a harrowing kindergarten tale of being lashed to a tree, spray-painted with slogans and pelted with rocks by racist sixth-graders. Thirty years later, the teacher came forward to debunk his account. Long before she did, I asked Earl, "Do you believe that really happened?"

"What makes you doubt it?" he asked.

"I don't know, it sounds a little like the settlers and the Indians."

"Tiger never lies," he said.

"Earl, he's the biggest liar on tour. He tells one player he'll be at this tournament, another player he'll be at that tournament, a third player he won't be at either tournament. Then he sits back and enjoys the confusion."

"That's not lying," Earl said. "That's verifying which players you can trust."

There would come a time when Tiger would be heard on the subject of his own truthfulness, and he would not come down on his father's side. He would confess, "I lied to a lot of people, deceived a lot of people, kept others in the dark, rationalized, and even lied to myself. . . . When you live a life where you're lying all the time, life is not fun."

On racial sensitivities, Tiger showed an obvious preference for white girlfriends over black, and would eventually marry the whitest woman almost anybody had ever seen. Of course there weren't many black females—or black males for that matter—in Tiger's orbit. Still, it's more than possible that Earl talked him out of black women specifically.

In front of me, so I presume in front of Tiger, Earl referred to his first wife as "Super Sapphire" after The Kingfish's loudmouthed shrew of a wife in the radio and television minstrel show *Amos 'N Andy*. Is that what he meant when he said, "Even when he was young, during our trips around the nation to golf tournaments, we had in-depth conversations about relationships"?

On the radio version of *Amos 'N Andy*, cast with Caucasian actors only, the voices of both Amos and The Kingfish were provided by Freeman Gosden, a prominent member and frequent playing partner to club chairman Clifford Roberts and President Dwight Eisenhower at Augusta National. Black actors brought in for the TV series had no difficulty memorizing the faulty grammar, but they struggled to re-create the exaggerated dialect and fractured pronunciation of Gosden and the man who played Andy, Charles Correll.

> *The Kingfish:* "Where is you, Sapphire? Holy mack'l, Andy! Sumpin' done happened to Sapphire!"
> *Andy:* "Maybe Sapphire done run off with some other man."
> *The Kingfish:* "Who'd run off with dat ugly ol' battle-axe? Da onliest peoples I can think of is under lock and key."

"I wanted Tiger to have black friends," Earl said. "I would have liked it if he had a black caddie. But hell, he's a suburban kid. As for Super Sapphire, I was too young when I married the first time. My sisters warned me, but I thought I knew everything. I told Tiger exactly that. I didn't tell him what to do as far as black women are concerned. I just told him what to expect."

Tiger first played Pebble Beach with his father. "He was twelve," Earl said. "Thirteen," Tiger corrected him, "in the rain. Even on a dry day, the course would still have been way too long for me." A few years later, competing in the State Amateur, Tiger started to appreciate Pebble not just for what he called "its pristine beauty" but also for its mystery. "After I finally got the mystique of the place," he said, "that's when it became important to me. I was only six and a half when Watson chipped in at seventeen to win the Open, and to be honest with you, I don't remember the chip-in. In fact, I didn't understand at the time how much it meant, how big a chip-in it was. I just have this vague memory of Tom making the putt he didn't need at eighteen and raising his arms in victory. I don't even remember the putt. I remember the arms."

Victory.

Getting better and better, Woods was also becoming luckier and luckier. His side of the draw was almost always the charm. Early Thursday, late Friday—Tiger's tee times for the 100th U.S. Open—again represented the winning ticket. By the time a fogbank—practically a cloudbank—rolled in to stop and start and make a general shambles of the first round, Tiger was already in front of a TV set with his feet up, decompressing from a bogey-free 6-under-par 65. "In California, we call this 'June gloom,'" Earl said brightly.

Tiger privately considered his score to be 7-under-par. The USGA's decision to reclassify par on the 2nd hole from 5 to 4, redrawing the course as a par 71 instead of a 72, offended his sense of continuity. "Don't they understand historical references?" he griped to his father. "Some of us out here want to compare our scores to the scores of all of the past champions." One of them did, anyway.

In the press tent postmortem, Tiger dissected his first round using the golfer's rapid-fire birdies-and-bogeys shorthand:

I birdied four, hit a two-iron off the tee. I hit a sixty-degree sand wedge to about a foot; made that.

Seven, I hit a pitching wedge to about twenty feet left of the hole and made that.

Ten, I hit a driver and an eight-iron to about fifteen feet and made that.

Thirteen, I hit a driver and a nine-iron to about a foot and made that.

Fourteen, I hit driver-driver, pitched up to about a foot, tapped that in.

Eighteen, I hit a driver, four-iron into the left bunker, blasted out to about a-foot-and-a-half and made that.

Interestingly, when he rattled off his day for Earl later, the highlighted holes were entirely different: 5, 9, 11 (where "the catcher called for a pitchout," their slang for a tee ball shoved to the right), 15 and 17. These were the greens he missed, or, in one case, nearly three-putted, where par had to be rescued with a nine-footer, an eight-footer, a twelve-footer, a six-footer and a ten-footer. "The par saves, not the birdies," Earl said, "are what win U.S. Opens."

"They even *feel* better than birdies," Tiger concurred. "It's not necessarily about making putts. It's about making the right putt at the right time."

In practice rounds before the tournament, Tiger didn't like the way he was putting, even though he was making everything. The balls were going in the hole, but "improperly" by his lights. They were scooting in, skidding in. They weren't rolling in, tumbling in. "Is that the definition of a perfectionist?" Earl asked. "They're not going in the hole the way he likes it? Past dusk Wednesday, Tiger was still out there working on his posture and release. How many one-putts did he have Thursday?" Twelve. (How many one-putts would he have in all? Thirty-four.) "Has anyone in the history of golf ever putted better," Earl asked, "including Nicklaus?"

"Butch and I were out on the practice putting green Friday afternoon," Tiger said, "impatient to get going. The field was becoming more and more backed up. My tee time had been four, then it was four-twenty, then it was four-forty. . . . We heard a roar at eighteen. At first I thought someone had holed out from the fairway, but then I recognized it was a Jack roar. 'Jack's due right about now,' I told Butch. He went over to a TV technician, who, after checking with somebody on his radio, called out to us, 'It's Jack.'"

Far off the cut line, Nicklaus had reached the last par 5 in two shots, but then three-putted for par to close his final U.S. Open, a record 44th, that included four victories and four seconds. "I'd have loved to have seen him finish," Tiger said, "but I had more important things on my mind."

For the same reason, he ducked the ceremony and conversation around the Open's absent defending champion, Payne Stewart, who died in a plane crash four months after winning at Pinehurst in 1999. Twenty pros plus Stewart's caddie, Mike Hicks, fired a 21-driver salute into the Pacific Ocean to open the Open. Tiger was invited but demurred.

"I'm sorry," he said, "but I can't be thinking about Payne right now. If I do that, I'll remember our fishing trips, our stops in Ireland on the way to the British, and I'll transport myself back to some pub late at night in County Down where he's singing a drinking song. I just can't afford to be there right now."

Only enough sunlight was left Friday for Tiger to complete eleven holes, the last two of which he birdied to stretch a one-stroke lead to three. Rising at the crack of dawn on Saturday, he finished off a 68, the low round again, but not without incident. At the 18th tee, the catcher called for another pitchout, this time to a left-handed batter, and Tiger's drive crashed into the ocean. Reacting like a carpenter who had just nailed his thumb, Tiger shouted into the TV boom mikes, "God damn you fucking prick!" The whole Monterey Peninsula went still.

Three-time major winner Nick Price, not known as a scold, said, "If you have enough control over your emotions to play this game, you ought to have enough control over your mouth." Admonitions of a similar kind would be aimed Woods's way for at least ten years to come.

"Well, it was the heat of the moment," Tiger said in the press tent. "I'm one of those guys who plays pretty intense; and, unfortunately, I let it slip out. And I regret doing it. But unfortunately it happened. And I can apologize until I'm blue in the face. But when you're a competitor and you're fighting all day—and it was early in the morning—and I just went ahead and hit probably the worst shot I hit all week on a hole I can get to in two. And I proved that. It was just very frustrating, and I let it go a little bit."

Earl said, "My father could swear for thirty minutes and never repeat himself. Tiger has the gene. He can really let go, especially on the golf course. But you can't have it both ways. You can't praise his charismatic abilities to execute the marvelous shots and then chastise him when that same passion causes him to overload when he hits a bad one. Tiger's not perfect. I'm not perfect. You've never heard him curse like that off the golf course, have you?"

"Yes."

"When?"

"I don't know, sometime when you were smoking, which could have been anytime at all. Tiger and I were leaving you at the same moment, heading out in different directions. The second we were outside, he cursed the cigarettes at the top of his lungs. You must have heard it inside the house."

Earl nodded. "I know," he said. "But do you realize how much he respects me? I'll tell you exactly how much he respects me. I can light up in front of him and he won't even seem to notice. No look. No remark. You know, I don't inhale. And I could quit if I wanted to. I have tremendous willpower. It doesn't bother me one bit to fly across the U.S. or to Europe and not have a cigarette. I can shut it out. Tiger'll tell you. California to Hong Kong. No cigarette, no gum, nothing. But once we land, Tiger and I have an understanding. He'll take care of the luggage and I'll be outside smoking a cigarette."

"Did you ever try to quit?"

"Sure. I quit for a year and a half once, but then I went to my daughter's graduation and got stuck in a house with all of Super Sapphire's relations. That was all she wrote. Now I consider smoking to be my right and my privilege. It's my choice. Don't mess with my choices." Following a pause, he said, "Oh, hell. It's a full-blown addiction. You might as well say, 'Try to give up water. Try not to go to the bathroom.'"

Tiger's 71 Saturday afternoon was the second-best score to Ernie Els's 68. Ernie took fifty bucks off playing partner Colin Montgomerie, but also won the bleak privilege of accompanying Woods in Sunday's coronation from a full ten strokes back. Two months earlier, Els had finished second by himself to Vijay Singh at the Masters, when Tiger was fifth. Before Ernie's year was out, the main casualty of the Woods era would make it three-quarters of the way to the Bridesmaid Slam.

"No bogeys today," Tiger informed Steve Williams Sunday morning, and made good. A fifteen-foot par putt at 16 that rolled in, tumbled in, was his favorite moment. At 18, while Els was calculating his second shot, Woods nudged Williams to the seawall to make a memory. Two days earlier, Nicklaus straddled the fence by the last tee because he knew someone would take a picture of that and he wanted a picture of it. "I told Stevie," Tiger said, "there comes a point in time when you feel tranquil, when you feel calm. You feel at ease with yourself. And, no matter what you do, good or bad, it really doesn't get to you. Even on the days when you wake up on the wrong side of the bed, for some reason, it doesn't feel too bad. It's just all right."

Leading the field in driving distance (299.3) and greens in regulation (51), Woods became the first Open champion to post double-digit figures in red, a 12-under-par [16, he reckoned] 272 that left runners-up Els and Miguel Angel Jimenez fifteen strokes behind. "I looked at the scoreboard," Irishman Padraig Harrington said, "in total wonderment."

Willie Smith's winning margin of 11 lasted only 101 years. With his eight and ten-stroke 36- and 54-hole leads, Tiger also erased the ninety-seven- and seventy-nine-year-old records of Willie Anderson and Long Jim Barnes. Young Tom Morris's major mark of 13-under was history, too. Pretty much everything and everybody was wiped out at Pebble Beach, and the summer had just begun.

"Tiger," someone in the pressroom asked, "when you first came on the scene, your father made some statements about your potential that many of us felt were probably a little outrageous. Given what's taken place today, is it possible that even Earl underestimated your potential? And can you talk a little bit about the Father's Day angle that always takes place at the Open?"

"Well," Tiger said, "I think my dad has always had a big belief in my abilities, and so have I. The only difference is, he stated them and I didn't. I let my clubs do the talking. And I guess that's—as a father, I'll probably be that way, too. To my kids, I mean. Be a proud parent. And I guess that's what my dad was. When asked, he would give an honest answer. It's just that sometimes too honest an answer can be twisted in the press and blown out of proportion, which happened occasionally with all of you here.

"I guess today is a very special day. It's Father's Day. And I can't tell you enough about what my dad meant to my golf. And to me as a person growing up. And for all the times I had questions in life, and for all the guidance he's given me, I can't thank him enough. Both my parents were always there for me. My dad always took me out, and we practiced and played and had a lot of fun competing against each other. Those are the times you look back on and you reminisce about and you miss. And to have my dad still alive while I won this championship, on Father's Day, it's very important to me. He was actually—

he should have been dead in ninety-seven, with the complications he had after the heart surgery. And for him to come back against doctor's orders, go to the Masters, give me a putting lesson—I putted great that week and won by twelve. And this week, to have him here witnessing this, it's very special to me."

"Tiger has always been a most appreciative child," Earl said, "but no three-putts in four days helped, too."

CHAPTER FOURTEEN

Major No. 4, the 2000 British Open

On one of the walls at the Tiger Woods Foundation, a short drive from Earl's house, hung the iconic image of father and son in each other's arms by Augusta's 18th green. As I was looking at it, I realized Tida was standing beside me. On the Sunday that the picture was taken in 1997, she was just outside the viewfinder. "There's that poor motherless child," I said.

She laughed. She cackled.

Tida had a fleet of writers. She would preface her remarks to them, "This for friend," meaning if they repeated or wrote what she was about to say, they were dead. "I cut you off forever," she swore. Her manifesto was, "Old man is soft. [Referring, obviously, to Earl.] He cry. He forgive people. Not me. I don't forgive anybody." Kultida Punsawad Woods was Don Corrado Prizzi.

She proved it early on when one of Tiger's corporate negotiators was about to be let go. Worried for the man's emotional state, Earl wanted to save him, but Tida told Tiger, "Do what you have to do, honey. Do what you feel. If you can't trust this man, he gone." When the ex-employee called up, crying, she told him coldly, "Take care of your own children. Tiger not your son."

By protecting her, the writers weren't working their passage with Tiger; not really. She could offer no access to him. And, while her broken English, punctuated with "Gah-damns," was delightful, it wasn't especially quotable. ("What the hell the matter with your ass?") They just liked her. They found her secretly sweet, generous and lonely.

I did quote her once in passing, calling Phil Mickelson "Plastic Phil." She complained vehemently to the editors at *Golf Digest*. "Tom Callahan a liar! He a liar! I tell him to his face! I never say 'Plastic Phil.' I say, 'Three Dollar Phil.' I say, 'Fat Phil.' He's a *fat* Phil. But I never say 'Plastic Phil.'"

Once, after seeing Earl in Thousand Oaks, California, I bumped into Tida in the lobby of a hotel. I wanted to ask her about Thailand and her own childhood. She was the daughter of a teacher and an architect, who reportedly had some tin holdings. They lived near the bridge on the River Kwai. But she said, "You've got the two. You don't need the third. I raised Tiger the Asian way, that's all you need to know. Tiger knows. I don't care if anybody else knows."

That essentially applied to everything.

And her decision, of course, was final. "Tiger never changes his mind," she said. "I never change my mind."

For instance, she never changed her mind about Tiger's girlfriends (none of whom she particularly championed, including ultimately his wife). "Only one star in Woods family," Tida said of the last blonde eliminated before Elin. By the way, in a room of golfers' wives, you could tell at a glance which players married before they were famous. Their wives were the brunettes.

Tiger said, "You think about Green Berets and all that, but I was never scared of my dad. He was a softy. I could talk to him. I was scared of my mom. She didn't want to hear it. And she had a heavy hand."

The most memorable punishments resulted when he misbehaved in public. "You will not embarrass me," she said. "I will not have a spoiled child."

What could be seen in Tiger was Earl. What couldn't be seen was Tida.

She was an offspring of divorce, a relative rarity in Thailand. Shunted up, down and around both of her half families and a Gothic boarding school, she felt displaced and unloved, the proverbial step-child. As new spouses and children were added to the blends, she was washed away in the current.

She told writer Jaime Diaz, "I am a loner and so is Tiger. We don't waste time with people we don't like. I don't have many close friends. Never have. I am independent and strong-willed. That way, you survive. When I was a girl, my mother would always be worried, 'What will people say?' And even then, I would think, 'I don't give a damn.' I always tell Tiger, 'You can't do things just to please other people. It will waste your energy, and you won't be happy in yourself. You have to do what is right for yourself.' And, on that, he does a good job."

When Earl's girls descended en masse, she cut him off at the knees but didn't divorce him. Because, to Tida, divorce was unthinkable. After that, some of the things she said about Earl were so hard that they could only mean she still had feelings for him. At the same time, she had no sympathy for the kind of weakness that a cigarette represented to a man with a diseased heart. In addition, she suspected her own chronic cough was a secondhand result of Earl's second-biggest weakness. Understandably, she resented it.

"Dad want to check out first?" she said. "Fine with me. I want to stay longer."

Nonetheless, she dropped in to Cypress to fire at least one of the young handmaidens serving Earl when he had the old house to himself. Tida was still involved.

By "the Asian way," she meant Tiger was raised to have and show respect for his elders. "I enjoy the things that are old more than the new," she said. "You know, the test of time. In Thailand you always respect the elders and history, which is what I taught my son. I know he liked Byron Nelson very much; he was my favorite of all the golfers I meet. Just the way he looked at me and shook my hand. I hardly talk to him. But I liked him."

And Tiger received at least a basic grounding in Buddhism. When he arrived on tour in 1996, he wore a string bracelet around his left wrist, signifying protection and strength. It disappeared for a long while, but reappeared in 2010. "Every night," she said, "I pray to the Buddha that in the next life Tiger will be my son again. Hey, you gotta believe in something, honey. I have strong belief in Buddhism. Like Tiger believing it will go into the hole, and then it does."

Christmas week every year, Tida and Tiger made a pilgrimage to a temple in Los Angeles to worship with a Thai monk. In Escondido near San Diego, Tiger found an American Buddhist to whom he could more easily relate. Tiger was keen enough to underwrite the completion of a few half-built pagodas, which, considering his well-known frugality, was keen indeed.

For a Buddhist, Tida had a bloodthirsty way of describing the opposition. "Tiger kill Davis Love's heart!" she said ecstatically. "He take Davis's heart!" Then she asked again, as she was forever asking her writers, "What you think of my Tiger now?"

CBS's *60 Minutes* asked him this question about his mother: "You've said that she gave you that competitive drive, and that she also gave you a killer instinct. What did you mean by that?"

"Yeah, you have no idea how competitive my mom is," Tiger said. "She would watch me compete, and you could see her over there on the side, and she would be living every moment. Live? I mean die. On every shot."

"What about that?" the interviewer asked Tida. "Step on their throats? Fight till the death? Show no mercy?"

"That's sport," she agreed. "You have to. No matter how close friend you are, you must kill that person. When it is over, you can shake hand, be friend again."

Over their careers, Gene Sarazen (slickered down and knickered up), Ben Hogan, Gary Player and Jack Nicklaus were the only four players to win all four majors. For want of a Masters, Lee Trevino; for want of a U.S. Open, Sam Snead; for want of a British Open, Raymond Floyd; and for want of a PGA, Arnold Palmer and Tom Watson, never quite made it to paradise.

Now, at the unfledged age of twenty-four, Tiger had achieved the rank of blessed and needed one more miracle for sainthood. Ladbrokes and William Hill, the Coke and Pepsi of London's legal bookmakers, didn't rate a Woods victory at St. Andrews very high on the miracle scale. Neither did Sir Michael Bonallack, five-time British Amateur champion turned Royal and Ancient secretary, whose happy duty it was to proclaim "the champion golfer for the year" at the tournament's conclusion. This time he proclaimed it in advance. "Who's going to beat him?" Bonallack asked.

Tiger agreed with them, but of course didn't say so. Spotting sun-baked and cotton-haired John Anselmo in the horde of Scottish spectators pressing up against the practice putting green, Woods thought back to his Anselmo years, age ten to seventeen, when the soft-spoken teacher would introduce some fresh technique and say, "You might want to try this, Tiger." To which the student customarily responded, "It's a done deal."

"I didn't know you had come over," Woods said.

"I came over to see if you were going to win the British Open," Anselmo told him.

"It's a done deal," Tiger whispered.

On the side of the draw opposite from Woods, never a good

omen, Ernie Els watched on television as Tiger kicked off the championship with a 5-under-par 67. Then Els went out and shot 66. But the first pressroom question put to Ernie had to do with Tiger, and the tournament leader seemed to despair. "Are we going to go through all this again?" he asked sadly.

And again, and again, and again, and again.

Thomas Bjorn, a dour Dane who eventually would split second place with Els, said, "When Tiger pops up on the leaderboard, everybody else seems to back off. I don't think players like Els, Duval and Montgomerie are so very far behind him, if they only knew it."

Farewell tourist Nicklaus, three-fourths done with his victory lap at the majors, said, "Everybody has thrown up a white flag and surrendered. Right now, I don't think there's anybody contending, and if they don't, the game's really going to suffer. He has to have challengers for the whole thing to be right."

In that sweepstakes, most of the betting action was on David Duval, caretaker of the No. 1 ranking while Tiger's swing was in the shop. Earl agreed, to a point. "He's a psychological study," said the former psychology minor at Kansas State, "and you don't have to be Sigmund Freud to psychoanalyze David."

His talent was eye-popping. In 1999, he eagled the final hole at the Bob Hope Chrysler Classic to shoot 59 and win by a stroke. At Pebble Beach once, he stood at a tee more strokes under par (8) than the number of holes he had played (7). Like Howard Roark, he laughed.

Ayn Rand's iconoclastic architect was Duval's beau ideal. Setting aside how dangerous it is for a twenty-eight-year-old man to be reading *The Fountainhead*, David distinguished himself from most of the industry just by the fact he read books. "Some of the best authors of some of the best books," he said, "leave something to your imagination. Sometimes you have to wait until the last chapter. Sometimes you have to read between the lines." Hiding more than his eyes behind reflective sunglasses, he added, "I don't think people have to know everything about me."

Almost all they needed to know was that, when Duval was nine, his father held him down while he screamed, as marrow was drawn from his hip bone and injected into his twelve-year-old brother, Brent. The transplant was rejected, and Brent died. David said he didn't blame himself, but behind those mirrors was the look of somebody who blamed something and, in all the books he read, just couldn't find the word for what it was. "It's almost like I've had two separate lives," he said. "Maybe I drew inside myself a little more after that. My dad thinks I threw myself more into golf. But I don't know, I was nine. I can't say something changed me, because I don't know what that means. What did it change me from? I only know me as me. I'm me."

Shooting 66 and 67 in the second and third rounds, Tiger held a six-stroke lead over Bjorn and Duval, his playing partner Sunday. Birdie-ing four of the first seven holes, David hacked the margin in half. And it might have been tighter yet. He three-putted the 5th hole for par, first singeing the cup with his eagle try, then missing a two-footer for birdie. "He was four-under on the day; I was one-under," Woods recapped, "and three strokes aren't very many at the Old Course, considering all the trouble lurking out there. But then David hit some good shots that ended up not in the greatest spots. He had to pitch out a couple of times. You need a few lucky bounces to win anywhere, but especially here."

You don't get lucky bounces, Nicklaus always said, for four straight days.

But Tiger wasn't sure he agreed with that. "I hit bad shots every day," he said, "that ended up all right. For instance, I hit a terrible tee shot Friday at ten that landed next to the pot bunker on the right. What did it do? It bounced past it instead of kicking into it, and I had a perfect lie. I made par instead of bogey or double. On thirteen today,

I was trying to draw a three-wood back up against the wind, down the left side, left of the bunkers. I lost it straight right. It came down alongside the last bunker and somehow skirted it again. David flew his ball straight into that bunker. Some of this is just karma, I think."

As well as destiny can be calculated, the statistic of the week, the year and maybe the millennium was the fact that Woods didn't land in any of St. Andrews' 112 bunkers, half of them invisible from either the tee or the fairway. Every group had its own raker assigned. The workman marching after Tiger looked a bit bored.

"Oh, I was in one bunker every day," Tiger said, "the same one. The practice bunker."

Duval spent about fifteen minutes and more than a quarter of a million dollars in the Road Hole bunker at 17. His first two sand shots slapped the steep face and came back to him. The third, a backhanded wedge, just moved his ball away from the beveled wall. The fourth tickled the lip before squirting onto the green. Two putts made eight, a quadruple bogey. "I felt bad," Tiger said. "David had worked so hard all day, and I wanted him at least to finish second." He tied eight others for 11th.

Genuflecting at Granny Clark's Wynd and the Valley of Sin, the last two stations of the cross, Woods putted out for an eight-stroke victory (67-66-67-69—269) and turned immediately to Duval. "I just basically said, you know, he's a true champion. 'It was a lot of fun competing against you,' I said, 'and we'll have numerous battles in the future. But, most important of all, know that you're a true champion. Walk off like a champion. Conduct yourself like one.' And, to his credit, he did."

To Bjorn and especially Els, second in a third-straight major, Tiger shrugged and mugged during the speeches, telling them, "Sorry, but I made some putts." Earl said, "Tiger spoke afterward about all the good breaks he received, all the bad shots he got away with, all the putts that just happened to go in. But to me on the phone he mentioned only one shot, somewhere on the back nine Sunday, a five-iron he drew about two yards into the wind exactly where he was aiming, with absolutely no margin for error. It thrilled him. Absolutely thrilled him. 'Dad,' he said excitedly, 'all of our work was worth it.'"

Flying home together on Tiger's jet, Woods and Duval smeared their fingerprints up and down the sacred names on the silver chalice, from Willie Park in 1860 through Tom Morris Sr. in 1861 and Tom Morris Jr. in 1868 and Jamie Anderson in 1880 and Robert Ferguson in 1890 and John H. Taylor in 1894 and Harry Vardon in 1896 and James Braid in 1905 and Ted Ray in 1912 and Jock Hutchinson in 1921 and Walter Hagen in 1922 and Bobby Jones in 1926 and Tommy Armour in 1931 and Gene Sarazen in 1932 and Henry Cotton in 1934 and Sam Snead in 1946 and Bobby Locke in 1949 and Ben Hogan in 1953 and Peter Thomson in 1954 and Gary Player in 1959 and Arnold Palmer in 1961 and Jack Nicklaus in 1966 and Lee Trevino in 1971 and Tom Watson in 1975 and Johnny Miller in 1976 and Seve Ballesteros in 1979 and Greg Norman in 1986 and Nick Faldo in 1987 to Tiger Woods in 2000.

Golf's career slammers had become a fivesome: Nicklaus (aged twenty-six years, five months, nineteen days), Player (twenty-nine years, seven months, twenty days), Sarazen (thirty-three years, one month, nine days), Hogan (forty years, ten months, twenty-eight days), and Woods, the youngest as usual (twenty-four years, seven months, twenty-four days). Tiger's four majors came just slightly out of sequence: Masters, PGA, U.S. Open, British Open. "Not repeating in any until he had won all four," Earl said, "is just like him, isn't it?"

A year later, at Royal Lytham & St. Annes, England, Tiger handed off the Claret Jug to Duval, who, having finally won his major championship, almost immediately began to sing "Is That All There Is?" and tumbled 880 rungs in the world rankings, nearly to oblivion.

CHAPTER FIFTEEN

Major No. 5, the 2000 PGA

"Jack Nicklaus is a great guy," Earl said. "Yes, he's a nice person.

"He's very dogmatic. Typical Germanic approach to life. Tenacity of a bulldog, and a will to go with it. Knew his strengths. Knew his weaknessees. And he utilized his strengths, maximized them. The mistake he made was that he never corrected his weaknesses. As a result, he grew up—and thrived—as a professional without a great short game. Some say he didn't have even a good one. I don't agree with that. He just didn't have a great one. Unfortunately, he was taught that way. Bang the ball out there, past the Quonset hut, into the Ohio snow. Bang! Bang! Bang! Bang! Bang! I taught Tiger to play the game from the green backward, emphasizing that the most important skill in golf is being able to get the ball up and down.

"Tiger respects Jack completely—why the hell wouldn't he?—and likes him, too, I know. He was the standard, obviously. His marks were the ones Tiger taped up on his bedroom wall. But Jack was never his idol or hero growing up. I realized this when Tiger was ten and the two of us were watching Jack win that sixth Masters at forty-six, the eighteenth major. 'Now it's Seve Ballesteros's and Greg Norman's to lose,' I told Tiger, getting a little caught up in it, 'but the tournament is Jack's to win.' Tiger was just as engrossed as I was, but he wasn't rooting for anyone. I could tell. That day, he was probably the only person watching on TV who was completely neutral."

"The funny thing," Tiger said, "which kind of shows you how my mind works, is that I remember only one shot Jack hit that day. I mean, I've seen a lot of the clips since then, like the birdie putt at seventeen [that was made]. But the one I actually remember was the putt for birdie at eighteen [that was missed]. Up the shelf, left to right. He left it about six inches short, dead in the middle of the hole. Leave it to me to remember one that he missed."

"Everyone talks about Tiger's goal being Jack's eighteen majors," Earl said. "But do you want to know something interesting? I've never once heard him mention it. Around me, he has only ever spoken of one goal. The same one. Over and over. To get better.

"Growing up in Kansas, I never had a sports hero. Logically mine might have been Joe Louis. I knew him, believe it or not. At least, I saw him, talked to him, during the early forties, when he was stationed at Fort Riley. He often came to Yuma Street, to the USO. He generally stayed with neighbors of ours, the Harrisons. Joe liked children. He was good with us kids. We knew how important he was to black people. All of the children were allowed to stay up late for his radio fights. Then there were the glorious celebrations in the street after he'd win. But, as marvelous an athlete, a fighter and a man as Joe was, he was inarticulate. He was uneducated. He couldn't be my hero."

So a man without a sand wedge couldn't be Tiger's?

Earl laughed and said, "All I can tell you is that, whenever Tiger filled out a form or questionnaire, under 'role model in golf' he always wrote 'none.'"

"I don't consider people like Jack Nicklaus as heroes," Tiger said.

"I admire them for their golf. I've tried to pick fifty players and take the best parts of their games and make one super player. But that's just golf. My role model in life is my dad."

According to Earl: "There was a junior player Tiger looked up to for a long, long time, who was sixteen or seventeen, I think [seventeen], when Tiger was ten. This kid was winning every junior championship in Southern California going away. He was the match-play king. His name was Bob May."

Tiger and Jack first met at the Bel-Air Country Club in Los Angeles when, in a mirror image, one was fifteen and the other fifty-one. Famed teacher Eddie Merrins, known as the "Little Pro" at Bel-Air, introduced them. The occasion was a clinic they co-conducted before a Friends of Golf (FOG) tournament, where Jack called the tunes and Tiger demonstrated the draws and fades.

Sometimes it seemed to Nicklaus, in a slightly wearying way, that he had played golf with absolutely everybody in the world when they were children. As Jack had been a teenager when he first shared a tee with Arnold Palmer, Tom Watson was a teenager when he first walked a fairway with Jack. That's the hand-me-down culture of professional golf. Tour pros were forever rushing up to Nicklaus to remind him of their day together way back when. Jack always pretended to remember.

His impression of boy Woods ("Nice-looking golf swing; I didn't think a whole lot about it") was typical. So was Tiger's impression of the Golden Bear. "I couldn't get over," he said, "how small he was." But by the time of the 2000 PGA Championship, when one was twenty-four and the other sixty, they knew each other well.

"It's weird," Tiger said, "but I've had several lunches with him and I've talked with him on the golf course. But we've never once talked about playing golf. You'd think I'd try to pick his brain, wouldn't you?

But I already know what he'd say. I've always felt that if he wants to offer something, he'll say it. I've never been one to press somebody or try to dig something out of anybody. Anyway, it's like Jack and I both know what we both know. There's no need to put words to it. If you aspire to greatness, you have to have a clear picture of greatness. Jack and I have an understanding of each other, just because of the way we play. The passion and the competitive drive we both have—it's inherent. I definitely sense something when I'm around him. We're a lot alike."

By pairing Woods and Nicklaus together for the first two rounds at Valhalla Golf Club in Louisville—for the only time in competition anywhere—the PGA of America effectively sawed the tournament in half: first, Tiger and Jack; then, Tiger and Ben. Having swept the summer Opens by twenty-three strokes, Woods looked more than ready to become the first golfer since Hogan in 1953 to win three majors in a calendar year and in a row. But Bantam Ben hardly got a call on Thursday or Friday.

Woods opened with a 6-under-par 66 to share the lead with Scott Dunlap, two strokes ahead of Darren Clarke and Davis Love III, a full eleven better than Nicklaus. Jack didn't take his usual time over every shot. Something else was on his mind. Six back of the leaders, as no one noticed, was junior-phenom-turned-journeyman-pro Bob May, who had three 66s and three extra holes to go.

Asked to update his opinion of Tiger, Jack said simply, "He's better than I thought he was. He shot just the easiest sixty-six today. Phenomenal control. Phenomenal concentration. Most of his shots were so well within himself that sixty-six was just a piece of cake. He doesn't have to extend himself at all to do what he is doing. Throughout the day, I kept saying, 'I don't understand why we don't have anybody else playing that well.' Now I understand why they aren't. He is that much better."

The day before, in the middle of a practice round, Nicklaus received word that his mother Helen had died at ninety. He started to withdraw from the tournament ("I had no desire to play, I promise you") but changed his mind. "Mom would have said play. My dad passed away thirty years ago. He was always in the forefront. She was always in the background."

During lulls in their game, Jack told Tiger a little bit about Helen. "She was a tough old girl," he said. She attended two Masters in her life, Jack's first in 1959, when his father, Charlie, drove the family from Columbus, pausing at Ohio State to pick up Jack's future wife, Barbara Bash. In 1986, of all years, Helen decided to return. Maybe that's where Jack got his sense of history.

"I know how much you love your father," Nicklaus told Woods as they walked. "Don't forget your mother." Tiger replied, "I never do."

Friday, Tiger shot 67 to take the lead alone, one up on Dunlap (five on May, still not registering on radar screens). Back in rhythm, Nicklaus broke par this time (71) but reached Valhalla's par-5 finishing hole needing an eagle-three to survive the cut. "Walking off the tee at eighteen," Tiger said, "I told him, 'It's been an honor and privilege to play with you, Jack. I've enjoyed it. Let's finish off on a correct note.' And he said, 'You got it. Let's go.'"

After a sound drive and sensible second, Nicklaus had one of those half wedges left that, as Earl was saying, had never been his specialty. Tiger said, "I put myself in a perfect vantage point, pin high. The sun was setting. The gallery was up on its toes, up on an embankment. It was kind of neat just to take it all in, the whole panorama. Jack and I both knew he needed to hole out to make the cut. When he hit it, I didn't watch the shot. I watched *him*, watched him swing. I said, 'That's perfect tempo. That's going to be pretty good.' Then I saw the ball land. 'It's got a chance,' I said. I don't know how it *didn't* go in, to be honest with you. I just thought, *Great fight, Jack. Cool.* Then I remembered my ball was buried in the bunker and I was pissed off again."

Both made birdies. "Years from now," Tiger said, "that's what I'll remember."

Bob May was not from a golfing family. His parents, Jerry and Muriel, owned a gas station in La Habra, California, about twelve miles from Cypress. An aunt bought little Bobby a single golf club. A few years went by before he had two. When May's quality began to show, his parents made the usual sacrifices. Every Sunday at 5:30, Jerry May rose to drive his son to Bel-Air for a 7 A.M. lesson with the Little Pro.

It seemed to Bob that the first time he ever saw Tiger and Earl was on television. *"The Mike Douglas Show,* I guess," he said. He first spotted Tiger in person at the Los Alamitos Country Club, contending in an age group drive-chip-and-putt contest. Mostly May followed Woods in the newspapers when Bob was an All-American at Oklahoma State University and Tiger was chainsawing a jagged swath through all of his junior glories.

Reading that the sixteen-year-old Woods had been handed a sponsor's exemption to play in the L.A. Open (exactly like Joe Louis many years before), twenty-three-year-old May telephoned *The Orange County Register* to register a complaint, or at least to make a point. He had *qualified* for the L.A. Open at sixteen. Bob May, not Tiger Woods, was the youngest golfer ever to *play* his way into a PGA Tour event.

Never growing beyond junior stature, five-foot-seven, May earned his PGA card the hardest way, via the Triple-A Nike Tour, then lost it the surest way, missing twenty-four of thirty-one cuts. Wandering in the wildernesses of Geneva, Gibraltar and Japan for four winless seasons (posting twenty-two second-place finishes along the way), he finally broke through at the 1999 Victor Chandler British Masters, a big tournament in Europe, overtaking playing partners Colin Montgomerie and Eduardo Romero the last day. That bought him another chance in America, which he was discreetly making the most of (23rd in the U.S. Open, tied with Duval for 11th in the British) when his second 66 at the PGA put him in Sunday's final twosome a stroke behind Woods.

"There was a time," Tiger said before they teed off, "when I dreamed of winning as many golf tournaments as Bob May did."

"On the front nine," May said, "we chatted quite a bit, just catching up on Southern California days. 'Yeah, I remember so-and-so. Do you remember such-and-such?' That kind of stuff." May couldn't get over the sound and sweep of Woods's gallery. "'Is this what you draw every week?' I asked him. 'You got it,' he said [dismally]. The way Tiger deals with what he has to deal with is really something when you think about it. I can go out to the sand dunes where I like to hang out with my off-road car, and nobody has any idea who I am. He can't even go to the mall."

On the back nine, the light conversation stopped. "It was business time," May said. By then, they were tied. Bob's fourth birdie in five holes gave him a one-stroke lead going to 15, where Tiger overshot the green to a stubbly swale and, using a putter, hammered the next one fifteen feet past the cup. Meanwhile, Bob had hit an inspired 7-iron to six feet. If Tiger missed and he made, his advantage would be three shots with three holes to play. Of course the opposite happened.

"You know what?" May said. "I hit that putt right where I wanted to. It just didn't break. Later, looking at the taped replay, I saw Olazabal had the exact same putt. His dove right. Mine stayed out on the high side. A bad putt would have missed on the low side. It's hard to explain to people how there are some misses in golf that you never regret. I've never regretted that putt."

He saved a stout par to match Tiger at 16, but a huge drive by Woods followed by a lob-wedge to four feet tied them at 17. After both reached the par-5 18th in two (in May's case, a testament to adrenaline), Bob ran his seventy-footer at least fifteen feet by the hole while Tiger's fifty-foot eagle attempt left him a birdie putt of 7.

"Mine was one of those concentrate-on-the-line, speed-will-take-care-of-itself putts," May said. "I played it outside-left. As it started to break across the hole, I thought, *It's not enough. You've left it short.* But it kept rolling and rolling. It seemed to be moving slowly—in fact it was screaming-fast—and every little dent in the green, every old corner of a footprint, altered its track, until the ball caught the right side of the hole and fell in."

So Woods had a seven-footer to tie or lose. If he missed, May would be a major champion. Obviously he didn't. "Not by any means was his an easy putt," Bob said. "It didn't have to go in, you know. That's the first time all day I looked at the scoreboard. I saw that we were five shots clear of everyone else. That's also the first time I heard of the three-hole aggregate playoff. That caught me completely off guard. I thought it was sudden death. In fact, I had kind of geared myself up for sudden death at eighteen. I figured he'd go for the green in two for sure, and maybe that would be good for me. Instead we went to sixteen. It shouldn't have mattered at all, but hearing the play-off was three holes took me out of my game plan, threw my one-shot-at-a-time mentality right out the window."

Tiger birdied the first extra hole from twenty feet, quick-stepping to the cup to scoop out his ball, and that pretty much was that. It was Woods's third birdie in a row, making him 8-under-par for the last fifteen holes. Driving adventures involving portable toilets and cart paths couldn't stop Tiger from parring in. May was beaten by a stroke.

"The moral, I guess," he said, "is that, when you're up against the greatest player in the world, and you're spotting him more than twenty yards on every drive [305.0 to 283.9, to be precise], maybe you better not give him a one-shot lead going into the day."

Many of the news accounts likened Woods's rally to his comeback over Steve Scott in the thirty-eight-hole final of the third U.S. Amateur.

But neither Tiger nor Earl saw it that way. "Tiger will tell you," Earl said, "that Scott played really good in the morning round and just good in the afternoon, while Tiger played terrible in the morning and great in the afternoon. Here, he and May were playing at the absolute highest level at the exact same time."

Tiger said, "This was different. This was special. Both of us shot thirty-one on the back nine with no bogeys. That's not too bad."

"What he won't tell you," Earl said, "is that the closest competition is his favorite thing by far. When he wins the U.S. Open by fifteen, he'll smile and say he wished it was twenty. When he wins the British Open by eight, he'll say he would have preferred twelve. But the truth is, Tiger loves to do battle even more than he loves running away, and he dearly loves running away. To be challenged, though, that's what he lives for."

Returning to the shadows, May had his moments in the summers that followed, but no triumphs. He was 29th on the money list in 2000, 94th in 2001, 138th in 2002, 193rd in 2003. While finishing up a shiny 64 at Byron Nelson's Texas tournament in 2003, he came to an unexpected stop. "When I walked off the eighteenth tee, I was fine," he said, "but when I went to swing in the fairway, my back hurt." He didn't play in another event for three years.

"It was a mystery. I could jump up and down. I could run. But I couldn't do anything rotational. It was like the only thing taken away from me was golf. I could do anything but play golf."

A dizzying stream of MRIs, CAT scans, EMGs and discograms failed to nail down a diagnosis. After eight months' total abstinence, he tried to swing again. The pain was overwhelming; it started at the base of his spine and radiated through his groin. "When the surgeon finally opened me up, he found it was ten times worse than any of the X-rays showed. My spinal nerve canal was twice as small as the normal man's spinal nerve canal." During ten days' bed rest—from the bed to the shower and back to the bed again—he steeled himself for what he knew was going to be a siege.

In December of 2005, on the strength of just nine holes' practice over thirty-two months, May started his career all over again at the PGA Tour Qualifying School. The first round represented the first eighteen holes he had walked since the original flash of pain. He won his card. At Verona, New York, in 2006, he shot 64 on Sunday to finish 2nd by a stroke in the B.C. Open, a tournament played opposite the British Open (won by Tiger). But by 2010, as May turned forty, he was back in Triple-A on what was now called the Nationwide Tour.

"What keeps me going," he said, "is I love the game. I love it for the same reason I always have, for the challenge it gives you. You can hate golf when you're not playing well, but when it's almost taken away from you, you can never hate it again."

That Sunday with Tiger in Louisville, May had no sense or sensation of lasting significance. "After they signed off the telecast," he said, "Jim Nantz and Ken Venturi came up to me excitedly, calling it one of the greatest days in the history of golf. I'm like, 'C'mon guys.' 'Oh yeah!' they told me. 'You don't understand!' 'I guess not,' I said."

But he came to understand.

Tiger's successful defense at the 2000 PGA Championship, a feat last accomplished by Denny Shute in the match-play days of 1936 and 1937, gave him the seventy-two-hole record to par in all four majors. But only the Masters, U.S. Open and British Open marks were Tiger's alone. Eighteen-under at the PGA, he shared with Bob May, maybe forever.

CHAPTER SIXTEEN

Major No. 6, the 2001 Masters

Earl lived, and pressed Tiger to live, by something he called The Now Principle. "By definition," he said archly, "time is a linear measurement to infinity of successive increments of now. So, wherever you go on that line, it's now. There are no yesterdays. There are no tomorrows. There's only now. You have one shot at every single day, just like a golf shot in a tournament. You'll never get another swing at it. So, you have to maximize the experience. It'll be one o'clock in the morning some time, and I'll say to myself, 'I'm enjoying this day too much to let it end.' So I'll stay up till three or four o'clock just because I know I'll never see a day like this again."

When Tiger was a young boy, he would sometimes stay up, too, just to keep his father company in this curious attempt at holding on to a good day. "I hope it isn't the reason," Earl said, "that Tiger can only sleep a few hours a night now." They discussed many issues, like athletes' obligations. "I don't know that great athletes have a responsibility to be role models," Earl said, "but the fact is, they are. And I can remember telling Tiger this, in the middle of the night. 'You're going to be one,' I said. 'Now, if you don't care, that's on you. That's your choice. That's what you think of yourself.' 'No, Daddy,' he said, 'I want to be a role model.'

"At one of our clinics—in New York, it was—we entered the field as we always did, with all our carts and fanfare, and the dust flying, and the kids screaming. Tiger just stood there at the microphone and waited. The kids got the message and quieted down. And he waited some more. You know how silence can take on a sound? Finally, slowly, he began to talk. 'Today,' he said, 'I'm going to speak to you from my heart.' I'd never heard him say that before. I've never heard him say it since. 'This is just for the kids here,' he said. About three thousand kids were there with their parents. 'You've selected me as your role model,' Tiger told them, 'and I accept the position. I'll do the best I can. But I ask you to remember something. I'm not perfect.'

"'OK, parents,' I said when my turn came, 'if it's good enough for the goose, it's good enough for the gander. You heard Tiger challenge himself to be a role model and challenge your kids to follow him. Now I challenge you to be role models, too.' Ever since that day, when we're giving our speeches, I always go first. Don't mess with me. I'm not about to follow that."

Another regular theme of those late-night talks was honesty.

"Actually, dishonesty," Earl said. "I told him lying is stealing, and cheating is stealing from yourself. Cheating on a golf course is the worst cheating of all, because you're not only taking something for nothing, you're throwing away the best part of who you are. You can never go back. From day one, I told Tiger, 'If you're in tune with truth, your life works. When you're not in tune with truth, that's when you get into trouble.' Love of self comes only with truth. I expect that this knowledge will see Tiger through the hard time, when I'm gone. At his age now, you're bulletproof. I thought so too once, but I have reason to know otherwise now. My heart attacks took care of that. When some variation of my experience comes along for Tiger, I hope I've prepared him for it."

W hat to call a grand slam was always a question. In 1930, at the age of twenty-eight, Bobby Jones won the U.S. Open and Amateur and the British Open and Amateur; then, with nothing left to win and nobody left to beat, withdrew from formal competition forever. Some of the newspapermen in their fedoras and cups liked the sound of "Impregnable Quadrilateral." Tiger, describing the pro equivalent, preferred the unvarnished term: "Grand Slam." "Calendar year or not," he said, "if you've got all four trophies sitting on your mantel, to me, that's a Grand Slam."

Jack Nicklaus tended to agree, but Earl, surprisingly, did not.

"I don't think what you call it is important," Nicklaus said. "If he does it, it will be the most amazing feat in the history of golf, that's all. He'll have done something that may never be done again. If he lines up all of those trophies on one table, it'll be better than anything I've ever seen."

Earl said, "You have to do it in a calendar year for it to be a real slam. I'm old school. In all sports, records should be kept on an annual basis. But if Tiger can win four in a row, he can win four in the same year. That's somewhere up ahead. It's just a matter of time and timing. You have to leave a few things for somewhere up ahead."

Already Tiger was being measured against 2000, even by himself. "My bad shots this year have been worse than they were last year," he acknowledged, "but my good ones have been really good. It comes in spurts. I'll play four, five, nine, twelve holes like I did in two thousand. Then there'll be a few off-holes. It's not quite there, but it's good enough.

"I think I played too much at the end of the year. Eight consecutive weeks, traveling more than twenty-seven thousand miles to four different continents. That took a toll on my body. When I came back out, I didn't feel appreciative enough about being there. I hadn't taken enough of a break. Unfortunately I wasn't as energetic as I should have been. That's not saying I wasn't trying. I was really trying to play. But when your energy level isn't quite what it should be, sometimes it's a little more difficult. That's one of the lessons I've learned, but the problem is, I had a lot of defending to do at the end of last year. It was kind of a catch-twenty-two. I'm fresher now, working on shaping the ball a little more. That's been fun."

If expectations kept growing, wouldn't he inevitably reach a crushing point? Woods was twenty-four years old but he had been conducting mock press conferences since he was a toddler. So, how old was he now really?

"Expectations are personal," Tiger said. "If I tried to live off other people's expectations, I don't think I'd be a very happy guy. My own expectations are high enough. Win or lose Sunday night, I guarantee you one thing. The sun will come up Monday. It's not life or death. I just enjoy competing. Take it as that."

On the first hole of the tournament, trying to hit what he called "a little bleeder," Tiger overcut his drive and had to punch out with a 2-iron from some newly planted trees. He aimed for a bunker and hoped for the upslope, eventually making a bogey. Of all the great golfers in history, Woods may be the worst man at transporting his game from the range to the first tee. "I knew right away," he said, "this was going to be a blue-collar day."

Just like in 1997, Tiger started with a 2-under-par 70, but this time he was five strokes and twelve players behind.

Friday was better. "Even though I three-putted twice," he said, "would you say I made my share of putts today?" Evidently. He shot 66 to join Phil Mickelson in second place, two strokes behind Chris DiMarco. Soon David Duval and Ernie Els would come to the top as well. A nice tournament was shaping up.

Nearly finished a third-round 68, Woods and caddie Steve Williams were stalled in the 17th fairway, gathering wool. "You guys know Stevie," Tiger said in the pressroom. "He's a pretty mellow guy, right? [What?] Backed up in the fairway, we're just standing there. It's quiet. All of a sudden he says to me, 'You know something, this is my sixteenth Masters [including tours with Raymond Floyd and Greg Norman] and I've made the cut in every single one.'"

"Oh, really?" Tiger told him. "How many green jackets do you have?"

That shut Williams up.

But in a softer voice, Tiger said, "Don't worry, Stevie. We'll get you one tomorrow."

Sunday morning. "Michael Jordan, Magic Johnson, Larry Bird, Abdul-Jabbar," Tida said under the clubhouse oak. "The bigger the moment, the better they are. My Tiger, best of all." Just then, her Tiger burst from the locker room. "Good luck, Tiger!" she called out from under her red bonnet. He didn't seem to hear her.

Three months before his British breakthrough, Duval would put up the strongest challenge. Standing on the 11th tee, the gate to Amen Corner, David was 5-under-par for the day and 14-under for the tournament. A little later, on that same spot, Tiger would also be 14-under. Mickelson, alongside Woods, would be 13-under. But only Tiger birdied 11, and neither Duval nor Mickelson could make a par 3 at 16. Phil lost by three, David by two.

A five-foot birdie putt Duval missed at 18 might have mattered. From behind, Tiger said he listened for the result. Listening was an Augusta tradition.

By the time Nicklaus notched that last major at Augusta, 1986, he had lost the horizon. It would be an exaggeration to say that son/caddie Jackie had to lead the old man around the National like a blind ward, but only a slight one. Color-blind to begin with, Nicklaus kept asking Jackie, "Did it stay on the green?" But his hearing was still good. "I heard a funny sound behind us," Jack said later that day. "It wasn't the sound of a cheer exactly. But it *was*." He told his son, "Seve is in the water at fifteen."

OK, Tiger thought, *David didn't make birdie up ahead.* [No roar.] *You've got a one-shot lead. Here's your last drive. There's the fairway. Trust it now, Woody.* He finished with a birdie.

"There isn't a leaderboard on every hole," Tiger said in the interview room, "so you have to wait a couple of holes to see exactly what's going on. But I've been here enough years now to be able to decipher generally what's happening by the roars around me, or the lack of them. You know what they are. You know who they are. It's neat. For instance, on seventeen, I hit my tee shot down the left side and, being blocked out by the tree, I had to aim right. It rolled off the green. Walking to my ball, I heard a roar. *David's stuffed it at eighteen,* I thought. When I didn't hear anything after my chip—and I was waiting for Phil to putt before I could putt—I said to myself, *Well, David missed it.*"

After making his own last putt at 18, Tiger said, "I walked over to the side of the green and I—I kept thinking—I was in such a zone today, working on, you know, every shot, working so hard on every shot. I just started thinking, 'You don't have any more shots to play. You're done.' When you're focused so hard on each and every shot, you kind of forget everything else. Looking up and realizing you have no shots left takes you a little by surprise. It's weird. You're finished. I started losing it a little bit, thinking about some of the tough shots I had hit, some of the big putts I had made, and, I don't know, all of these different images came through my head real quick: the leaderboard, thinking of David, watching Phil, hearing the roars. Everything played back in my head at that moment, at full speed. That's why I pulled the cap over my face, to get it together. So that, when Phil putted out, I was able to shake his hand."

This was different from '97, when, as Tiger said, "I hadn't been a pro a full year yet. I guess I was a little young, a little naïve, and didn't fully understand what I accomplished. This year, I understand. I've been around the block. I've witnessed a lot of things since that first year. I have a better appreciation of winning a major championship. To win four of them in succession is just—it's hard to believe, really. You have to have your game peak at the right time. That's the first part. Then you have to have some luck. You have to get some good breaks, and you just have to have everything kind of go right. To have it happen four straight times, some of the golfing gods must be looking down on me the right way."

Where were the four trophies going?

"On my coffee table," he said. "Haven't you been paying attention?"

Three of the four courses in 2000 were classics. The fourth, Valhalla, was selected for free rent. The PGA of America owned the property.

Tiger said, "Pebble Beach is probably the greatest golf course we have over here, and St. Andrews is probably the greatest golf course in the world. Valhalla is a benign course, but to win the way I did there, making birdie after birdie after birdie, that was tough enough. And then to do it back here, at one of the most historic places in all the world—well, it's perfect."

Near the end of his news conference, he decided to ask a question of his own. "Am I young or old?" he wondered.

Seasoned, he was told.

"Seasoned, but not grizzled yet, right?"

Not yet.

"Good."

CHAPTER SEVENTEEN

Major No. 7, the 2002 Masters

"This is a Masters of change," Earl said, sitting at an umbrella table with his back to the practice putting green. He motioned toward the first tee far off to his left. "Starting right there," he said.

The opening hole was one of nine that had been stretched significantly for 2002 (not exactly like Frankensteins, more like pituitary cases) in an obvious reaction to Tiger. "Tiger-proofing," some called it. On Thursday, forty-eight players would pass through number one before the first birdie was recorded. On Sunday, Woods, Ernie Els and Phil Mickelson would be snared one after another in the same fairway bunker they all used to carry routinely.

"We recognized that we had to make some changes to some of the par fours," said Augusta National Chairman Hootie Johnson. "We had to strengthen them. [Architect] Tom Fazio and I were down on eleven last year, and we saw Phil Mickelson's drive come down there. We thought somebody had chipped out of the woods! After he hit his next shot, I went under the rope to measure it, and Phil was ninety-four yards from the green. I told Tom, 'Heck, man, no question about it, we have to be more aggressive here.' Take eighteen, for another example. A three-wood and a pitching wedge just won't do for a finishing hole. What would Mister Roberts say?"

He wasn't referring to Henry Fonda; rather, to Clifford Roberts, the original "massa" of the plantation, who called every Masters shot from 1934 to 1977, including the final one. With his pajamas sticking out from underneath his trouser legs and his bedroom slippers on the wrong feet, Roberts walked out to Ike's Pond in the middle of the night and put a bullet in his brain.

In 1974, a year away from Lee Elder's breakthrough, Mr. Cliff brought up the subject of "our dark-complected friends" before anyone else could.

"One of our former caddies, Jim Dent," Roberts said, "is hitting the ball so far that Jack Nicklaus told me he's out-driving him by twenty to sixty yards. And I'm told Jim has been improving his short game, too. He might soon win a tournament and be eligible to play here. If he does, you'll find a lot of people around here very happy about it."

Technically, Dent never caddied in the tournament, but one year he did wave a fairway flag. Asked if he remembered Jim, Roberts replied, "very indistinctly," but guessed he would recognize him if he saw him. Jim stood six-foot-two and weighed 230 pounds.

"He's got a brother who was a caddie here," Roberts said, "a cousin who was a caddie, and another cousin who's a maître d' here still."

Dave Anderson of *The New York Times* requested, "The maître d's first name, please?"

After rocking between committeemen on his left and right, Mr. Roberts straightened up and said sweetly:

"We just call him 'Dent.'"

"I think the committee did Billy Casper, Gay Brewer and Doug Ford a favor," said Earl, referring to three former champions whose "lifetime exemptions" had run out. They were reminded of their mortality by letter. (Brewer took particular umbrage, boycotting the Champions Dinner.) "Come Friday afternoon," Earl said, "Arnold Palmer will envy them."

Palmer may not have waited that long. Thursday, finding his ball in a tangle of pine straw at 15, the seventy-two-year-old four-time champion said jokingly, "With all of my friends out here, how can I have such a bad lie?" A regretful voice in the ranks, speaking for the entire division, said, "You should have seen it before."

"Arnie's Army" was formed at Augusta in 1958, the year Palmer won his first green jacket in the fourth of what would be fifty consecutive starts at the Masters. Tiger couldn't break that record before 2045. The military reference was inspired by soldiers in khaki from nearby Fort Gordon who tended the scoreboards and cheered for Arnold. "Hell, I know everybody in the gallery by their first names," he said after signing for his 17-over-par 89. "I'm kidding a little, but not too much. I could probably tell you the first names of thousands of them."

Among all golfers, only Palmer had the ability to make eye contact with the entire world. But, when he couldn't reach the 18th green with his two best hits, some old campaigners averted their eyes. Of course, after he got up and down to avoid 90, they reenlisted.

"I think this is my last Masters," Arnold told the reporters. It was his second from last. "I don't want to get a letter." Leaving the press center with his head down, he felt a muscular arm loop around his waist and looked up to see Tiger embracing him. "How did you do?" Palmer whispered. But Woods didn't say 70, or anything at all. He just held on.

As Tiger stepped up to the microphone, he was asked if he could see himself playing in the Masters at seventy-two. "At seventy-two," he said, "I just hope I'm on this side of the grass."

Hard rain from Wednesday through Saturday morning combined with the new distances to eliminate all but the longest hitters, like first-round leaders Davis Love III (67), Angel Cabrera (68) and Sergio Garcia (68). Tiger's 70 gave him a piece of seventh place. In the second round, bombers Vijay Singh (70, 65), Retief Goosen (69, 67) and Els (70, 67) moved to the top of the board while Woods bided his time two strokes back. But measuring by rounds was misleading. By days was clearer.

Tiger's Friday was a squall-shortened ten-hole affair. His twenty-six-hole Saturday settled everything.

"He was up before dawn on Saturday," Earl said. "He's always up before dawn at Augusta, not just when he has to resume playing at seven-thirty. He was up and out in what seemed to be the middle of the night on that first Sunday in ninety-seven, too. I don't know whether he's walking or he's running or he's thinking or he's talking, or where the hell he goes. But he always leaves nervous and comes back relaxed."

As he teed off on the 11th hole at 7:30, Tiger was six strokes behind Singh, who had finished his second round early and could sleep in. In what amounted to a marathon mud ball battle—with no lifting, cleaning or placing allowed—Woods read the clumps and smears better than the others. While Mickelson in particular was howling with frustration, Tiger shrugged off a few knuckleballs to negotiate his twenty-six holes in 8-under-par. Meanwhile, Vijay awoke to misjudge a caked ball spectacularly at 15. Zigzagging like a Frisbee, it flew the green and one-hopped into the backwater. Suddenly he was two behind Tiger and coleader Goosen, and two ahead of Els, Garcia and

Mickelson. All of Woods's regular foils were lining up practically by their world rankings.

They fell in sections. Els, starting birdie-birdie Sunday, finally a dry day, improved by a third stroke to 10-under-par to get within two of what would be the winning number. But then he made the traditional miscalculation at nine, sometimes referred to as "pulling a Greg Norman," sucking a short approach shot back off the green for a bogey. From then on, Ernie felt obligated to overreach.

"Tiger wasn't doing much, playing percentage golf," he said, which was probably how all of them were thinking. "I figured he wasn't going to shoot lights out, but I had to."

At 13, the first par 5 on the back, a hooked drive left Els a choice between a chip-out to a 6-iron third shot or going through a small window that held out at least the possibility of a sand wedge approach. Caddie Ricci Roberts begged his man to come out sideways, but Ernie couldn't make an eagle that way and probably wouldn't even get a birdie. Two water balls later, he had a triple-bogey 8. Tramping up 18, Els told Ricci, "You were right, man. I should have listened." To the writers, Ernie went even further with his trademark honesty. "I don't know what it is about professional golfers," he said, "but sometimes we think we're better than we are."

Vijay outdid Els's 8 with a 9 at 15, where he was long on Saturday and short (twice) on Sunday. "I wasn't thinking about Tiger," he insisted. "I was just trying to play my own game."

Beginning bogey-par-birdie-bogey-birdie-bogey, Sergio said, "Look at my card. That's the picture of what trying to force something looks like." Mickelson, who had followed his two-birdie start with two of the clumsiest bogeys, spoke peculiarly afterward of "how very lucky" he felt to be able to "play this game for a living." Goosen, who went out in 39 but came back for second place, said something even stranger. "The way I was swinging this week," he said, "didn't allow me any chances for birdies." With twenty-one of them, he led the field in birdies.

As a young player, Retief had been struck by lightning on a golf course. It had knocked him out of his shoes and burned his clothes off. According to friends, Retief went to sleep as an overbearing loud-mouth and woke up as Chance The Gardener.

Tiger's calm 71 gave him a 276 total and a three-stroke victory over the fourth (Goosen, 279), second (Mickelson, 280), fourteenth (Jose Maria Olazabal, 281), third (Els, 282), ninth (Padraig Harrington, 282), seventh (Singh, 283) and fifth (Garcia, 284) players in the world. "All those guys were right there behind me," he said. "When you beat a field like that, it's satisfying."

That made three Masters in the last six, six majors in the last ten, twenty-three conversions for twenty-five fifty-four-hole leads, seven for seven when carrying a lead into a major Sunday. And with seven grand slam titles, he joined Harry Vardon, Bobby Jones, Gene Sarazen, Sam Snead and Arnold Palmer on the list of saints. Tiger was twenty-six years old.

"He's learned to scale it back," Butch Harmon said. "He'll par you to death in these things, if that's the smart play. Everything Tiger does is based on Nicklaus. Nicklaus would wait for you to make a mistake, too. When Tiger was first starting out, he made what I call young decisions. Not bad decisions, just young decisions. Since then, he has learned how to play golf. He knows when to be aggressive and when to scale back. Majors are usually won by scaling back."

"This was a Jack Nicklaus kind of win all right," Earl said.

Asked to compare the Augusta National layout of 2002 to the one he first played in 1959, Nicklaus said, "Well, it's green."

Edged on the driving chart by both Mickelson and Els, Woods placed sixth in distance (293.8). But the leader, John Daly (297.8), finished thirty-second in the tournament. "I'm not that long anymore," Tiger said with a smile. "I just kind of dink it around. Seriously, there are a lot of college and high school players out there who can hit it as far as I can, or farther." He was just twenty-second in fairways hit, twenty-first in putting (Els was first). Almost none of the statistics said three-stroke victory, though Tiger was number one with 54 greens in regulation, compared to Ernie's 39.

"The more he wins," Earl said, "the easier it becomes for him. They are the trees. He is the forest fire. They don't have anything to stop him."

CHAPTER EIGHTEEN

Major No. 8, the 2002 U.S. Open

Earl's granddaughter, Tiger's niece, was a prospect. In 2002, she was twelve. Earl traveled to Phoenix to install the old fundamentals, and she came to Cypress for finishing school. "I did it once," Earl said, "and I can do it again. I'm Shawnee, twenty-five percent, but she's Cheyenne." After laughing at that awful joke, he turned serious. "Cheyenne has everything that Tiger had," he said, "and I mean everything. She's skilled, she's fast, she's athletic, she's intelligent, she's personable, she's gorgeous and she's competitive as hell."

By the end of the decade, she would be a scholarship golfer at Wake Forest University, leading the team in stroke average. Though she grew up in Arizona, home of the most logical golf schools, she elected Winston-Salem, North Carolina, for a reason that described her. Of all the campuses she visited, Wake's was the smallest one that had world-class athletes. She didn't want to attend a college so huge that the football team had its own closed dormitory. She wanted to live and eat and talk and grow in the company of great players.

In a closet-size room off Wake's golf offices, Cheyenne was waiting, and Earl was certainly right about one thing. She was gorgeous.

"Do you putt to the picture?" I asked her right away.

"Of course," she said.

"You know, Hank Haney thinks that's genius."

"I think so, too."

On the team Web site, she was described as a four-time letterman and three-time MVP at Xavier College Prep in Phoenix, the winner of back-to-back Arizona State Championships among some thirty amateur titles. She was named high school golfer of the year by *The Arizona Republic*. "The daughter of Earl Woods Jr. and Susan Woods," it said. Under the heading "Getting to Know Cheyenne," here were some of the entries:

What I love most about the game of golf is . . .
   "Being able to travel and see different courses."

I wish I were better at . . .
   "Singing!"

Describe your style of play in one word . . .
   "Steady."

Favorite athlete to watch in another sport . . .
   "LeBron James."

Person who most influenced your golf game . . .
   "My mom because she was my chauffeur every day for golf lessons and junior events."

If I could bring something with me from my hometown, it would be . . .
  "The weather!!! Or my dog."

The best golfer you have ever played with . . .
  "Charles Barkley."

Your pre-round superstitions or habits . . .
  "I always have to listen to a good song before I tee off or else I feel like I will play bad."

One thing you couldn't imagine living without . . .
  "Music."

Favorite golfer . . .
  "Lorena Ochoa."

Favorite course you've played . . .
  "The Castle Course in St. Andrews, Scotland."

Favorite pre-round meal . . .
  "My dad's spaghetti."

Favorite song to sing in the shower . . .
  "So Fresh, So Clean—Outkast."

Favorite Wake Forest athlete . . .
  "Tim Duncan."

No mention of Tiger Woods.
"It was in there at first," she said, "but I asked them to take it out.

Nothing against him. He's been very nice to me. It's just, you see, I don't want to be Tiger Woods's niece."

They played golf together only twice. "Once with Barkley and those guys," she said. "The other time, just Tiger, Elin and me. When I fluffed a chip, we stopped for a while and practiced chipping. He was very generous. It was fun."

Her ambition was to be an LPGA pro, but she wasn't in a rush to get there. She was a sophomore and liked being that. On her list of attributes, Earl should have included wise.

"I've got a daughter," Den said, "and, being divorced from her mother, I know I haven't done everything right by her. But I've tried. We talked last night. We cried last night. We laughed, too. 'You are my daughter,' I told her, 'and I want you to know we'll always be together.' Purposely I've stayed away from her golf. When she was a little girl, there was a bunch of little girls, their mothers and me. I backed off.

"Above all I want Cheyenne to have a balanced life. I want her to have another side besides golf. So I decided that I would represent the other side. Ever since she was young, we fished together. She loved digging for worms, even after a while hooking up her own worms. About a month ago she sent me a text. 'Guess what, Daddy. The golf team is in Georgia. And do you know what we're doing right now? We're fishing.' She told me how she was the only one baiting the hooks, the only one taking the fish off the lines. Without saying the words, what she was really telling me was, 'I got this from you, Dad. Thanks.' I didn't give her a driver, but I gave her this. She's such an amazing daughter.

"Wake Forest was strictly her decision, by the way. Her mom and I were worried about it. Cheyenne doesn't have a lot of world experience, and of course we wanted her to be safe. ASU and USC were closer to home. I have to say, we were rooting for them. But her opinion was the only one that mattered. I think I had something to do with that, too. After the divorce, when she'd come to visit me, I'd ask, 'What do you want to do today?' 'I don't know,' she'd say. 'What do you want for dinner tonight?' 'I don't know.' I finally told her, 'Your opinion matters, baby. Don't ever forget that.' She gets it now."

About the only golf advice Den ever gave Cheyenne could have been channeled from Tida.

"Go out there," he told his daughter, "and make those little girls cry. Make them cry."

Favorite course you would like to play but haven't . . .

"Bethpage Black."

Instead of hello, the voice on the other end of the line said just, "Stud."

"Hey, Earl. Are you in New York?"

"No, I'm home. I wanted to tell you something."

"Shoot."

"The harder it is," he said, "the better it is, for the better players." Then he hung up.

The Black Course at Long Island's Bethpage State Park was going to be hard all right. It was the first publicly owned facility to host a United States Open Championship, and the tweedy men of the USGA with their shooting sticks, rugged pipes and dandruff were in an especially punitive mood. They might have felt they owed something to the municipal golfers who queued up all night in their pajamas and cars to pay $31.00 to take on the Black. Not that any of these sleepy dreamers could have finished eighteen holes in the conditions awaiting the professionals in 2002. "If the wind really blows," Jesper Parnevik said, "none of us will finish either."

On a chilled, wet Friday, half the field was unable to carry the trouble at 10, just to reach the fairway. One hundred and forty-four of the 155 contestants missed the 7th green (489-yard, par 4) in regulation. The other eleven missed the putt.

A few pros were bitter but most were philosophical. At least most of the big hitters were. Davis Love III said, "I've heard more people this week in the gallery asking, 'How are you liking my golf course?' I love that. Country club people don't say that, not the same way. These people think the course belongs to them, because it does."

So it became "The People's Open."

And Tiger started off with a 3-under-par 67.

"I think it's special to be holding our country's national championship on a muny," Tiger said a couple of days before the tournament began. "That's how some of us grew up. I've fished a few balls out of the water in my time. I hawked more than my share of public courses searching for X'ed out specials. This is pretty cool. I'm psyched. If Carnoustie is the hardest par seventy-one we play, I have to think Bethpage Black is the hardest seventy. I'm probably not hitting the ball quite as close as I was in two thousand. I was flagging a lot of shots then. But I feel every other facet of my game is pretty close to that. It's just, instead of having a lot of eight- and ten-footers, I'm drawing a lot of fifteen- and twenty-footers. When I'm not feeling completely comfortable over the shaft, I'll often bail to the center of the greens and just give myself a putt at it. Two thousand was different, as you probably remember."

One stroke back after the first round was Sergio Garcia, who, in a nervous affliction that would turn out to be temporary had taken to gripping and re-gripping his club before every shot, milking the handle as many as 17, 18, 22, 27, even 30 times. This fidgety spectacle brought to mind sewer worker Ed Norton teaching bus driver Ralph Kramden how to address the ball.

Inevitably Garcia's New York gallery began counting along. *Fourteen, fifteen, sixteen . . .*, like a circus crowd egging on an aerialist. And the sprawling Bethpage property had enough space for fifty thousand spectators a day, twice the capacity of Pebble Beach or Shinnecock Hills. At the People's Open, the largest section of the herd came by rail from Manhattan—in the Club Car.

"Even if I don't win," Sergio said, "I'll be leaving with a lot of new nicknames." Such as "Waaaaa," "El Grumpo" and "While We're Young." But the winning entry seemed to be "Wagglepuss." Shooting 74 in the worst of Friday's rainstorm, Wagglepuss compounded his misery by charging afterward, "If Tiger had been out there, it would have been called off." The next day, New York really let him have it.

Meanwhile, with a second-round 68, Woods upped his advantage to three strokes over Padraig Harrington. The highlight so far, Tiger said, was the ovation he received as he emerged from a portable toilet. "Are you guys clapping because I'm potty-trained?" he asked. "I've made it this far, haven't I? You'd think I'd know how to go."

Earl said, "People who have no idea what they're talking about say Tiger's problem with Sergio goes back to the Battle at Bighorn, when Sergio celebrated too much." Earl was referring to a made-for-television match in 2000 won by Garcia under the lights. "That isn't the reason Tiger dislikes him," Earl said. "In the clubhouse once, he saw Sergio looking up at a TV monitor and rooting somebody's golf ball out of the hole. That's why Tiger has no use for Sergio."

If he wasn't quite as wet as Garcia, Tiger spent his own time in the rain and professed to enjoy it. "When he was a little boy," Earl said, "Tiger had only one problem in the rain—talking his mother into letting him go out in it. In Southern California, you had to take whatever rain you could get when you got it. As soon as the sky opened, Tiger would grab his clubs and run. He was the only kid in the world who broke out into a grin anytime the weatherman said 'possible Santa Ana winds.'"

Saturday, shooting even-par, Woods lifted his lead to four strokes, over Sergio again. "Today was a long day," Tiger said, "and it seemed I was over par for most of it, but I hung in there, birdied fifteen and seventeen, and none of the guys made a run at me." He was unusually proud of a three-putt par at 13.

"Before I hit my second putt," he said, "I saw the footprints, the heel marks, on the other side of the hole. So I knew the guys had been missing it long. But then I did the same exact thing. Standing over that third putt was kind of my whole day. I thought to myself, *If you miss it, the ball's going back to the original spot. If you try to die it in, it might not go in. But at least that would eliminate the possibility of a five-putt.* Finally I said, *No. Bang it in there with pace. Let's get out of here with a good three-putt.* That's how my mind works out there, and that's what happened. A good three-putt."

When Woods started with two bad three-putts for bogeys on Sunday, missing a seven-footer at the first and a two-footer at the second, Mickelson took heart. "For just a moment there," Phil said, "I thought he might be catchable." But the putter was Tiger's only undependable club. He needed thirty-six putts, a great many for him, but hit almost all of the fairways and greens to beat the people's choice, Mickelson, by three. For the week, Tiger was first in greens in regulation, 53 of them, the only player who reached the 50s.

Playing partner Sergio said, "He didn't miss a full-shot all day. That's what kills you. I had him. I had him at the beginning. Unfortunately, I let him get away. He only did what he had to do. That's him, isn't it? If he's leading by four or five, he doesn't need to pull too hard, so he doesn't. If he needs to play a little harder, he does. He's able to do whatever it takes. I never had the chance to watch Nicklaus in his prime, but I'll tell you one thing, if he was better than this guy, he was unbelievable."

Nicklaus took 35 starts to win eight majors. Woods needed just 22 to gather his eight, seven of them in his last eleven tries. Jack's eighth was the 1970 British Open after a dull stretch of more than three years. Nicklaus said, "When Dad died suddenly in nineteen-seventy [of cancer, at just fifty-six], I realized two things. How short life is, and how much I'd let him down. The last three years he was alive, I didn't work at it as hard as I should have. I just sort of went along, winning a bunch of tournaments but no majors. When I analyzed it, I could see that my dad had lived for me, for what I did. That was what he really enjoyed, what brought him his greatest pleasure. I sort of kicked myself in the rear end, got to work again and won the British Open at St. Andrews."

Immediately after that victory, someone said to Nicklaus, "That's your tenth major, Jack," counting two U. S. Amateurs. "Only three more to tie Bobby Jones."

"The number had never even registered before," Nicklaus said. "Tiger wins the Masters in nineteen-ninety-seven and everybody says, 'Seventeen more to go, kid.' Almost everything has been tougher for Tiger than it was for me."

It would get a little tougher in 2003 and 2004. In fact, thirty-four months and ten majors would go by before Tiger won another.

In October of 2004, he took a wife, Swedish model Elin Nordegren, former nanny to the children of Jesper and Mia Parnevik. Earl arrived at the Barbados ceremony in a silver Rolls-Royce and cried on cue. Though Earl had long counseled against marriage, he claimed to have changed his mind. "The phone rang once," he said, "and it was Tiger on his cell. 'Where the hell are you?' I asked. 'Australia,' he said. 'What the hell for?' 'I'm scuba diving.' 'Don't you know there are Great Whites down there?' 'I won't bother them if they don't bother me.' He thought nothing of it. We laughed. But when I hung up, I felt a little sad. I thought, *Does he have to go all the way to Australia to get out from behind that gate at Isleworth and away from all those damn twenty-million-dollar houses?* You know why he scuba dives, don't you? Because the fish don't know who he is."

Earl worried that Tiger's life of golf and celebrity and "his surgeon's degree of concentration" might be costing him some human dimension. "So I'm glad he has found a wife, a great wife," he said. "You know, it's hard for a caveman to go out on a hunt, bring the damn food into the cave, light the friggin' fire, do every other damn thing, and then sit there and eat alone. Thank God, Tiger's not alone."

CHAPTER NINETEEN

Major No. 9, the 2005 Masters

Near the end, Tiger and Earl had a falling-out: a serious splintering that lasted about a year. Earl didn't say it had to do with a woman. He didn't have to. All he said was, "Tiger's mad at me."

"Are you sure *you're* not mad at *him?*" I said.

"Why would I be mad at him?"

"For kicking you to the curb."

"That was the plan all along."

This was a stock answer Earl applied to almost every disappointment.

The issue that split them couldn't have been just a garden-variety dalliance, because Tiger had been aware of those since high school, according to his original sweetheart, Dina Parr-Gravell. Among a legion of hard-looking women who would someday come forward to testify against Tiger, she was the only sweet-looking one who took the stand.

"He would just call, crying," she said, "and say, 'My dad is with another woman,' and that would be all he *could* say, he would be so upset. So, I just tried to be there for him and listen to him."

Earl didn't volunteer any particulars, but he implied that Tiger had to buy him out of some kind of sexual jackpot, and that the same cleaners who would be dispatched to Florida later had to come to California to take care of whatever it was. Anyway, Tiger was furious.

Of course the possibilities ranged from hideous to heinous with hilarious in between. Earl didn't shoot blanks. But the trouble might have been nothing more than a harassment claim. Any woman who ventured within fifty feet of Earl was a potential plaintiff.

Tida, of all unlikely peacemakers, did the most to repair the rift between her son and husband. Though she had her own trouble forgiving Earl, she prodded Tiger back to his father.

Once again, underneath Tida's gruffness was that tenderness, so often missed. Like when she tried to talk Royce into a smaller, less-expensive free house from Tiger. Tida wasn't being venal or selfish. She was being thoughtful and practical. She knew two things Royce didn't: that the annual taxes on a big-ass California house can amount to a mortgage, and that Tiger would never pay La-La's taxes.

"Tiger," Tida said, "you got to forgive your dad, for your own sake. Because he's going to be gone and you're going to be sorry."

Earl and Tiger reunited in plenty of time. Well, not plenty of time. In time, though. They were back in each other's arms at the end.

At a Players Championship one May, Tida's unmistakable voice could be heard in Tiger's gallery shouting at the sky, "Dad! Help your boy! He needs you!"

Earl made it to Augusta for the 2005 Masters, but was too ill to come to the course, even just for the kiss. He had a year and a month to live. In 2002, Tiger had been the first man after Nicklaus in 1972 to win both the Masters and the U.S. Open in the same season. Since then, he had been performing nice wonders but gaining no ground on Jack.

In 2003, Tiger broke Byron Nelson's musty record for consecutive cuts made on the PGA Tour, when he cruised past 114. He also became the first player ever to win at least five tournaments in five consecutive seasons. During 2004, Tiger surpassed Greg Norman's total number of weeks as the world number one, 331.

Arriving at the 2005 Masters famished for another major, Woods opened with a 2-over-par 74 that left him seven strokes and thirty-two players behind Chris DiMarco.

This was Nicklaus's forty-fifth and final Masters—he was sixty-five and missed the cut by five strokes—but the melancholia surrounding him had nothing to do with golf. A little more than a month before, seventeen-month-old grandson Jake Walter Nicklaus—Steve and Krista's boy—crawled into a hot tub and drowned. His five-year-old brother Stevie saw the emergency workers put Jake into the ambulance. "We told Stevie," Barbara said, "that Jake had gone away to be an angel. He's not old enough to understand. We hope." Jack said, "Jake was just starting to develop a personality. I loved holding him. His mother and dad couldn't get him out of my arms."

Tiger and Mark O'Meara sought Nicklaus out for a lunch on the Tuesday before the tournament. They talked around the heartache, mostly about fishing. "Mark and Jack reminisced about all these great fly-fishing places they'd been to all around the world," Tiger said, "all the fishes they hooked and landed in Russia, Iceland and Canada. You know, just shooting the bull. I mostly listened, watching Jack."

At the Champions Dinner, Tiger looked around the gradually emptying room and felt the same sensation of time passing by. Nelson, who was ninety-three, couldn't make the trip this year. "I'll never forget my first Masters dinner," Tiger said. "Just to be looking at the real Byron

Nelson and the real Gene Sarazen. I'm over here with Mr. Nelson on my left, Ben Crenshaw on my right, and here we are with dinner knives in our hands demonstrating our grips. Mr. Nelson is telling me how he changed his grip back in nineteen-thirty-three. I'm thinking, *My dad was just born.*"

Byron would die in 2006, four months after Earl.

"Pop's struggling, he's really struggling," Tiger said. "He's here, but he's unable to come out to the course. His health has been pretty bad all year. That's why Doral was so great a few weeks ago, when I shot sixty-three, just to give him something for his birthday, a birthday wish. He's had his moments this year where he's turned it around and other times where it hasn't been so good, like this week."

With a 66 in the second round, Tiger climbed twenty-nine places but made up only one stroke on DiMarco. Lightning flashes broke up the weekend, turning Sunday into a twenty-seven-hole day for both Tiger and Chris. In the morning nine that topped off his third round, DiMarco needed forty-one strokes to finish a 74. Meanwhile, Tiger birdied seven, eight and nine before the horn blew, then returned the next day to birdie 10, 11, 12 and 13, a record-tying seven in a row. From the 15th hole of his second round through the 13th of the third, he made 11 birdies in seventeen holes. That third-round 65 built Tiger a three-stroke lead.

"I hit a pretty good six-iron at ten," he said, relaxing between rounds, "made a nice little putt down the hill. I got a great break on eleven. My tee shot wasn't very good, but I had a nice opening to the green, made birdie; you know, kept it going. After the rain, the greens were soft and receptive. There usually aren't so many birdies out there on a Sunday."

In the afternoon, a surprisingly taut Woods-DiMarco duel had a false finish: Tiger's stunning chip at the par-3 16th that everyone except Earl was calling the best shot of his career. DiMarco stood only one stroke behind and fourteen feet from the hole as Tiger addressed his ball from ten yards over the green. In generally the same location six years earlier, Davis Love III had tossed his ball up on a high bank and reeled it straight down into the hole. Tiger thought of that.

"If Chris makes his putt and I make bogey," he said, "all of a sudden I'm one behind. I remembered Davis chipping in from over there, but I wasn't necessarily thinking about holing it myself. Just throw it up on the slope and hope it feeds down, you know, just hope to have a makeable putt for par."

Hitting a dot twenty feet or so above the hole, he watched the ball slowly slide all the way to the rim of the cup and then stop. After thinking it over for a moment, the ball dropped in. "It looked pretty good," Tiger said. "Then, all of a sudden, it looked *really* good. Then, how could it not go in? Finally, an earthquake happened."

The aftershocks included DiMarco's miss, two closing bogeys for Woods and a sudden-death playoff at 18. One 3-wood, one 8-iron and one fifteen-foot putt later—impeccable shots, all of them—Tiger's majors total reached nine, exactly halfway to Nicklaus. Leaving Tom Watson behind, Woods pulled up alongside Gary Player and Ben Hogan on the majors list. "The three-wood was perfect," he said. "The eight-iron was cool. My two best swings of the week. The putt was nice, too." DiMarco said, "I went out and shot sixty-eight for a twelve-under total, which is usually good enough to win around here. The way I look at it, I didn't lose it. I was just playing against Tiger Woods."

At the green jacket ceremony, Tiger tearfully thanked Earl, who, watching on television, said, "We may have seen the awakening of a sleeping giant."

On the telephone quite a while later, Earl said, "That chip-in at sixteen wasn't Tiger's best shot ever. Not even close. I put it about tenth. The ninth best one was that curling putt at the Players, when the announcer said, 'Better than most. Better than most! BETTER THAN

MOST!' The eighth best one was a thirty-five- or forty-footer Tiger holed at the ninety-six U.S. Am at Pumpkin Ridge. Seventh was at the Canadian Open in two thousand, the six-iron out of the bunker and across the water to get up-and-down to win. The top six, however, are all shots he hit playing with me, just the two of us, that nobody else in the world ever saw."

CHAPTER TWENTY

Major No. 10, the 2005 British Open

On July 7, 2005, a coordinated series of London bombings protesting Britain's involvement in the Iraq War killed four terrorists and fifty-two innocents, injuring seven hundred others. At 8:50 A.M., the crunch of the morning rush hour, three homemade devices packed in rucksacks were detonated within fifty seconds of each other in the Underground. At 9:47, a fourth explosion took the top off a double-decker bus in Tavistock Square. Noon, one week later, the Open Championship interrupted its first round for two minutes of silence. Tiger and Jose Maria Olazabal stood on the fourth green with their hats off and their heads down. Only the day before had Tiger learned that Tida, on an English holiday, was in a hotel right across the street from the last blast.

"I didn't know," Tiger said later. "She didn't tell me. I found out from Hank [Haney]. She doesn't tell me anything. That's kind of how our family is. If you're injured or you're hurt or you're sick or anything else happens, you don't tell anyone. You just deal with life and move on. 'Are you OK, Mom?' 'Yeah, good. What are you going to do on the golf course today, honey?' Typical Mom. She likes to change the subject real fast."

She didn't say anything at all?

"We don't do that in our family."

But it was quite a—

"My family doesn't do that. When my dad had cancer, he didn't say anything. When I had my knee surgery, I didn't say anything. This is how we are. It's one of our deals of probably being a Woods, I guess. Kind of deal with things and move on."

Did she return to the States or did she—

"No, she's out here following. Didn't you see her out there? I heard a couple of 'nice putts' from her."

He did have a couple of nice ones, shooting 66 to take a one-stroke lead. Bobby Jones decreed that no golf career is complete without a victory on the Old Course at St. Andrews, Scotland, so Tiger was the only contender not feeling the heat of history, having won the Open Championship the twenty-sixth time it was conducted at the home of golf in 2000. That year, he missed all of the bunkers. Thursday, he hit three.

"Two thousand, two thousand, two thousand," Tiger sheeshed. He was sick of hearing about 2000. "I couldn't care less. Thinking of two thousand is not going to help me hit a golf shot out here, hit a draw, a high fade and keep the ball on the ground. I have to be in the present, here and now. I won in two thousand, but we had totally different conditions. The wind here switches two or three times an hour, you know.

"I was still using a forty-three-and-a-half-inch steel-shafted driver and using a ball that spins a lot. I'm still using probably one of the spinniest golf balls out here, but even the spinners go a little bit farther now. I've changed to a graphite driver with a bigger head. There's fifteen, twenty yards right there, maybe a little more, just in those two combinations."

Jack Nicklaus was finally dropping the curtain on the longest death scene since the one in *Camille*. Tiger hadn't minded it. "No, it's been good," he said. "Every time he's retired, I've won. I wish he'd keep retiring. I won at Valhalla when he said good-bye to the PGA, and at Pebble Beach [when he said good-bye to the U.S. Open], and at the Masters this year. Now we're here. Hopefully, we can do it again."

Shooting 75–72 to miss the cut by two strokes, Nicklaus said, "I played well for me, it's been a blast. But it's time to get on with life. I'm a competitor, not a monument. You know, with me not playing on Sundays anymore, all the family comes over for dinner. Kids, grand-kids. I love this game, but the family is more important than trophies." Jake's dad, Steve, caddied.

When Jack was walking the final fairway in the heart of the gray town, rooftops creaked under the weight of all the citizens who came out of their garrets to applaud. On a balcony of the Rusacks Hotel, overlooking the Valley of Sin, Ernie and Liezl Els stood, clapping. Counting practice rounds, it was Jack's fourth straight day with Tom Watson. "Watson was really choked up and emotional all week," Nicklaus said. "When we crossed over the Swilcan Bridge at the end of our first practice round, I said, 'Tom, it's only Tuesday.' Just a couple of sentimental old fools, we are."

The legal bookmakers at William Hill offered 4-to-1 odds that Nicklaus wouldn't birdie his last hole of the tournament. That was like handing out free money. They paid off in new five-pound notes engraved with Jack in 1970 holding up the Claret Jug.

"He's the greatest champion that's ever lived," Tiger said. "There's nobody that's been as consistent for as long a period of time as Jack. Just look at this championship alone. Over years and years at the British, almost his worst showing was a tie for fourth. *A tie for fourth!*"

Actually, from '63 to '80, Nicklaus finished 3rd, 2nd, 12th, 1st, 2nd, 2nd, 6th, 1st, 5th, 2nd, 4th, 3rd, 3rd, 2nd, 2nd, 1st, 2nd and 4th.

"It's hard to imagine being that consistent, isn't it?" Tiger said.

"Sooner or later, you're going to find yourself on the bad-weather end of the draw, aren't you? But he played straight through whatever there was, always in contention. He's been the benchmark for every player that's played the game, at least in my generation. When I started playing, his prime was already over. But he was certainly our benchmark, just like Bobby Jones was his."

In round two, Tiger shot 67 and now led by four strokes over Colin Montgomerie. That old feeling of inevitability was once again settling in. But Saturday was a tougher, breezier day. Against Tiger's 71, Olazabal shot 68 to get within two. "When I hit that last putt in the wind," Woods told Montgomerie as they walked away from 18, "I could actually feel the shaft flex in my putter. That doesn't happen very often." "Over here, it does," said the Scot.

"Monty's done everything *but* win a major," Tiger said, "and this is his best chance in quite a while. Obviously the people were rooting for him; they should. But they were gracious to me, and I appreciate that. They applauded when I hit quality shots, even if the ball ended up thirty feet away from the hole. I'd still get a pretty nice cheer. That's all you can ask for. People over here really understand the game of golf."

His Sunday march to a five-stroke victory (over Montgomerie), giving him two St. Andrews routs by a combined 13 shots, was an ode to ball-striking. As the players say, Woods putted like an idiot. "I putted to a seventy," he said, "but I made only one bad full swing all day, my second shot at thirteen. I yanked it left by about ten feet. I may have slightly overshaped a three-iron a couple of times, too. But every other ball I hit was struck solid, dead flush. This is a round of golf I'll be thinking about for a long time."

So, to his first place at the Masters and second place at the U.S. Open ("when you rank eightieth in putting, you can't complain about second place"), he added another first at the British. Almost unnoticed, Tiger's tenth major championship gave him a second career slam. Only he and Nicklaus had won all four majors twice over, and Tiger was the younger and quicker to do it. Jack was thirty-one years, one month and seven days old when, playing in his thirty-seventh pro major, he won the 1971 PGA. Woods, playing in his thirty-fifth, was twenty-nine years, six months and seventeen days old.

After Ted Ray (1912), Bobby Jones (1927), Gene Sarazen (1932), Henry Cotton (1934) and Tom Weiskopf (1973), Tiger became the sixth player in 134 Open Championships to lead wire-to-wire. "These are things you don't even dream about doing," he said.

Earl was on Tiger's mind, naturally. "Dad is hanging in there," he said. "He's fighting, as always. He's being stubborn. *If I can fight and grind through this, why can't he?* That's what I kept thinking today, hoping, you know, to give him just a little extra motivation. It's a silly comparison, but I'm trying to do everything I can to help him stay positive."

A month later, the PGA went to Phil Mickelson at Baltusrol. Tiger tied for fourth.

CHAPTER TWENTY-ONE

Major No. 11, the 2006 British Open

In December of 2005, Earl's daughter Royce paused her career as a marketing specialist in San Jose, taking family leave under California law to move back in with her father. His many maladies were racing each other now, but cancer was out in front. "I had visited Cypress the month before," she said, "and he'd just had a gamma ray—gamma ray?—behind his eye. Dad was OK then. But in December we got word that he wasn't doing too well. Neither Tiger nor Tida called. That just wasn't them. Although in ninety-seven, when Dad had his heart attack, Tida did call us. I have to give her credit for that. But generally, Den, Kevin and I were excluded. We were nonexistent."

She found her father entirely cogent; Earl was, in most ways, himself. But he had fallen a few times and was burning things with his cigarettes. And, in a boiling house, he was freezing. The Kansas boy who had kept his windows open throughout the wintertime was requesting more and more layers of clothing. Earl sent Royce out to buy new sweaters. He asked the male nurses to climb up to the ceiling ducts and bend the heat in his direction. Mostly he sat in his easy chair in the living room, watching movies. Sometimes they could get him to go to bed.

Of the radiation treatments, he spoke confidently. "Oh, they zapped this" or "They zapped that." He'd tell her. "Don't worry, I'm good."

"Then something would show up in his stomach," Royce said, "and he'd just shrug, 'Oh, they'll zap that, too. I'm fine.' When the doctor stopped at the door to say 'See you later, Earl,' Dad called out to him, 'Toodle-oo!' He loved his doctor."

Old father-and-daughter teasing games came back into play. "Royce," he said, "when I get old, I want to be put in a senior home with gorgeous nurses who are all twenty-one years old." "Yeah, right," she said, "like a twenty-one-year-old nurse would give you the time of day." He started laughing.

"I had him up walking a little, in the backyard, on the patio," she said. "He was gun-shy about that, unsteady on his feet.

"'Dad, can't you move any faster?'

"'Shut up.'

"'Is this your idea of a hundred-yard dash?'

"'I'm going to run after you in a little bit.'

"'Big talker.'"

But, at a point, he said seriously, "Royce, I'm really glad you're here," and she answered, "I wouldn't be anywhere else."

She said, "Being in denial—my brothers say I live in denial—I started thinking, *Dad's getting better*."

Tida took Earl's two dogs, chocolate and yellow Labs, to the big-ass house. On their visits, Tiger and Elin brought along a black-and-white puppy, Taz. "Dad got such a kick out of that little dog," Royce said. "He'd say, 'Hasn't anybody even *tried* to discipline this animal?' I'd hear Tiger and Dad laughing and talking in the bedroom; they were having so much fun. I went in there and sat down off to the side and just listened to them. Tiger gave him a big burst of energy. But that evening Dad said to me, 'Royce, I think I did too much today. Let me take a Tylenol.' This was unusual."

On March 21, the Tuesday before the Players Championship in Florida, Tiger abruptly stopped hitting balls in Ponte Vedra Beach and flew cross-country to Cypress. When Earl looked up and saw his son standing over him, he grumped, "What the hell are you doing here?" Tiger said later, "It was great to hear that."

Back at the tournament, where he played listlessly, Woods spoke again of how "stubborn" his father was and how well he was "hanging in there and fighting, which he always does." But this was a smoke screen. Tiger had hurried home because of reports that Earl wasn't eating, that he was saying good-bye to his caretakers, that, in actuality, he was quitting. "We don't quit," Tiger told him in a pep talk. "Remember? You taught me that."

The Sunday night of the final Players round, Tiger was profiled on *60 Minutes*. Asked in the press tent if he intended to watch, he said, "No." Why not? "I'm sorry, no offense, but being around you guys, I don't watch anything anymore."

To *60 Minutes*, Woods's house, boat and wife were all declared off-limits. But Elin did come up in the conversation with correspondent Ed Bradley.

"I have found a life partner, a best friend," Tiger said, now eighteen months into his marriage. "She's brought joy and balance to my life. We love doing the same things."

Bradley: "How do you think having children will affect your day job?"

Tiger: "Family always comes first. It always has been in my life, and always will. I may sleep a little bit less, and we have to work on that as a team."

Bradley: "Can you see yourself giving as much time to your kids as your parents gave to you?"

Tiger: "As best I can. I always want my kids to know their father."

By April, Royce decided Earl was approaching the end as though on a classified mission. "He was like a POW," she said. "He had trained for this. 'Are you in pain?' I asked him. 'Nope,' he said. Sure. He had cancer, but he wasn't in pain. Mind over matter." Because she was complicit in small deceptions, like hiding his medication in the applesauce, Earl stopped looking at Royce with total trust. She became one of his handlers. "That hurt my feelings," she said, "but it was OK."

Two nights before May 3, Royce sat on the edge of his bed and asked softly, "Can I rub your back, Dad?"

"Yes," Earl said, correcting her grammar, "you *may* rub my back."

"Am I ever going to graduate from the school of Earl Woods?"

"Evidently not."

"I love you, Dad."

"I love you, too."

The last time he went to the door, the doctor called out, "Is there anything you want, Earl?"

"Yes."

"What?"

"I want you to leave me the fuck alone."

"Dad would fall into a deep sleep," Royce said, "and for some reason they didn't want him in a deep, deep sleep. So the nurse would go, 'Earl? Earl? Mister Woods? Mister Woods?' And Dad would finally say, 'Yeah, yeah, what is it?' 'Just checking, making sure you're OK.' 'OK, thanks.' So on May second, I was in the front room and I heard the nurse going, 'Earl? Earl? Mister Woods? Earl? Earl?' There was no response. I ran back there in a panic. 'Mister Woods? Mister Woods?' I jumped on the bed, and now I'm right in Dad's face. 'Dad? Dad?' At this point, I'm hysterical. His eyes were open. Like, looking straight through me. 'Dad?' And all of a sudden he said, 'What?' I'm crying. 'Are you OK, Dad?' 'Yeah, honey, I'm fine.'"

The next day, Earl went on oxygen for the first time. "His kidneys were shutting down," Royce said. Everything was. "The doctor left, Tida left, Tiger left. [That was the last time Tiger saw him.] I was on the computer in the next room, listening to the oxygen machine. I'd go in and check on him. *OK, he's all right.* A little while later, I went back. Dad was rolled over on his side. I sat behind him and started rubbing his back. He took three weird breaths and that was it."

She said, "After my father's service in Cypress—open casket—I'm walking in and out of rooms, crying, crying, crying, and a couple of times Tiger grabbed me and held me. 'It's OK, it's OK,' he said. I thought at the time it was genuine. But ask me today. I just don't feel, I just don't believe, he's genuine. I think he pretends. With Tiger, you always ask yourself later, 'Was it real?'"

Ann mourned, too. "My regret," his first wife said, "is I never got to see him. My kids, they just felt it wasn't a good idea. I wish I had made a real quiet secretive trip, just rang the doorbell. Behind that pompous wall he put up, he could be normal and natural. He could be very loving. Earl had a heart, a sentimental heart. But he could break your heart, too. He broke mine. I guess he broke Tida's as well. And maybe his own."

Had she rung the doorbell, he probably wouldn't have been any kinder to her than he was to Tida, who came over with bowls of soup. In Tida's hearing, he thanked everyone else but her, which was hurtful. Maybe Ann and Tida represented the same thing to Earl.

In mourning for more than two months, Tiger retreated from golf after tying for third in the 2006 Masters. He didn't resurface until the U.S. Open. So it shouldn't have been too surprising that he missed the cut at Winged Foot, his first cough in nearly ten full seasons of majors. Maybe even Tiger Woods better not go straight from early April to mid-June without competing in between. "The Masters loss was bitter," he said, "probably the most disappointing loss I've ever had, or ever will have. I knew it was the last major my dad was ever going to see. Just one more time, I wanted him to feel it. Why couldn't I have sucked it up and got it done on the back nine at Augusta, when he was around?"

Having retrieved his game at the Western Open, Woods moved on confidently to the Open Championship in Liverpool, England, to defend his British title. In the days leading up to the tournament, Fleet Street took its turn to talk about Earl. Tuesday in the interview room, one of the Brits wanted to know, "Do you still think of him every day?"

"Well, there's not a day that I don't think I'll ever go through life without thinking about my dad," Tiger said. "I love him dearly. And everyone I've ever talked to who has lost a parent, they think about them every day and they always miss them, and especially with the bond we had, you know. I believe it transcended just a normal parent-child relationship. I think about him especially when I'm playing and practicing, because he taught me all of the fundamentals. You have to understand, when you return to golf after a break, it's always to the basics that you go. And they were all from my father. Grip, posture, stance, aim. You can't start in again without going back to younger days. How can you ever get beyond something when everything you're doing is such a vivid reminder? That made it really hard at first. It's still hard. But I've come to terms with it. He's not here anymore. I can't pick up the phone and say, 'Pop, what do you think about my putting stroke?' But I have so many wonderful memories. I'll look back on them with smiles every time."

Someone asked seriously, "Does your mum offer technical advice?"

"No, no, no, no, no, no, no, no," Woods said, and everybody laughed. "She usually gives words of encouragement. As you all know, she's pretty fiery. So it's more from that side of it than from a technical side."

This would be an Open Championship played in black armbands

Earl at K-State • *Courtesy Kansas State University*

Hattie Belle Woods • *Courtesy Geraldine Walton*

Woods's Kansas home • *Courtesy Pat Patton*

Tiger with and Earl • *Courtesy Mabel Woods Moore*

Earl and his three sons: Den *(middle)*,
Kevin and Tiger *(front)*

• *Courtesy Barbara Woods Gary*

Earl, Tilda, and Tiger with actor James Stewart c
The Mike Douglas Show • *Courtesy Mabel Woods Mo*

Tiger with golf club • *Courtesy Mabel Woods Moore*

Vuong Dang "Tiger" Phong

Most of the grave markers were made of wood and had rotted. Tiger Phong's was made of concrete.

Tiger Phong's widow and five of his nine children clean his bones, retrieved from the woods outside a Communist reeducation camp in the north.

The Stanford student in 1995,
a year before turning pro

Tiger with Arnold Palmer and Jack Nicklaus at the 1996 Masters Tournament,
Tiger's last as an amateur.

The "Hello, World" press
conference, as Tiger turns pro.

• *Courtesy* Golf Digest/*Bill Fields*

Woods Clinic, 1997

• *Courtesy* Golf Digest/*Stephen Szurlej*

he Masters, 1997 • *Courtesy* Golf Digest/*Stephen Szurlej*

Earl and Tiger in Miami, 1997 • *Courtesy Golf Digest/Stephen Szurlej*

Jack Nichlaus and Tiger at the 2005 President's Cup • *Courtesy Jim Mandeville*

Tiger in Spring 2000. He's on his way to winning the U.S. Open by 15 strokes, the British Open by 8, and the PGA and Masters to follow—"The Tiger Slam."

• *Courtesy Mabel Woods Moore*

Elin at 2007 Buick Invitational • *Courtesy Golf Digest*

Tida Woods • *Courtesy Golf Digest/Dom Furore*

Tiger and caddie Steve Williams after winning the 2006 British Open, his first major victory after Earl's death. • *Courtesy* Golf Digest/*Stephen Szurlej*

all around. Chris DiMarco's mother, Norma, died suddenly of a stroke on the Fourth of July, sixteen days before the tournament. "A couple of weeks ago," DiMarco said, "reality set in. The reality is, I'm playing a game. It's not life. Life was two weeks ago."

Saddest of all was the lost expression on the face of Ulsterman Darren Clarke, normally the most optimistic stout-drinking and cigar-puffing pro in either of the Irelands, whose wife, Heather, was in the last throes of a five-year siege of cancer. Sons, Conor and Tyrone, named for the county, were five and seven. "Have you seen D.C.?" Tiger whispered on his way out of the press building. "I need to talk to him."

In 2000, the peak of Woods's graph, when he was 53-under-par in the majors (among the players who made it through all sixteen rounds that year, Ernie Els was second-best, 35 shots worse), "D.C." or "Clarkie" upset Tiger—and stunned everyone else—in the thirty-six-hole final of the Accenture Match Play, one of those World Golf Championships that seemed to be Woods's private preserve. After seeing to the winner's media responsibilities, Clarke returned to his locker to find a note from Tiger. "You're still a fat fuck," it read.

At a subsequent tournament, Darren was warring with his swing on the practice tee when a gentle voice behind him reset his stance, straightened his posture and quieted his arms. Clarke hit the next couple of shots flush and turned around to smile at Tiger.

A dusty English summer had made the Hoylake course not just hot and dry but literally flammable. It was more brown than green. Scoreboard signs warned, FIRE RISK. SMOKERS PLEASE TAKE CARE. Tiger saw that and smiled sadly.

Two holes into his first practice round, Woods began to formulate a plan of attack that made sense only to him. Australian Hall of Famer Peter Thomson, who won one of his five Open Championships at Hoylake, described the course well on Wednesday. "When I came to practice in nineteen-fifty-six," he said, "I couldn't make head nor tail of the place. I built up a fair amount of pessimism that I wasn't going to win because always when I played I had a plan to play a course. I found out where the trouble was and figured out how to keep out of it and make the most of opportunities elsewhere. But this course, I never really got the hang of, even after I won. You can plot your way around St. Andrews or Birkdale. But it's a very complex and difficult course, this. As no doubt the players are finding."

The first thing Tiger noticed was that his driver was flying, bounding and rampaging 350, 370 and 420 yards. He shoved a 2-iron in his bag and, with one exception in seventy-two holes, benched the driver. Tiger ended up scalding that 2-iron off forty tees. "The fairways are difficult enough to hit as it is," he said, "and now you add a driver that's going so far. How impossible is *that*? Nobody can control that. The guys who'll hit those long drives, and take on the bunkers, they may end up with some wedges to the greens. But, the thing is, most of these pin placements can't be attacked even with wedges."

His short stingers off the tee left a lot of long 4-irons to the green. Hitting many of them pin high, Tiger aimed almost none of them directly at the flags (although he did hole one of those 4-irons Friday for an eagle).

"A good shot here might be thirty or forty feet away," he said. "Then, if I putt just respectably, I'll be right there on Sunday afternoon." He sounded excited. When this was brought up to him, he said, "It's going to be a fantastic challenge playing a course this fast. I love links golf. Back home, we're handcuffed by target golf. I prefer creating shots, playing all the options. Starting the ball way out here, carving it back way over there, throwing it up on top and spinning it. Seeing all of the possibilities. Using every bit of your imagination. I don't have to tell you, Dad didn't much care for the weather over here, but he loved the golf. The links. The shaping of shots. All these weird, weird shots. Playing the ball on the ground instead of in the air. He always got a big kick out of that. This is going to be Pop's kind of week. Mine, too. Because we've never played a golf course like this before. None of us."

For companionship in the first two rounds, Tiger drew Shingo Katayama of Japan, recognizable by his singular cowboy hat, and semi-retired television broadcaster Nick Faldo. Thirty-nine majors back, at the 1997 Masters, Tiger spoke of his comfortable relationship and easy conversations with Nick. But since then, some swing criticism Faldo leveled on TV ended their rapport. They shook hands and smiled at the start and at the finish. But they didn't really talk, except at the very end, when Nick said, "Since you won't be using it anyway, can Matthew [Faldo's son, age seventeen] have your driver?"

In effect, Woods stepped back and let fifty-two players go in front of him on the tee, starting with Andrew Buckle (Andrew Buckle!), who averaged 320.8 yards a drive (and tied for sixty-first place in the tournament), followed by Robert Karlsson (314.0), Andres Romero (313.4), Retief Goosen (311.4), Angel Cabrera (310.6), Adam Scott (309.5), Ben Crane (309.0), Robert Rock (308.8), Gonzalo Fernandez-Castano (308.4), Phil Mickelson (308.0) and forty-two others. Tiger averaged a meager 290.9, but he was first in fairways hit (48) and second in greens in regulation (58).

Squinting to see the back of Katayama in the distance, Woods still saw no reason to alter his scheme. Tacking a Friday 65 on to a Thursday 67, he led at the halfway point by one stroke over Els. Saturday, just moments before he and Ernie teed off at the back of the field, Tiger looked up from a practice putt and spoke to Hank Haney. I was standing right next to Haney, but Tiger must have seen only his teacher, or he wouldn't have said, "If I can break this big guy's heart one more time, maybe he'll go away and stay away."

Both Woods and Els shot 71s. In Tiger's only shaky putting day of the week, he stroked a 68 into a 71. Meanwhile, Ernie short-gamed a 74 into a 71. Els would finish third by himself.

Tiger's Sunday partner was Sergio Garcia, still struggling to retrieve his youthful joy, coming off a 65. When Gary Player wanted to signal strength and power, he dressed all in black. Sergio showed up in yellow, a regrettable choice. He looked like a 160-pound canary. On a 73, Garcia slipped to fifth.

DiMarco, the other brokenhearted son, shot 68 to Tiger's 67 and lost by two. Jim Furyk, who finished fourth, said, "When Chris birdied and Tiger bogeyed, it was down to a shot. But then Tiger birdied the next three holes. That's kind of the way it is with him. Put a little heat on and he'll birdie three straight holes. What are you going to do?"

After he putted out at 18, Woods collapsed into the arms of caddie Steve Williams. Tiger didn't just cry; he bawled. *"Tiger was taught at a very early age," Earl had said, "that it was all right for a male to cry, to have feelings and to let them out."*

"You know me," Tiger said later. "I've cried before, but never like that, not in public. I guess everything we've gone through of late just came pouring out. I'm kind of the one who bottles things up a little bit and moves on, trying to deal with it in my own way. But at that moment—all that my father has meant to me and to the game of golf—I just wish he could have seen it one more time.

"I was calm out there as long as we were playing because, if you looked at the board, only Ernie and I had won this championship. Sergio hasn't won it. There's a certain calmness that comes from being able to say honestly, *I've done this before.* Dad would have been proud, very proud. He was always on my case about thinking my way around the golf course and not letting emotions get the better of you, because that's so very easy to do in this sport. Here was one of the all-time thinking-your-way-around-the-golf-course weeks. Just use your mind to plot your way, and if you deviate from the game plan, make sure it's the right deviation. I adjusted a few clubs off the tees, just because wind conditions kept changing, but as far as the overall game plan, I never changed."

Coming down the home stretch, he seemed to be muttering something to himself.

"Yeah," he said. "I was saying, 'Thanks for keeping me calm, Pop. Thanks for everything.'"

CHAPTER TWENTY-TWO

Major No. 12, the 2006 PGA

Going around and around on the rota of major championships reminds a man he is graying and gets him to reminiscing easily. First, you're with Johnny Miller at Oakmont in 1973. Then the world turns around and you're with Larry Nelson at Oakmont in 1983. Then the world turns around and you're with Ernie Els at Oakmont in 1994. Then the world turns around and you're with Angel Cabrera at Oakmont in 2007.

Dan Rostenkowski of Illinois, former chairman of the House Ways and Means Committee, was in the particular embrace of this wistfulness several years ago, probably because he was in jail. At a federal correctional institution in Wisconsin, the chairman wasn't taking any phone calls about mail fraud or politics, but this was about golf.

"Were you at Medinah in nineteen-seventy-five," he asked the caller, "when Lou Graham won the U.S. Open?"

Yes. Graham played off against John Mahaffey, who three years later *won* a playoff in the PGA (at Oakmont). Tramping after Graham and Mahaffey for eighteen holes was like following any two guys playing golf on a Monday. You wondered if they would stop at nine for a hot dog. In the gallery, a wife whispered to her husband, "Where does Lou Graham get all those faded shirts?"

"Do you remember," Rostenkowski asked, "the dramatic electric storm that came up Saturday at Medinah?"

No, not really. The wetness of the course was unforgettable, though. Walkways were covered with straw. It smelled like a circus.

"You don't remember that incredible flash of lightning that struck the seventeenth green?"

No. Sam Giancana being whacked in his basement was more memorable. That story led the *Trib*.

"Maybe," Rostenkowski said, "we better not talk about that over a tie-line to a penitentiary."

Back at Medinah, seven years after his second major victory, Tiger went looking for that 17th green where lightning often struck, and couldn't find it. "I wanted to relive that eight-footer I made to beat Sergio," he said, "but it's gone. The green's been moved, rebuilt. It's gone. They're already ripping up my memories. Am I getting old?"

Yes. He was thirty.

"I've changed quite a bit as a person," Tiger said. "My life has changed on and off the golf course, and I think obviously it's a maturation process. [In 1999] I was still very young to the tour. I didn't really know a whole lot about the business yet. I was in my third year, but it takes probably a good five years to really and truly understand. I was still new and fresh to the whole idea of being a professional golfer. Things have changed quite a bit since then."

Rain had softened Medinah; he knew that much. The easier it is, the worse it is, for the better players. "They're not going to be able to quicken up the greens now," Tiger said. "They're slow enough where you're not really afraid of any downhill putts. You don't have that roll-out after a good putt. Everything seems to be stopping. This isn't going to be your typical major where par is a good score. Usually you're just trying to make pars and survive. Not this week. Par's no good this week. Of course I prefer it when the winning score is in single digits. Shoot 1-under-par for seventy-two holes, that's the way I like to play. Do that here, though, and you'll be run over. They're going to need a longer leaderboard."

As predictions go, this one was pretty good. At one point on Saturday, ten players were tied for the lead, about 14 percent of the remaining field. Tiger opened with a 69 to share tenth place, followed by a 68 for a piece of fifth. Then he switched on his putter, and turned it up to full throttle.

For the first two rounds, Woods played with Phil Mickelson, who matched Tiger's opening 69 but then fell off with a 71 on his way to a tie for sixteenth. "I get along with some players better than others," Tiger said, answering the unspoken question, "and that's just the way it is. Sometimes I talk, sometimes I don't. Sometimes I'm in the mood to talk, sometimes I'm not going to say a word even if my best friend is out there. It's a major championship, and I don't usually talk a whole lot in major championships. I'm trying to put my ball where I need to put it. I stay in my own little world and try to handle my own business. I may not even talk to Stevie very much, but that's just the way it is in majors for me. You know, I played with Mark-O [O'Meara] in a major once and didn't say a word to him all day except, 'Here's your card.' That's just the way it is. I'm trying to win the golf tournament."

Mickelson's method, according to Phil, was to try to hold on to the good shots. "It all depends on your personality," Tiger said. "For me, I tend to remember how I could have been better. That's kind of how I am. It's probably a good thing and a bad thing at the same time."

Saturday's 65 tied Tiger with Luke Donald at the front. Then, on Sunday, as the golfers say, Tiger made every putt he looked at (including a pair of forty-footers, at six and eight) for 68 and a five-stroke victory. He became the only player to win two PGAs at the same venue, the only one to win multiple majors in consecutive years. Tiger suffered just three bogeys all week. "That's good at the Bob Hope," Williams said, "let alone the PGA."

Shaun Micheel, the 2003 PGA champion, who had six straight birdies and a 30 on the front nine Saturday, finished second by himself and became the twelfth man in Tiger's twelve major victories to collect at least a share of the runner-up position. The others were Thomas Bjorn, Chris DiMarco (twice), David Duval, Ernie Els (twice), Sergio Garcia, Retief Goosen, Miguel Angel Jimenez, Tom Kite, Bob May, Phil Mickelson and Colin Montgomerie.

Tiger equaled the 18-under record he and May set in 2000. Bob was still in the books.

"Sunday was the most special day," Tiger said. "I just had one of those magical days on the greens. I started to feel that if I put the ball anywhere on the green I could make it. It's not too often you have days like that. On the television last night, I was watching the highlights. I saw how the putter went back, and I didn't like it very much. That's the kind of thing my dad used to catch for me. I rehearsed my stroke late into the night, and everything came out fine. It's rare, but sometimes you just have the feeling that, if you read them right, they're going in. I just had that feeling today. It's special when you can have that going for you at a major."

In the interview room, some deep thinker wanted to know what Tiger thought was his impact on golf in the last decade.

"My impact?" he said. "Fifty wins on tour. W's. Just getting W's. That's why I play. To win. To beat everybody in the field. That's fun. I've got my name on trophies fifty times here in the States. I think that's all right. That's a good impact, I think."

Sensing this might not be the right answer, he took a mulligan.

"Truthfully," he said, "I hope I've spurred on some young kids to play the game of golf. I know, when I was growing up, golf was not a cool sport to play. You were considered a wuss for playing. Now I think it's more of an accepted sport and a viable sport as well. I think you're seeing a lot more juniors out there hitting the golf ball around more than when I first came out here on tour. Maybe that's my impact."

CHAPTER TWENTY-THREE

Major No. 13, the 2007 PGA

On the day of the second round of the 2007 PGA Championship in Tulsa, a memorial was held at Candlestick Park in San Francisco for the former Forty-Niners and Stanford football coach Bill Walsh, who was seventy-five when he died of leukemia eleven days before.

Some months earlier, Walsh was on the telephone discussing, among other things, the quarterback Tiger Woods.

Talking about his illness, the same disease that took his forty-six-year-old son Steve in 2002, Walsh said, "My attitude is positive but not evangelistic. I've had a number of blood transfusions; they're exhausting. I have a bad stomach all the time. But otherwise I'm functioning pretty normally. I'm pragmatically doing everything the doctor recommends, working my way through it. Thank God for Stanford. Not only are they giving me the best treatment, they have a lot of basketball and volleyball games going on out there every day, and I'm enjoying watching these young people play. For a while there, I thought I was dead. I put all of my stuff in order. But I'm not dead. I'll accept my fate as it unfolds. I've always felt that way. I have no regrets."

During the mid-'90s, when Walsh was transitioning from the football field to the athletic director's suite, student Woods haunted his office. "We had one coach," Walsh said, laughing, "who walked in on us a couple of times, just sitting there shooting the breeze, and later said to me, 'Can't you get rid of that fucking kid?' I said, 'I don't want to. I like having him around.' If I had known Tiger was going to be this successful, I'd have had somebody take our picture. No, seriously, I knew he was going to be great. He was already awfully good. Tiger was insatiably curious about everything having to do with competition. He looked at sports—at *his* sport certainly—not as a sport at all, but as an art form. Conversing with him, I could tell he was my type. Tiger wasn't a hope-for-the-best, depend-on-heroics kind of competitor. He was convinced, as I was, of the beauty in a well-rehearsed plan. That's why he was hanging around our offices. I'll tell you, he reminded me of my quarterbacks."

The best ones included Ken Anderson in Cincinnati, Dan Fouts in San Diego and Joe Montana and Steve Young in San Francisco. "The West Coast offense," Walsh said, "actually started to develop with Kenny. Well, initially with Greg Cook, until he got hurt. But Anderson first and foremost. I guess 'Midwest Offense' didn't have the same magical-mystical ring to it. Kenny showed up with the purest mechanics. When I worked him out at Augustana College, he already had them. Paul Brown asked me, 'How can anybody from a jerkwater school like that have mechanics like this?' I think it had something to do with living right next door to [Kentucky basketball star] Dan Issel. Ken knew the correct way to play any sport.

"Beyond the requisite skills, Fouts's great asset was courage. It's a sin that Dan didn't win a championship, but he made it to the Hall of Fame and certainly deserves to be there. Charlie Joiner went with him. [The wide receiver in the playing card on Tiger's wall.] Remember, we had Charlie in Cincinnati, too. What a hitter.

"Montana's starting point was agility, or so I thought. I worked

Joe out at UCLA with the hurdler James Owens, then drafted Owens first and Montana third. Genius. But I couldn't see Joe's football instincts yet, his terrific touch and timing, and that wonderful sense of anticipation. I just saw his feet. He seemed far too shy, and he didn't have exceptional size. His arm strength wasn't classic, either. Plus he had an in-and-out career at Notre Dame; he didn't even dominate his own locker room. But he was light on his feet. The son of a gun could dance. That day at UCLA, his spikes didn't even seem to touch the ground.

"Tiger walks a little like a quarterback; I think you know what I mean. He isn't the athlete Young was. Who is? That was Steve's great gift. But Tiger reminds me of all of them just a little. If he talked with any of them, I promise you this. They would understand each other."

Walsh and Woods seldom discussed the game of golf itself, though the coach did tell Tiger that, on his eclectic list of personal inspirations (the lightweight boxer Lauro Salas, the high hurdler Harrison Dillard, the Jewish residents of the Warsaw ghetto, Stonewall Jackson, the U.S. marines on Guadalcanal), one golfer was included: Ken Venturi persevering in debilitating heat on the thirty-six-hole final day of the 1964 U.S. Open at Congressional.

Bill said, "One time, when Tiger and I were together, I told him I had the shanks really bad—well, nobody has them very good—and I started whining to him, 'The only club I seem to be shanking is the wedge.' All he said was, 'Get a different wedge.'"

"Yeah," Tiger remembered. "Coach was—he still was the coach my freshman year, and obviously continued to be there after that. He said, 'Just stop by anytime you're at the building, or in the area. Come up and see me, and we can just chat.' I mean, to me, that was incredible. Super Bowl champion. Hall of Famer. There were so many things he had to do, yet he would sit there with me for two hours and we'd talk about anything. He was, in a sense, basically a father away from home my freshman year, and we kept in touch quite a bit after

I left college and turned pro. I can't tell you how much I got out of it, how much I learned from him. He was just a great human being."

On the day of the Walsh memorial, Tiger shot 63 at Southern Hills to climb from a tie for twenty-third place to the lead alone, by two strokes over Scott Verplank. Woods was the twentieth player since Johnny Miller in the 1973 U.S. Open to shoot a 63 in a major championship (Greg Norman and Vijay Singh did it twice). That was the record.

In the first round of the 1980 U.S. Open at Baltusrol, Tom Weiskopf and Jack Nicklaus shot 63s within minutes of each other. Weiskopf was in the press tent telling his birdies-and-bogeys when an explosion went off at 18, stopping him. What happened? Someone outside the tent shouted, "Nicklaus has a two-and-a-half-footer for sixty-two!" He missed it, but the look on Weiskopf's face would never go away. He was a dead man.

Tiger's own putt for 62 wasn't much longer than Jack's had been, but it lipped out. What did that mean to him? "It means I have a two-shot lead," Tiger said, "instead of three."

Saturday, he struck the ball just about as well, but never made a putt to speak of, and yet with a 69 extended his lead to three strokes.

In the 101-degree heat, John Daly, who was enjoying a momentary renaissance, was on a new physical-fitness regimen. "I've been staying indoors," he said, "playing slots over at the Cherokee Casino. I didn't play a practice round here. Too hot. I played the Cherokee course Wednesday, by myself, in a cart. I keep waiting to make a seven or eight near the end, when I'm really dripping wet. That's the way my year has gone. If golf courses were only fourteen holes, I'd have won seventeen tournaments in the last year and a half. Look at my scorecards."

But he never shot worse than 73 in Tulsa and finished in a respectable tie for thirty-second. He may have even lost a few pounds. By the end of the tournament, only about half of the putts were breaking toward John Daly.

"In this kind of heat," Tiger said, "that's when fitness really pays off. It's a huge advantage. The less you're worn down physically, the less you're going to be worn down mentally. At home it isn't as hot as this, but it's humid. All those miles of roadwork I do build up my confidence. Make me feel I deserve it maybe more than some others. In golf, feeling deserving is underrated. If you've paid the price already, you're way ahead. You can see some guys' shoulders slumping and dragging a little bit. I have to admit, I don't mind seeing it. Train hard. Bust your butt. That's what sport is, doing that. I know not everyone considers golf to be a sport, but I do."

On Sunday, Woody Austin (67) and Ernie Els (66) made spirited runs, but Tiger held them off with another 69 to win by two and three. "When I three-putted fourteen," he said, "I felt like I gave all the momentum back to Ernie and Woody. But I was still leading. I wasn't about to forget that. If they birdied up in front of me, well, I get to play those holes, too. I just told myself, *You know what? You got yourself into this mess. Now get yourself out of it.* I was yelling inside my head going to the tee at fifteen. *Just get back to what you do, will you? Put it where you need to put it. Bear down.* I hit a four-iron off the tee to where I needed to put it and a seven-iron on the green to where I needed to put it. Then I made that fifteen-footer, and it felt great."

His overall performance was notable for a basketful of little trouble shots Tiger pulled off every day. "My dad thought I was crazy as a kid," he said, "because I used to enjoy going out in the evening and throwing golf balls in the trees. I always played three balls; the average had to be par. I loved creating shots that way. I didn't enjoy standing out there beating balls on the range; I still don't. Too boring. I've always preferred practicing golf to playing golf, but only if you make it interesting. Only if it's fun. I'd much rather chip, putt and create. That's the joy of golf. Maybe just because my last name is Woods."

His fourth PGA Championship, second in a row, left him one PGA behind Nicklaus and Walter Hagen among the collectors. "It turned this into a great year," Tiger said. "I felt like I played well most of the year [seconds at both the Masters and U.S. Open, a twelfth at the British], and just didn't quite get it done. This time I did. So anytime you win a major championship, it's always going to be a great year."

For the first time, daughter, Sam, was along. "That's a feeling I've never had before," Tiger said, "having Sam there and having Elin there. It feels a lot more special when you have your family with you. It used to be my mom and dad. Now Elin and I have our own daughter. So it's evolved. And this one feels so much more special than the other majors. The British Open last year was different, but this one was certainly so special and so right to have Elin and Sam with me. I wasn't really paying attention when I saw them there at the end. I was so excited and just wanted to give Elin and Sam a kiss and get back to signing my scorecard."

CHAPTER TWENTY-FOUR

Major No. 14, the 2008 U.S. Open

In 1995, under the influence of champagne, Earl publicly declared that, before Tiger was through, he would win fourteen major championships. Tiger blanched. They were in a merchandising tent at the Newport Country Club, toasting the second U.S. Amateur championship, and a crowd of civilians was listening in. Earl never explained how he settled on the number 14, but he always resented the fact that it was written. As did Tiger, who excommunicated the writer.

Jack Nicklaus once said, "Maybe not everyone was meant to win the U.S. Open." He said it years before the 2008 Open, so he wasn't referring to Rocco Mediate necessarily. But he could have been. With faint apologies to Lee Westwood, Robert Karlsson, D. J. Trahan, Carl Pettersson, John Merrick, Miguel Angel Jimenez, Heath Slocum, Eric Axley and Brandt Snedeker, who finished third to eleventh on one of the least compelling leaderboards in the history of the tournament, this was a two-man drama from the jump, that lasted ninety-one holes.

At Torrey Pines in La Jolla, California, Robert Dinwiddie led the field in putting, Derek Fathauer in fairways hit, Ian Leggatt in bogeys, Brian Bergstol in others, but none of the statistics in the 108th Open meant as much as Rocco's good nature and Tiger's bad leg.

Two thousand two hundred and forty-one days removed from his most recent PGA Tour victory, just 1,645 days away from being eligible to join the Champions Tour, Mediate would have been the actor least likely to be cast in this role even if he hadn't had to go extra holes after a thirty-six-hole qualifier just to get into the tournament. "Come on, children," he said to the troop of twentysomethings he led back out into the gloaming, all of whom outdrove him by fifty yards, none of whom made their putt. He did.

After shooting a 2-under-par 69 to start, Rocco said in the pressroom, "Nobody's watching me. Everybody's watching Tiger, including me. Why not? He's the best player that ever walked on grass. It's hard for me to have expectations on a course like this, set up for an Open. All I can do is go back out there tomorrow and see what I got again. Hopefully it's something similar. This is the greatest test there is. I love it."

The next day, as he took the same seat following a 71, Mediate said, "I bet you're surprised to see *me* here again."

Meanwhile, to his own 72 Tiger tacked on a 68 (including a back nine 30) to join Rocco and Karlsson in second place behind Stuart Appleby, who was about to shoot 79. Lighter in knee cartilage since a post-Masters scoping, Woods teetered around the course like an uneven table.

"It's about dealing with things and getting out there and giving it your best shot," he said. "There's never any excuses. You just go play. That's the beauty of it—enjoying the opportunity to compete whether you're a hundred percent or not."

For helping him pass the dullest days of the recuperative process, Woods thanked daughter, Sam Alexis. "There's no way I could have gotten through this without Sam being there," he said. "Spending so much time away from golf and training, I needed someone to help get my mind off the surgery. She was incredible, just watching her grow. She's running now. So much fun. The greatest thing in the world."

On Thursday Tiger double-bogeyed his first hole and, as he put it, "three-whacked" the last. "But at least I didn't need a cart," he said, and obviously Friday was better. "Making fifteen- and twenty-footers can do wonders for an aching knee," he said. Was he taking anything for the pain? "Oh, yeah."

Lagging behind Tiger on Saturday, 72 to 70, Mediate said, "The stuff he does is unreal. He's completely out of his mind. Watching him makes me nervous, but it's a good nervous. Plus the world is watching, which is really cool. I love that."

Though a forty-five-year-old journeyman with but five tour victories, two of them at Greensboro, Rocco was respected in the industry for his clean contact and his generous nature if not for his driving length or putting stroke. And just recently he had stopped trying to putt with one of those long logger's pikes that fairly shout yips. "I've been putting with a conventional, short putter since when? Friday of Hilton Head? I guess that's right, a couple of months. I put the Sabertooth in, nice name for a putter, and started making some. It's mostly a head game, of course. I'm not the top anything in the world right now. But you never know. You never know."

By the stuff Tiger did that was unreal, Mediate was thinking of three shots during a six-hole stretch at the end of the third round. Twice in that push, Woods's left knee buckled, almost sending him to the ground. At the 13th hole, trying to hit his second shot into the back bunker, he somehow kept it on the green sixty-six feet from the hole, and made that. "I was thinking," Tiger said, "if I could get the speed close to right, I might have an outside chance at two-putting. And then it went in." At 17, having just avoided a greenside bunker, he slapped his uphill chip far too hard, but it one-hopped into the hole. "Wasn't that lucky?" he said. Then he closed the round by making a forty-foot eagle putt that caused his playing partners, Adam Scott and Phil Mickelson, to look up and stare.

Tiger had a one-stroke lead over Westwood. They would play together on Sunday with Rocco tottering along in front of them.

"I wish I was with him," Mediate said. "It's the greatest to be part of the era that Tiger's in, a dream for me. Sure, he's probably going to win, but he might not. I'm ecstatic. This is the best I've played in this kind of situation consistently for—maybe ever, maybe ever, in a major event. I'm fortunate to do what I do, especially in a theater like this. I'm going to enjoy the heck out of it."

Hitting three different trees on the first hole Sunday, Tiger double-bogeyed to change places with Rocco. From two up, he moved to one down. Also, Woods's limp appeared to be worsening. "But the pain only comes after impact," he said, "so I kept telling myself, 'If you get that shooting pain, you get it. Just go ahead and make the proper swing. You might as well. If the pain hits, the pain hits. So be it. It's just pain.'" Was the doctor telling him anything? "Yeah," Tiger said. "Don't play golf."

Rocco took his one-stroke lead to the 18th hole, but neglected to birdie that par 5. "He could have all but closed me out there," said Tiger, who needed a birdie to tie and was odds-on to reach the green in two if he could put his drive in the fairway.

"I tried to play a cut off the tee," he said, "but ended up kind of hitting a pull cut, into the bunker. Absolute perfect lie. If it was a practice round, I'd have gone for it. Instead I stuck a nine-iron into the sand and the ball went straight right. That left me ninety-five to the front, a hundred and one to the hole." Now he had to get up and down or lose.

"It was just a perfect number for my fifty-six [degree wedge], but I didn't think I could stop a fifty-six in there. So, if I hit the fifty-six, I'd have to hit it short of the green and bounce it up. That didn't seem like a smart play. Stevie and I decided to go with the sixty, hit it hard, and make sure we stay to the right, just in case it doesn't get there. If it does, it should land on the front and skip past, and I should have a putt at it. It turned out perfect. The putt [a twelve-footer] was probably about two and a half balls outside right. The green wasn't very smooth. I kept telling myself, 'Make a pure stroke.' If it bounces in or out, so be it. At least I can hold my head up high if I make a pure stroke."

Waiting in the cart barn, Rocco asked the room, "Well, does he make it or not? Anyone want to bet?"

Under these circumstances, all of the merely good golfers who ever played could stand out there for the rest of their lives and never make that putt. As television showed from a ground-level camera, the ball bounced like a basketball, all the way up to the right edge and in.

"I have nothing left right now," Rocco said. "I'm toast."

In the TV age of sudden-death and three- or four-hole aggregate playoffs, the U.S. Open was the last major holdout for eighteen-hole deciders. Would Rocco have preferred to get it over with then and there?

"I don't know if I could," he said.

Anyway, a night to absorb all that had happened so far was welcome. "Heck," Rocco said, "I missed the cut in eight of the first ten tournaments I played this year on tour. Come on. Seriously. This week has been a total dream."

"How bad," he was asked, "do you want to win tomorrow?"

"Fairly," he said.

After the laughter, he added, "It would be the story of my life, I can tell you that."

Tiger was a stroke up after 1, a stroke down after 3, even after 5, a stroke up again after 6, two strokes up after 7, one stroke up after 8, two strokes up after 9, 35 to 37. Rocco was three strokes down after 10, two strokes down after 11, one stroke down after 12, even after 14, one stroke up after 15, and even again after 18, 71 apiece. A tap-in for par on the 1st hole of sudden death won Tiger Earl's fourteenth major.

"This guy is impossible," Mediate said, "ridiculous. He is who he is. There's nothing else to say. But, oh my God, I've never had so much fun in my life. I can't give any more than I gave out there, I really can't. I hit a bad tee shot on the extra hole, but that's OK. Some of those shots that I hit today came off so perfect—I had him scared there for a minute, didn't I? He had to birdie eighteen to tie me again, and he did it again. That's him. I'm disappointed, sure. But I just can't be upset. Everybody thought he was going to hand me my ass today, but he didn't. He just beat me, that's all. I can take it."

"This week had a lot of doubt to it," Tiger said. "All things considered, I don't know how I've ended up in this position. But now I understand why my dad was so emotional in two thousand and two [Bethpage Black] when I won and I brought it back to him. Now that I'm a father myself, I get it. To have my daughter there, and to have Elin there, it means so much when you do it. Father's Day was yesterday, I know, but close enough."

One week later, he underwent full-blown surgery, not just arthroscopic, to repair a ruptured anterior cruciate ligament, a double stress fracture of the tibia (he had won the Open on a broken leg) and a frayed Achilles tendon that was contributing more than its share of the pain and obviously would have stopped him had it snapped entirely. In any case, his 2008 season was over.

Tiger returned in 2009 to win seven tournaments (five on the PGA Tour) as well as his tenth Player of the Year award in thirteen seasons, but no majors. Still, for Earl's prediction to have even a chance to be right, it seemed something unexpected would have to happen.

CHAPTER TWENTY-FIVE

Vehicle one was traveling in a southeasterly direction while exiting the driveway of 6348 Deacon Circle. Vehicle one entered onto Deacon Court and continued to travel southeasterly. Vehicle one crossed over the roadway (Deacon Court) and the concrete curb onto the grass median of Deacon Court. Vehicle one swerved to the left in an attempt to travel northbound on Deacon Circle. Subsequently, vehicle one crossed over Deacon Circle and the concrete curb onto the grass shoulder on the east side of the roadway. As a result, the right side of vehicle one collided with a row of hedges. Vehicle one then swerved back to the left (west) crossing back over Deacon Circle and the concrete curb onto the grass shoulder on the west side of the roadway. Vehicle one then traveled in a northerly direction and the front of vehicle one collided with a fire hydrant in the front lawn of 6348 Deacon Circle. Vehicle one continued to travel in a northerly direction crossing over the driveway of 6342 Deacon Circle and the front of vehicle one collided with a tree. Vehicle one came to a final rest facing northbound in the front of 6342 Deacon Circle. The driver of vehicle one received injuries and was transported to Health Central Hospital.

—*Florida Highway Patrol*

As a society, professional golfers were at least as unlikely as their fellow men to marry for life. Ben Crenshaw won his first Masters while Polly was on her divorce cruise and the weight of Texas had been lifted off Ben. After twenty-four years together, Tom Watson put Linda on the waiver wire to wed Zimbabwean pro Denis Watson's old wife Hilary, who didn't even have to change her driver's license. Because of a deep rut Hal Sutton's fiancées were wearing in the aisle, his tour nickname was "Halimony."

In a day as innocent as the expression "ladies' man," Arnold Palmer was a renowned romantic. But it must also be said that Arnold's forty-four-year marriage to Winifred was loving. Innocent phrases aside, golf always had its share of libertines. Doug Sanders, in his magenta clothing, wasn't ashamed to say he lost his virginity in a Georgia ditch at the age of eleven, and in the seventh grade, when the teacher stepped out of the classroom for a few minutes, he and a girl made love standing up behind a Hammond's Map of the World.

Two weeks after turning pro, Sanders married a hometown sweetie; they had a son and separated. Next he wed a performing water skier at Cypress Gardens. They also divorced. He went through a lot of women who sent him mash notes, who said to look for them in the gallery. They'd be wearing a yellow dress. Eventually, he found Scotty. She left, too, but only after twenty-seven years of hard marriage. He missed her. "She was solid," he said. Standing beside the 18th green at St. Andrews, she was the one with the hands over her face in 1970 when Doug pushed a two-and-a-half-footer that would have beat

Nicklaus and won the British Open. "I sometimes go as long as five minutes," he'd say for forty years, "without thinking about that."

In the 1990s, a caddie gave back one of the most lucrative bags in the history of golf because he was tired of passing notes to pretty girls in the gallery. He felt like a pimp.

But, all that being said, golf never needed a shower more than it did after Tiger Woods careered off a fire hydrant into a tree, shaking loose a multitude of cocktail waitresses, lingerie models and porn actresses, none of whom accused him of gentleness.

Forgetting morality, Tiger had done the absolute last thing anyone ever expected him to do. He made himself ridiculous.

T ida could be heard on the 911 call wailing, "What happened?" A couple of days later, an ambulance was summoned to Deacon Circle for Elin's mom, Barbro, suffering a momentary anxiety attack. So, both mothers-in-law were actors in the piece. Plainly this wasn't your average Thanksgiving weekend in Windermere, Florida. It was a play in three acts by Edward Albee.

I am deeply sorry.

Incidentally, Tiger's big brother, Mark O'Meara, had long since been written out of the production. He and Alicia didn't go the distance after all. With a new wife, Mark was living in Texas now and hadn't been available for Isleworth counseling in some time. He and Tiger hadn't talked at all since the British Open in July.

If by "What happened?" Tida was asking why Tiger was leaving (fleeing?) the house barefoot at 2:30 in the morning, her question was never answered. "Well, it's all in the police report," Tiger said over and over, following the advice of a task force of lawyers and crisis managers, joined briefly by former White House press secretary Ari Fleischer.

I have let you down.

Not even in the corkscrew route the Escalade took from hedgeto-hydrant-to-tree could the local constabulary find enough probable cause to test Tiger's system for alcohol or drugs. (Two of the cops, the *Orlando Sentinel* reported, were on Tiger's payroll as moonlighting bodyguards.) Elin handed over a couple of small pill bottles containing Vicodin and Ambien. First responders found her seated alongside her unconscious husband with her legs folded under her on the street. His bleeding lip would take five stitches. "Officers looked for evidence of domestic violence," according to the FHP report, "but found none." Still, there was enough of a whiff of that for the ambulance crew to deny Elin's request to ride with Tiger to the hospital.

I have made you question who I am.

Elin told investigators she heard the crash, hopped onto a golf cart and sped to the scene. And, to extricate Tiger from the wreckage, she smashed out the rear window with a golf club. A golf club. As irony goes, this one had a shot at first place. Two home-security cameras that might have corroborated her account weren't working.

I am embarrassed.

In a fall so fast and far that you almost had to be Pope Benedict, Queen Elizabeth, Barack Obama or Tiger Woods to accomplish it, Tiger monopolized the *New York Post's* front cover for a record twenty consecutive days, bettering by one the previous streaker, September 11.

I was unfaithful.

The True Confessions ranged from sad to sick, involving as they did menstrual cycles and tampons, but one account in particular begged for Tiger to step forward and shout, "That's a lie!" A Vegas model and blackjack dealer said she was in Tiger's bed when he left to see Earl for the last time and then returned to make love, or whatever it was that Tiger considered love. She claimed to be sleeping beside him when Tida called to say Earl was dead.

To all of the charges, Tiger stood mute.

I had affairs.

On February 19, 2010, fresh from forty-five days of undefined therapy at the Gentle Path clinic in Hattiesburg, Mississippi, Tiger issued a thirteen-minute apology (the networks went live) at PGA Tour headquarters in Ponte Vedra Beach, Florida. Many listeners thought they heard echoes of a 12-step recovery program. The studio audience, including Tida, was handpicked. Elin was absent.

About a month after the crash, just before Tiger's thirty-fourth birthday, December 30, mother and son made their annual visit to the Buddhist temple. To one of her writers, Tida said, "I tell him, 'Tiger, right now you are in a dark hole, and I know it's hard, but you can do it. You know Mom is strong and you have my blood. You are strong, too. You made a big mistake, but now you know the cost. So you are going to be much better and stronger, a good husband and a good father. Just go to work like you do.'"

I cheated.

The Tour, which normally ladled its logo thickly over everything, had the very good taste to leave the stage and rostrum blank. Tiger stood in front of a blue curtain with lush folds that brought to mind a funeral parlor or execution chamber. The only thing Woods ever had in common with Muhammad Ali, a certain quirk of complexion, was front and center. When on song, Ali glowed like a copper kettle. But on his off nights, he looked blotchy. Tiger's face was completely washed out. He appeared exhausted and depressed. Why wouldn't he be?

I thought only about myself.

Near the end of Ali's career, ringside judges handed him a number of specious decisions because they were afraid that, when he left, he might take boxing with him. For similar reasons, golf was staunchly on Tiger's side. Tour Commissioner Tim Finchem, a diminutive man anyway, somehow managed to make himself even smaller in the front row. He continued to call Woods "an American hero." Nike chairman

Phil Knight said, "When his career is over, you'll look back on these indiscretions as a minor blip, but the media is making a big deal of it right now." He didn't mean the golf media. None of golf's unctuous essayists considered Tiger's situation to be irredeemable.

Meanwhile, sponsors tied indirectly to the sport (Accenture, Gillette, Gatorade, et al.) headed for the hills.

I felt I was entitled.

After the speech, Tiger's earnestness was a subject of national debate. Certainly he was more animated in the sections of the talk dearer to him, like his children's privacy. But just the fact that he was in rehab spoke for sincerity. And two clipped sentences late in the presentation sounded like the truth. "I do plan to return to golf one day," he said. "I just don't know when that day will be."

"He will be away longer than people think," said friend and former Stanford teammate Notah Begay, seated in the front row. "My best guess is three months."

A better guess would have been three weeks.

I was wrong. I was foolish. I don't get to play by different rules.

The next step in the 12-step program (Fleischer's?) called for five-minute one-on-ones with Tom Rinaldi of ESPN and Kelly Tilghman of the Golf Channel. "I ask this question respectfully," Rinaldi tiptoed up to it, "but of course at a distance from your family life. When you look at it now, why did you get married?"

The questions behind his question, asked a little less respectfully, included:

Was it just time for you to get married? Was image a consideration? Did the image-makers order up a wife and two kids? Was it true you were with one of these hitchhikers when Elin was in the maternity ward? Are you aware Nicklaus fainted at the birth of every child?

"Why?" Tiger repeated the spoken question. "Because I loved her. I loved Elin with everything I have. And that's something that makes me feel even worse, that I did this to someone I loved that much."

Not wasting her powder, Tilghman said, "It's been reported that members of your team, your inner circle, were involved in your misdoings. Is it true?"

"That is not true," Tiger said. "It was all me. I'm the one who did it. I'm the one who acted the way I acted. No one knew what was going on. I'm sure if more people would have known in my inner circle, they would've stopped it or tried to put a stop to it. But I kept it all to myself."

This was a lie on its face. Someone knew what he was doing. Several someones. Maybe nobody except Tiger could recite the entire roster, but just before his handlers took to the barricades, one of them helped facilitate an extraordinarily uncharacteristic, not to say incredibly suspicious, favor of an interview and a cover shoot for *Men's Fitness* magazine, sister publication of the *National Enquirer*. If that wasn't a blackmail payoff, it sure smelled like one.

I brought this shame on myself.

In any case, Tiger had been circumspect only around writers, broadcasters and any other bystanders who could hurt him. In front of those who posed no risks, like the photographers and his regular posse, he didn't hide the leers.

My failures have made me look at myself in a way I never wanted to before.

Finally, Tilghman asked, "If your father were here today and looked back on these last four months, what would he say to you?"

"He'd be very disappointed in me," Tiger said. "We would have numerous long talks, and that's one of the things I miss. I miss his guidance. I wish I could have had his guidance through all this, to have him help straighten me up. I know he would have done it."

"What do you think he would say?"

"You can't say it on air. But he would have been very direct and basically said you need to get your life headed in the same direction again."

It's up to me to start living a life of integrity.

In announcing that the enablers had survived, Tiger might as well have said the marriage had not. If the friend who served as a mistress-es's travel agency was staying, then Elin was going. Jesper Parnevik, the player who introduced them, took Woods's betrayals personally. "I vouched for the guy," Parnevik told ESPN's *Outside the Lines*. "I told her this is the guy that I think is everything you want. He's true. He's honest. He has great values. He has everything you would want in a guy. . . . I was wrong."

It's hard to admit that I need help, but I do.

When Tiger stopped talking, he and Tida embraced. "I'm so proud of you," she whispered. "Never think you stand alone. Mom will always be there for you, and I love you." Then he dissolved into the blue background, and Tida called the few pool reporters to attention. "You know what?" she said. "I'm so proud to be his mother. Period. This thing, it teaches him, just like golf. Golf is just like life. When you make a mistake, you learn from your mistake and move on stronger. That's the way he is. As a human being, everyone has faults, makes mistakes and sins. We all do. But we move on when we make a mistake and learn from it. I am upset the way media treated him like he's a criminal. He didn't kill anybody. He didn't do anything illegal. They've been carrying on from Thanksgiving until now. That's not right."

In a less crowded setting and a gentler tone, she said, "Since a little boy, Tiger always loved competition—he born with that. So he will face himself, solve the problem, and when he comes back, he will still love to play and love to win. I think more than ever, because his closet will be cleaned out and his mind will be free. And I know he will break Jack's record."

Before long, Tida was calling around to editors and writers to warn them that she was monitoring all of the reports and in the end would not forget who wrote what. "I'm making a list," she said.

I am the one who needs to change. I owe it to those closest to me to be-

come a better man. I need to regain my balance. I need to make my behavior more respectful of the game.

If Elin did take a golf club to the Escalade in anger, the act wasn't without precedent on the PGA Tour. In 1998, Nick Faldo's Porsche was worked over "with either a nine-iron or a wedge," as color commentator Faldo reported the action himself. Wielding the club was Brenna Cepelak, a twenty-year-old American coed when Nick took up with her three years earlier while married to Gill Faldo. He took up with Gill while married to Melanie Faldo. Subsequently he married and divorced Valerie Faldo (the object of Brenna's grumpiness).

England marked Nick's untidy life in its traditional way. On her birthday in 2009, Queen Elizabeth II patted his shoulder with the flat of a sword and dubbed him Sir Nicholas Faldo, the purest knight-*errant* since Lancelot shagged Guinevere.

I ask you to find room in your heart to one day believe in me again.

Tiger had taken his place in the pantheon of athletes who swear like men and screw like boys, and gallery yahoos would never again yell, "You the man!" without at least a tinge of irony.

CHAPTER TWENTY-SIX

In the handicapping around Tiger's return, the smart money was on Arnold Palmer's Invitational at Bay Hill in Orlando. The smart money was wrong. By the time that end-of-March event rolled around, Woods had already declared for the Masters April 8.

The morning before Arnie's tournament began, its eventual winner, Ernie Els, was in his Lake Nona home having breakfast. He was recalling the 1996 British Open at Lytham, where Els came second to Tom Lehman and Tiger finished twenty-second, low amateur. That was quietly the start of everything. Ernie and Tiger had a short beer and a long talk.

"The bar in the old locker room," Els said, "is just behind the eighteenth. If you stand up on one of those benches, you can look out the window and see the green. It's right there. I was sitting alone, disappointed. I had bogeyed sixteen and eighteen. Wrong clubs. Two bunkers. I had to wait for Lehman to finish, to clap for Tom at the ceremony, and was having a beer, kind of blowing off steam. You know how I am."

His nickname, "The Big Easy," was the biggest lie since "The Merry Mex." Only when the cameras were on was Lee Trevino lighthearted. One time, while lacing up his spikes in a locker room, he was asked, "Who supplies your shoes these days, Lee?" "I buy my own shoes," the real Trevino answered. "Where were they when I needed shoes?"

"Tiger walked up to my table," Els said. "If it had been anyone else, I would have told him to give me some space. But I could see he had something on his mind. You know, in those days, he was a shy guy and he'd give you your space. He was very respectful. He would never have invaded mine for something that wasn't important. That's what I figured anyway."

They had been paired together at both summer Opens in 1995, when they were the U.S. Open and U.S. Amateur champions. Around the world, they had bumped into each other here and there, at Carnoustie for a Scottish Open, at Phuket, Thailand, for an IMG special. "We had a little friendship going," Ernie said. "We would talk, loosely."

So Tiger sat down. "And I said, 'Shit, you played really well,' and dah-dah-dah-dah-dah. I gave him my whole story, my sob story. But I finally looked straight at him and said, 'What's the matter, Tiger?' He just said, 'I'm thinking about it.' Of course, I knew what that meant. He was thinking of turning pro. I said, 'Why are you thinking so hard?'

"'I don't know whether I'm ready.'

"'Mate, I've never seen anybody readier than you are. You still have to learn a lot, but you can probably win right now without knowing too much. Sometimes it's better not to know too much. You have so much talent. Have you spoken to your father?'

"'Yeah, I've spoken to my father. We've discussed it. But I'm worried about how people are going to look at me. I haven't finished college.'"

Ernie laughed, then and now. "'Look, I didn't even go to college [not for a lack of offers; every American institute of higher learning with a good golf team saw tremendous academic potential in the South African]. You don't have to worry about that stuff. [Jack Nicklaus didn't finish college.] You've got your whole life ahead of you. If you're ready to go, you've got to go, Tiger. You're ready to make your own mark.'"

"Ernie was very helpful in my decision," Tiger told me a month later in Milwaukee, standing outside the press tent after delivering his birdies and bogeys. "He gave me a lot of insights from both sides of it. I shot sixty-six on Friday at Lytham, to either set or tie the amateur record, I think. Something kicked in that day. Almost like I'd found a whole new style of playing golf. I had heard that phrase 'playing within yourself' my whole life. I finally understood what it meant, and the game has been easier ever since. After playing that well in a major, it was at least worth a thought of moving on. Prior to that, honestly, I was in the process of getting my Stanford classes organized for the fall." When I called Els from Milwaukee to ask if Woods was ready, he said, "That's the dumbest question I've ever been asked. Have you seen him?"

"To me," Ernie continued, "it was one of the most human things about Tiger, that day at Lytham. He was twenty. I was a young guy, too, just twenty-six. I guess he wanted confirmation from a guy he was secure with. Maybe I shouldn't have talked him into it. Maybe I should have let him finish college."

Els didn't mean that. He was a sportsman in the old-fashioned sense. Modern players like Phil Mickelson or Vijay Singh, and players from a generation or so back, like Curtis Strange and Lanny Wadkins, would have a hard time relating to this, but even under the demoralizing circumstances, Ernie couldn't help but be a little thrilled by how good Woods was. And, to the disapproval of some, he said so out loud. ("He's from Mars.")

"You feel a little defenseless against this bloody guy at times," Els said, "when he's on. He beat me at Disney in nineteen-ninety-nine, by a shot. The day we played together, I think he shot sixty-six and I shot sixty-seven. He was just out of this world. The power. The accuracy. It was amazing how he was driving the golf ball. Now it's his weakness. Back then, it was his strength. He just drove it unbelievably.

"You know, I was basically the kid with everything once. When I started out, I just knew I could beat Greg Norman. I just knew I could beat Nick Price. But you have this guy come in and you could see the difference. I didn't want to see it. Even my dad kept telling me, 'Hey, you can beat this *fucking* guy.' I said, yes, I can. I know I can. But I don't think I can beat him more than he can beat me. I can win thirty percent, but he can win seventy. Against everyone else, it was almost the other way around.

"Then Curtis Strange started blasting me, saying how soft I am and I've got no balls. Even though I was the only guy really taking him on. No one else was, at least not consistently. Mickelson has stepped up over the last few years, but before that he wasn't even on the horizon.

"Strange and others couldn't see it," Ernie said. "They didn't get it."

Into microphones Els never mentioned his own moments versus Tiger, though he had them. He defeated Woods from behind at Riviera and from in front at Doral, while playing with him for the last thirty-six holes at Bay Hill, and when holding on in the same stormy weather at Muirfield, where Ernie won the Open Championship. In a two-man sudden-death overtime at a Presidents Cup, they dropped putt after putt on top of each other until darkness called it a draw.

"Most of the time, of course," Els said, "he was playing in his own country. If I was playing in my own country, that support and help I would have gotten might have pushed me over the line now and then. And I'm not saying that in a negative way. It's just the way it is."

In an early and unusual slip into candor, after Els beat him and the other '97 major champions (Justin Leonard and Davis Love III) in a two-day Hawaiian television show, Woods said, "Ernie sort of played an old man's game today to my kid's game. He's got those soft hands and gets it in play and lets me blow it all over the place. Then he out-thinks me and out-savvies me. I want to get a little more like that." And, of course, he did.

"He was such a great kid then," Els said. "I mean, a really great kid. *You* knew him. A *tough* little guy, but a shy, nice kid. You could see he had a lot of chip on him because of all of his father's influence. Earl was putting it on him to look the guys in the eye, and obviously he did an unbelievable job. Tiger's always had that killer instinct. My dad was also a tough guy, you know? A transporter [trucker]. You can ask him about the arguments we had. He wanted to run my life, too. I finally said, 'Listen, Dad, don't you *ever, fucking,* do that with me. I'll do it my way.'

"As I get older [forty, now], I see how much I'm like my father. I also have a temper. I'm also highly strung every now and again. As you well know, I'm different outwardly than inwardly. When I'm unhappy with myself, people better not come too close. There's a punch inside me. But I don't think you'll get anyplace without that punch. You can ask any athlete. It's in there, whether they show it or not."

When Tiger first moved to Isleworth, not so far from Lake Nona, Woods and Els got together a few times, for a barbecue or a tennis game. "You should see him play tennis," Ernie said. "He's hopeless, absolutely hopeless." But boxers don't go to dinner with their sparring partners. They may have to fight for real someday.

"I could see people were starting to stick around him, flock around him, and I just said, 'You know what? I'm not going to get in there.' It's not like it was a completely conscious decision on my part or Liezl's part. We just let it go. If you ask me whether I regret it, a little bit, yes. What started hurting him, what started changing him— I'm not sure Liezl and I could have made the slightest bit of difference." But they could have tried.

Every man has to go his own way, and how much help one can offer another is problematic. John Daly and Els were pals. They met in the late '80s, as kids essentially, playing South Africa's Sunshine Tour. On the second day of the 1997 U.S. Open at Congressional, Daly walked off after nine holes without a word to his playing partners, Els and Payne Stewart. Tying and untying their shoelaces, they did everything they could to postpone hitting their second shots at 10 and automatically disqualifying him. But he never came back.

"What do you think of your buddy now?" someone asked Els later in the pressroom. Ernie's reply was all you needed to know about Daly, Els and the nature of friendships between men.

"He's my friend," Ernie said. "I love John Daly. He breaks my heart."

In Els's opinion, the first half of Tiger's change was inevitable. "How he changed with people, I could see that happening, and I understood it. He turned inward, away from the world, because he had to. I do the same almost in South Africa. I try my best to be everybody's friend, to accommodate everybody. You can ask Liezl how much it frustrates me. Because, whatever you do, you can never do enough. There's no way. I think that's what started hurting Tiger. He does a lot of foundation stuff, he does a lot of good. But whatever he does, it's never enough."

As for the second half of the change, the darker territory, maybe Tiger reached back for something he thought he missed as a boy. "I asked him once," Royce said, "'Don't you ever want to do a little dirt, Tiger? Be a little bad? Spray graffiti paint all over a wall at school, or something?' 'You know, I probably would,' he told me, 'if I didn't know I was going to be famous someday.' I couldn't believe it."

Even before Tiger's secret life was exposed, the fear of him in the locker room had started to ease. Tiger, not Y. E. Yang, blinked at the 2009 PGA. The Korean was the one who made the putt at the end. Tiger was the one who overshot the greens. "The talk in the locker room now," Els said, "is that the two best players in the world [Woods and Mickelson] can't hit a fucking fairway. Guys who actually have no chance to beat Tiger are all of a sudden thinking they can. They're saying to themselves and each other, 'Hell, I hit it better than he does.'

Of course they're wrong. But, the point is, they're not as scared of him as they used to be. They're starting to have more courage, so to speak. After his speech, I stuck my bloody foot in there. Somebody asked me what I thought, and I said I thought it was selfish to do that on a Friday in the middle of the Match Play. Monday is the day for speeches. I promise you, everybody in the locker room was saying the same thing."

Ernie had an opinion about the world-shaking Masters coming up in two weeks. "I think he'll have a good Masters," he said. "I think he'll contend. I think so. He's that good. But, win it? No."

When asked why not, he said, "There's a guilt." Then he thought for a moment and added, "There's a conscience."

He said, "I know it's the worst cliché of all, but it's true. Golf, just as a game, is an animal that tests your character. It beats you down until you feel you're not a good person anymore. Things start piling up against you, and you say to yourself, 'You're a fucking asshole.'"

In 2004, Els came within inches of winning all four majors. He set a one-year record for scar tissue that may never be broken. Ernie lost the Masters when Mickelson holed a long putt. He lost the U.S. Open playing in the final twosome with the winner, countryman Retief Goosen. He lost the British in a playoff against Todd Hamilton. He missed a putt that would have put him in a playoff at the PGA. Then one of his knees came unstrung. Finally, Ben.

In late May of 2005, the day after Samantha's sixth birthday, Ernie was barbecuing in his backyard off the 16th fairway at Wentworth in England, where the European PGA Tour's BMW tournament was in progress. Ernie, Samantha and Ben, age two, had just popped out of the swimming pool, where they resembled a family of otters. Still in his swimming trunks and back in the peach golf shirt he wore on the course that day, Ernie was cooking the chicken and the chops and assembling the chutney and onion sandwiches. "I miss smelling the

African smells," he said. "I miss the smell when I get to George [east of Cape Town] on the beach, that's in the air, you know? I miss the smell of the food. It's the bush. We call it the bush. It's the breeze. It's the sound of the animals."

A commercial jet streaming over just then mesmerized Ben. "Look at him, he likes airplanes," Ernie whispered. "Look at Liezl and look at me. Ben is going to be a big boy, isn't he? He's going to be a rugby player." This was before the seizures and the diagnosis of autism.

"My boy Ben [seven, now]," Ernie said in Lake Nona, "is the reason we're in Florida more these days, usually in Jupiter, near the best treatment and facilities for autism. It's tough on Samantha, who had ten great years in England and had to leave all her friends behind and start what amounts to a new life. Samantha's a beautiful girl. She says she wouldn't want Ben to be any different than he is. She loves him just as he is. And Ben's a wonderful boy in his own right. He has a great sense of humor and a lovely disposition. His condition has changed me enormously. I have a whole new perspective on life."

Liezl said, "I think men and women react differently to these things. A woman asks, 'What do we do next?' A man asks, 'What did we do wrong?' Ernie was so hurt for so long. But watch them together now, when Ben's riding up on Ernie's shoulders. He idolizes his daddy."

To Ben, Ernie must have seemed twelve feet tall. Looking at them looking at each other, smiling as though they shared a magnificent secret, could make you cry.

Back on the subject of guilt and consciences, I told Els, "You know, not everybody has a conscience. There are robots out there." Before we knew who Tiger was, he knew who he was. It didn't seem to stop him from hitting splendid golf shots. "I still say," Ernie said, "you can't play your best without self-respect. Obviously Elin married the person she believed he was. If he sincerely wants to become that person, good on him. I'll support him. Absolutely. That's what I've done my whole career, supported him. But, to be honest, I wonder where he's going to put his energy now. Into fitness? More and more fitness? Tiger's going to be a very lonely guy, I think, unfortunately."

A number of Ernie's memories were set in bars. Like his father Neels, the tough guy (the tender guy, too), Ernie had a bit of a thirst.

"I was in the Old Road Hole Bar at St. Andrews—a really great bar," he said, "with a bunch of friends having quite a few beers during the Dunhill. It was nineteen-ninety-four, I think. Anyway, I had already won my first U.S. Open. A gray-haired woman was sitting in the corner there. 'Master Els, come over here!' she called. 'Come over here, Master Els!'

"So I walked over and said, 'How are you, ma'am? How are you doing?'

"She said, 'Do you know who I am?'

"'I've no idea, ma'am.'

"'Have you heard of Henry Cotton [Sir Henry Cotton, winner of the Open Championship in 1934 (St. George's), 1937 (Carnoustie), and 1948 (Muirfield)]?'

"'Absolutely, yeah, I've heard of him.'

"'Well, I'm his daughter, and I want to give you some advice.' I think she'd also had a couple of scotches.

"So, she looked at me and said, 'You are going to have a long career. You're going to be great. But let me tell you something. Don't let anybody ever fuck you around, OK?' Just like that. 'You do it on your own terms and at your own time. Don't let anybody fuck you around.'"

On your lips, mine, Tiger's, Earl's, and Ernie's, it's not the prettiest word. But sometimes it's the perfect word, and on the lips of a silver lady in a corner at the Old Road Hole Bar, it's perfectly charming.

"OK, ma'am," Els told her, "I'll keep that in mind." Of course, as with everything else, he would have to learn it for himself.

CHAPTER TWENTY-SEVEN

I would also like to, I guess, make another little comment before we start. I know that the players over the past few months have been bombarded with questions by all of you and the public as well, and I would like to tell all of the players that, hopefully after today, after answering questions at this press conference, the players can be left alone to focus on the Masters and focus on their game. Not only for this week, but going forward as well. And I certainly apologize to all of them for having to endure what they have had to endure the past few months.

A lot has happened in my life over the past five months, and I'm here at the Masters to play and compete. And I'm just really excited about doing that. I missed the competition. I missed seeing the guys out here. A lot of my friends I haven't seen in a while. It was great to play [a practice round] with Freddie [Couples] and Jim [Furyk], two of my best friends out here, and I played with Mark [O'Meara] yesterday for nine holes and I'm playing with him again tomorrow. So it's been just an incredible experience so far here at the Masters.

I didn't know what to expect with regards to the reception, and I'll tell you what, the galleries couldn't have been nicer. I mean, it was just incredible. The encouragement I got, it was just—it blew me away, to be honest with you, it really did.

Having to look at myself in a light that I never wanted to look at myself—that's been difficult. How far astray I got from my core fundamentals and the core morals that my mom and dad taught me. Having to break all that down, with all of the denial and rationalization. To cut through that, I had to really take a hard look at myself. And that's when I started finding strength and peace. The other difficult part I think over the past few months was the constant harassment of my family. My wife and kids being photographed everywhere they go, being badgered. That's tough. That's tough on them, because it's really hard for us to heal and try and get through this as best we can.

I'm actually going to try not to get as hot when I play. But then again, when I'm not as hot, I'm not going to be as exuberant either. I can't play one without the other, and so I've made a conscious decision to try and tone down my negative outbursts and consequently I'm sure my positive outbursts will be calmed down as well. Just try to be more respectful of the game and acknowledge the fans like I did today—that was an incredible reception today for all eighteen holes—and show my appreciation for them. I haven't done that in the past few years, and that was wrong of me. So many kids have looked up to me and so many fans have supported me over the years. Just wanted to say thank you to them, especially going through all of this over the past few months. It really put things in perspective for me, how much I have appreciated—or underappreciated—the fans in the game of golf.

Earlier in my career, I was at peace, and I've had some great years. Unfortunately what I've done over the past few years has been just terrible to my family. And the fact I won golf tournaments I think is irrelevant. It's the pain and the damage that I've caused, you know, my wife, my mom, my wife's family, my kids. Going forward, I'm going to have to explain all this to my kids. That's my responsibility. I did it. And I take full responsibility for it, and as I said, winning golf tournaments is irrelevant compared to the damage I've caused.

Well, [to a question on Canadian doctor Anthony Galea, arrested with performance-enhancing drugs in his possession] he did come to my house. He never gave me HGH or any PEDs. I've never taken that my entire life. I've never taken any illegal drugs ever, for that matter. I had PRP, platelet-enriched plasma treatments, and basically what that is, is they draw blood from your arm, spin it in a centrifuge and spin the plasma into the injuries. As you all know, in two-thousand-eight I blew out my ACL and part of my reconstruction with my LCL, it wasn't reacting properly, it was a little bit stuck. And so I had the PRP injection into my LCL. And then in December, I started to train, started running again and I tore my Achilles in my right leg. I then had PRP injections throughout the year. I kept retearing it throughout the year and throughout the summer. I used tape most of the year to play, and so—I also went to hyperbaric chambers after the injections—it does help you heal faster and I did everything I possibly could to heal faster so I could get back on the golf course going through the PRP injection.

[On the Augusta reception again] That first tee, I didn't know what to expect, I really didn't. It's one of those things where I've never been in this position before. To be out there in front of the people where I have done some things that are just horrible, and you know. For the fans to really want to see me play golf again, I mean, that felt great, that really did. Usually I kind of focus on placements of shots and getting ready, but today was a little bit different. I kind of took it in a little bit more, sort of more than I think I have in a long time, and it felt really good.

During the practice rounds, acknowledging the fans and their support for me is important. For them to still cheer for me is just incredible, it really is.

I've taken them [Ambien and Vicodin], yes. As everyone knows, I've had some pretty interesting knee situations over the years. I've had, what? Four operations now on my left knee? Then last year with my torn Achilles, it hurt quite a bit at times. And yeah, I did take that. Most of the time I was on the Ambien was when my dad was sick and when my dad died. That was a tough time in my life. So that's when I was still taking some of those things to help me sleep. And that's about it.

You know, my knee feels great. The only time it doesn't feel good is when a front comes through. Arthritis is there when you get a little older. But other than that, it feels great. It's strong. It's explosive again, which is great, and my Achilles is good now, so I'm training like I used to years ago.

He [Galea] worked with so many athletes. That's also one of the reasons why I saw Dr. Whiten for my eyes is he's worked on a lot of different athletes and there's a certain comfort level to that when a person has worked with athletes.

I was in [rehab] for forty-five days and it was to take a hard look at myself, and I did, and I've come out better. I'm certainly a much better person for it than I was going in. Does that mean I'm ever going to stop doing that? No. I've got to still continue with my treatment. And that's going forward. That's not going to stop in the near future for sure.

Part of the problem I had is that the way I was thinking was not correct. And as part of where I was at, I was rationalizing and denying and in total denial at times. Whatever I did, I lied to myself, I lied to others, and just because I was winning golf tournaments doesn't mean a thing. The way I was thinking caused so much harm with the people that I love and care about the most on this planet. After I started going to treatment, that's when they started stripping all of that away. [To be] more centered, more balanced, that's where I'm headed towards. That's what I'm working towards each and every day. I meditate religiously again like I used to, going back to my roots with my Buddhism with my mom. I need to do these things the way I used to do it. And unfortunately I got away from that, and I just lost that and unfortunately also lost my life in the process.

When I gave my speech in February, I had no intentions of playing golf in the near future at all. I just had barely started practicing two days prior to that. That was the first time I hit balls. And then I started hitting more balls and more balls and more balls and I started getting the itch again to start playing again. And Hank [Haney] came down and we started working again and that felt great. It felt like old times. So much has transpired, it felt like old times to have Hank out there working on my game for hours and hours and hours on end, and that's when I made the decision to come back and play. The reason why I didn't come back and play earlier than that, whether it was Tavistock Cup or Bay Hill, I wasn't ready for it. I wasn't even near physically ready to play at this level, and I needed more time. Hank has come down quite a bit. We've come up here on two different occasions, the last two Mondays and Tuesdays we have come up here to do some work on the golf course, and here we are.

I've had a lot of support, and that's been the great thing about it. Probably just prior to Christmas I made the decision to enter rehab. And having spent Christmas Day with my family was just incredible, and then having to go off from there into treatment, that was a very difficult time, because what people probably don't realize is that because of the time frame of it, I missed my son's first birthday. And that hurts. That hurts a lot. I vowed I would never miss another one after that. I can't go back to where I was. I want to be a part of my son's life and my daughter's life going forward and I missed his first birthday. I mean, that was very hard that day and something I regret, and I probably will for the rest of my life.

Elin is not coming this week, no. I certainly have everyone [agent Mark Steinberg, caddie Steve Williams, et al.] around me. I've lied and deceived a lot of people and a lot of people didn't know what I was doing, either. So I've had, again, a tremendous amount of support as well from others on the outside, and it's been a difficult time, but also I'm actually surprised how much support I've gotten as well.

I don't know [if part of him wanted to get caught]. All I

know is I acted just terribly, poorly, made just incredibly bad decisions, and decisions that have hurt so many people close to me. That's enough. You know, I fooled myself as well. As I said, I lied to a lot of people, deceived a lot of people, kept others in the dark, rationalized, and even lied to myself. And when I stripped all of that away and started realizing what I had done, the full magnitude of it, it's pretty brutal. I take full responsibility for what I've done, and I don't take that lightly.

My dad, it's amazing how he says things that come back. "In order to help people, you have to first learn how to help yourself." That's what he always used to say. I never understood that. When I was in treatment, I wrote that down. I looked at it every day. By learning how to help myself, I can help more people going forward, infinitely more, than I did prior to all this.

Well, to have Stevie [Williams] back, it's tremendous. It really is. He's a great friend, always has been and always will be. We are honest with one another. We've had a long talk, and it was a great talk as well. It's great to have him on the bag. He's excited to get back and compete again. He's been doing really well racing-wise. He won the New Zealand Championships. But also, this is another part of his life that he loves to do. He loves to be back here at Augusta, and for us to go back out there as a team together, it feels good.

When I went through that period when my father was sick and my father passed away, it put things in perspective real quick. And when my kids were born, again, it put it in perspective. And then what I've done here, it puts it in perspective. It's that it's not about championships. It's about how you live your life. And I had not done that the right way for a while, and I needed to change that. And going forward, I need to be a better man than I was before. And just because I've gone through treatment doesn't mean it stops. I'm trying as hard as I possibly can each and every day to get my life better and better and stronger, and if I win championships along the way, so be it. But along the way, I want to help more people that haven't quite learned to help themselves, just like how I was.

The police investigated the accident and they cited me a hundred sixty-six bucks and it's a closed case.

Do I understand why they [sponsors] dropped me? Of course. I made a lot of mistakes in my life. And I totally understand why they would do that. Hopefully I can prove to the other companies going forward that I am a worthy investment, that I can help their company, help their company grow and represent them well. I felt like I was representing companies well in the past, but then again, I wasn't doing it the right way, because of what I was engaged in.

[Golf-wise], nothing's changed. Going to go out there and try to win this thing. The fact that I haven't really played at all, that's a little bit concerning. I'm hoping I get my feel back quickly. You know, feel for the game, feel for shots, feel for how my body is reacting and what my distances are going to be. I hope I get that back, you know, relatively quickly. Hopefully the first hole. If not, please hope it's the second hole. But that's what I'm looking forward to. I'm looking forward to getting out there and doing that. I'm looking forward to the first tee and teeing off, getting out there and doing what I've done for a very long time.

As far as my peers, everyone's been great. It's amazing how many hugs I've gotten from the guys. This is only

Monday. So I've seen the guys here yesterday and today and then a couple of times that I've been up here prior to this, some of the other players have been up here as well. I'm actually surprised by how well received I've been.

[Before last December] I had not hit far enough on the bottom to make myself look at what I've done and what I was engaged in. Once that happened, then I went to rehab.

That first tee [Thursday], I'm looking forward to it. I haven't looked forward to that tee shot in a long time, not like this. It feels fun again. You know, that's something that's been missing. Have I been winning, have I been competing, have I been doing well? Yeah, I have. I've won numerous times the last few years but I wasn't having anywhere near the amount of fun. Why? Because look at what I was engaged in. When you live a life where you're lying all the time, life is not fun. And that's where I was. Now that's been stripped all away and here I am. And it feels fun again.

CHAPTER TWENTY-EIGHT

Augusta offered the most contained and civilized environment for Tiger's reentry, though golf audiences are known to be compliant pretty much everywhere. They root for everyone, even for anonymous balls that come flying over the hill. "Be right!" "Get in the hole!" "Awww!" For all they knew, Vijay Singh hit it. If Charles Manson was on the tee, somebody would holler, "Knock it stiff, Charlie!" Then the others would all shush each other so the little prick could concentrate.

In their times, Greg Norman and Tom Watson waded into U.S. Open crowds looking for whoever it was who muttered the word "choker." But that's the rare exception. At the 2010 Masters, the only tomato that came Woods's way was hurled at his head like a message pitch by Augusta National Chairman Billy Payne. And, really, who was in a better position to moralize than the overseer of sports' most historic bastion of racism turned highest cathedral of misogyny?

"Finally," Payne said to the assembled press, winding up his state of the Masters address, "we are not unaware of the significance of this week to a very special player, Tiger Woods. A man who in a brief thirteen years clearly and emphatically proclaimed and proved his game to be worthy of the likes of Bobby Jones, Jack Nicklaus and Arnold Palmer. As he ascended in our rankings of the world's great golfers, he became an example to our kids that success is directly attributable to hard work and effort.

"But as he now says himself, he forgot in the process to remember that with fame and fortune comes responsibility, not invisibility. It is not simply the degree of his conduct that is so egregious here. It is the fact that he disappointed all of us, and more importantly, our kids and our grandkids. Our hero did not live up to the expectations of the role model we saw for our children.

"Is there a way forward? I hope yes. I think yes. But certainly his future will never again be measured only by his performance against par, but measured by the sincerity of his efforts to change. I hope he now realizes that every kid he passes on the course wants his swing but would settle for his smile. I hope he can come to understand that life's greatest rewards are reserved for those who bring joy to the lives of other people.

"We at Augusta hope and pray that our great champion will begin his new life here tomorrow in a positive, hopeful and constructive manner, but this time with a significant difference from the past. This year, it will not be just for him, but for all of us who believe in second chances."

Coincidentally that evening, in an unwitting reply, Nike and IMG released a new television commercial that gave just about everyone the creeps. In it, Tiger stood silently by, looking thoroughly chastened. Nike's closing catchphrase, "Just Do it," was tastefully omitted.

"Tiger," said a spliced-together voice-over of Earl from the hereafter, "I am more prone to be inquisitive, to promote discussion. I want to find out what your thinking was. I want to find out what your feelings are. And did you learn anything?"

Really, two voices were coming from the grave, the other one belonging to the marketing genius who founded the International Management Group, Mark McCormack. McCormack made his living, a huge living, shaping images. His life ended in 2003, four months after a heart attack during a dermatology procedure put him in a coma. At seventy-two, McCormack had gone in for a face-lift. In a way, the great image-maker died of vanity.

A goatee Tiger was featuring at the start of the week was gone by Thursday afternoon, proving that, while Gillette was no longer paying him to shave, at least he was trusting himself again around razors. To shield his eyes from a lime-green pollen that was piling up by the inch on parked cars, Tiger wore dark glasses. They seemed appropriate.

"I always believed Tiger showed up in character," said Paul Azinger, America's Ryder Cup captain in 2008. "Almost like an actor, he played a role. On Sunday he'd show up in black pants and a shirt the color of blood and get out of that car and step right into character. *I'm invincible. I'm the most fit. I'm the most mentally strong. I'm the most prepared. I'm the most dedicated and committed and single-minded guy out here.* Well, all that's gone. Tiger has lost that invincibility about him. He's now painfully human. The sunglasses are just a way of saying, 'I don't want you looking in my eyes.' It's not the pollen. I mean, come on."

The 4-under-par 68 Tiger shot in the opening round, by the cold numbers his best Masters start ever, tied him for seventh place. Fifty-one-year-old Fred Couples was leading (66). Sixty-year-old Watson was one behind. For the moment, it was an old-timers' game.

What had Tiger expected?

"Oh, I expected to go out there and shoot something under par today. Looking at all the scores, I could see guys were just tearing the place apart. The tees were mostly up, the pins were mostly friendly, especially on the par fives."

Having gone 144 days between tournaments, did he feel more nervous than usual?

"No, it felt normal. Try to hit a little fade off the first tee, try to take something off of it and make sure I got it in play. That was about it. From there, I just went about my business."

And what was the reaction of the spectators, whom the Green Jackets refer to archly, and the broadcasters tamely, as "patrons"?

"The reception was incredible from the time I went to the practice green to putt, to the range, back to the green, off to the first tee, and pretty much all day. It was just incredible." He was exaggerating, but just slightly.

What about his pledge to tone down emotions, both negative and positive?

"I was pretty calm all day. I was just trying to plod my way along and not throw away shots. I felt like today most of the guys were going to shoot some good numbers, and they did. Unfortunately I didn't putt very good today. Otherwise it could have been a very special round."

When he eagled 15, was he consciously trying to rein himself in?

"No, I was just trying to make the putt. First putt I made all day."

So, it was largely business as usual?

"It felt like that, it really did. I got into the flow of the round early. The rhythm of just playing and hitting shots and thinking my way around the golf course; you know, ball placement. I got into that very early, which was nice. At Winged Foot after my dad died [a two-month layoff], I didn't get into the rhythm right away. It took probably three or four holes, and by then I was two or three over. You can't do that at the U.S. Open. Today I was one under through three."

Speaking of Earl, what did Tiger have to say about the grave-robbers' ad?

"Well, I think it's very apropos. I think that's what my dad would say. It's amazing how it—how my dad can speak to me from different ways, even when he's long gone. He's still helping me. I think any son who has lost a father who meant so much in their life, I think they would understand the spot."

Finally, what did his first day back mean to him?

"It meant that I'm two shots off the lead. That's what it means."

Nothing more?

"I'm here to play a golf tournament."

The tipped caps, the willing autographs, the ready smiles of the practice days were behind him now. He had his old crust back.

Meanwhile, Phil Mickelson started with a 67. Eleven months earlier, his wife, Amy, was diagnosed with breast cancer. A few weeks after that, his mother Mary received the same jolt. Phil had been having an indifferent spring, but both his mind and heart were understandably elsewhere.

Almost to a man, pro golfers are father guys, and Phil was close to his dad. They used to play a public course in San Diego, Balboa Park, near enough to the zoo to hear the growls. Phil Sr., an airline pilot, would pick his son up right after school, which left them enough light for twelve or fourteen holes if they hustled. Their walks in the dark through the canyons to the car were Philly's sweetest memories.

But, as devoted as he was to his father, he was more Mary's child. She was a champion mom, the family hoot, a basketball player on organized teams into her forties. She was the one who put a football helmet on him in the house, because, as she said, "He'd turn around and walk right into that pillar. He had those big hands and those big feet and he was just about the clumsiest kid you ever saw."

He threatened to run away a lot, to golf courses. Mary kept all the notes he left behind. Over a meatloaf dinner at their home once, she handed me one. "I love you," it read, "but I'm really going this time."

Nobody in life is more marooned than a teenage boy in Southern

California who isn't old enough to drive. "Come on, Mom, get up," Phil would whisper in Mary's ear on cool summer mornings. "Picture yourself in a silver Mercedes, Mom, a golden Cadillac. When I'm a famous golfer, I'm going to buy you a new car." And, of course, he did.

Few people ever took to parenthood as enthusiastically as Mickelson. "It's been fun, I got to tell you," he said over the phone in 2001. "The greatest thing about my job is that, when I'm here, I'm really here, all day, all week, morning till night. I took my daughter Amanda on a little date today. We went to the park and rode the train and had a picnic and stuff. It's funny now how she favors me. She doesn't want to leave me. No matter what I'm doing, if I'm just sitting and watching TV, she'll come and sit beside me."

The week before the 2010 Masters, Mickelson finished thirty-fifth in Houston, but his scores were misleading. He double-bogeyed three of the first ten holes on Sunday, hitting drivers when he shouldn't, boning up for Augusta. On the 14th tee, following three straight birdies, Phil yanked Dr. Tom Buchholz out of the gallery, took the bag off Bones Mackay and strapped it to Amy's and Mary's radiation oncologist from the M.D. Anderson Cancer Center in Houston. The man who performed their surgeries, Dr. Kelly Hunt, was along, too.

Buchholz was only going to caddie for one hole, but they birdied it. And the next one. And the one after that. Six in a row. Mickelson was ready for the Masters.

Tiger shot 70 on Friday (Phil 71; they were tied, two back). "I hit the ball a lot better," Woods said, "and I putted a little better. I had more control of the golf ball today from tee to green and at least hit the putts on my lines. That was something I wasn't doing yesterday."

But Saturday his warm-up was scratchy, and he battled his swing all day to a second-consecutive but far less-pleasing 70. Was Tiger still feeling normal?

"No," he said sullenly. "Three-putting three times does not feel normal."

The whole afternoon, and maybe the whole tournament, came down to a twenty-seven-minute interlude on the back nine, when at 13, 14 and 15 Mickelson went eagle-eagle-near eagle and Englishman Lee Westwood moved from four-up to one-down. When the third eagle try was spinning beside the cup, it seemed like an act of God. Or, as Westwood's caddie, Billy Foster, put it, "Bloody hell." Phil ended up one behind Lee and three ahead of Tiger going to the final round.

Tiger's Sunday was startling. It looked like he was having a nervous breakdown. His first tee shot nearly missed the golf course left. Then he began missing right and left. The best golfers usually err on one side or the other. Ernie Els's misses tend to be left. Tiger's tend to be right. But this was a day for everything, eagles and bogeys. Tiger had two eagles, holing an 8-iron on seven, and five bogeys. He made a fifteen-footer for the other eagle, but had a three-putt at 14 that would have embarrassed Orville Moody. With his mind obviously wandering, Tiger missed a tap-in there. His feet seemed to be on backward.

"I had another terrible warm-up today," he said. "I didn't have it." Hooked it left at one, popped it up at two, bladed a pitch at three, stuck it in the ground at four, hooked it again at five, and still shot 69 for an 11-under-par 277 total worth a share of fourth place.

No clubs were bounced angrily into the gallery, but, breaking his language pledge, Tiger had a couple of blasphemous moments and let go one "Tiger Woods, you suck!" For him, this qualified as a sanguine afternoon. In his time, he'd been known to shout, "Tiger, you're the worst fucking golfer who ever lived!" before turning to Steve Williams to add, "and you're the worst fucking caddie!"

CBS's Peter Kostis brought up deportment in one of those cringe-producing colloquies behind the 18th green. Because kneeling down and touching one's forehead to the ground was out of fashion, roving TV reporters always kicked off their Tiger interviews with parfaits of flattery before apologetically coming to the point. But on this Masters Sunday Tiger wasn't in the mood for even the softest soap.

"I think people are making way too much of a big deal of this thing," he said, snapping all the way back to his old curt self. "I was not feeling good. I hit a big snipe off the first hole and I don't know how people can think I should be happy about that. I hit a wedge from forty-five yards and basically bladed it over the green. These are not things I normally do. So I'm not going to be smiling and not going to be happy. And I hit one of the worst, low—kind of a low quack hook on five. So I haven't hit a good shot yet. I'm not going to be walking around there with a lot of pep in my step."

Kostis tried for a positive finish.

"Yeah, I finished fourth," Tiger said coldly. "Not what I wanted. I wanted to win this tournament."

Later, after Mickelson reached 18, reporters were unable to resist turning the contrast between them and their respective blondes into an oversimplified morality play.

For the first time in her ordeal, Amy Mickelson had made the trip to a tournament location, but Thursday, Friday and Saturday she was too ill from the chemotherapy to make it to the course. "At night they talk about every round, each shot he hits," said teacher Butch Harmon, Tiger's discarded pro, "and Phil doesn't have that when he's out on the road. That's why he tries to go home whenever he can. He was in a completely different frame of mind here, knowing she was coming, hoping she was coming. Everything about him changed."

Then there she was at the back of the green, with Mary, big Phil and the children. Mary looked exactly like herself, but Amy looked somehow different. Beautiful, but just a couple of degrees different. After completing his third 67 (for a 16-under-par total of 272) to beat Westwood by three and Woods by five, Mickelson couldn't let go of his wife as a tear rolled down Plastic Phil's, Three Dollar Phil's and Fat Phil's cheek.

"Having Amy and the kids here took a lot of the heartache away," he said. "It's been a tough time, but we have a lot to look forward to and a lot to be grateful for. Long-term we're in good shape. We just need to improve the quality of life and what [side effects] the medicines are giving her." At the green jacket ceremony, he told the assembled *patrons*, "We've really been through a lot this year. It means a lot to share some joy together. This is something we'll remember for the rest of our lives."

Asked what he and Amy said to each other at the back of the green, Mickelson answered, "I don't know if we said anything, we just hugged. We just hugged."

A couple of years before, Phil said something extremely smart:

"The reality is, even if I play at the top of my game for the rest of my career and achieve all of my goals—let's say, win fifty tournaments and ten majors—I still can't get to where Tiger is right now. So I won't compare myself with him. It makes no sense."

But, standing there in his third green jacket, he looked like he wanted to take it back.

Tiger *did* have a good Masters. He *did* contend. He *was* that good. But, win it? No. Maybe there *was* a guilt. Maybe there *was* a conscience. Not that either guilt or conscience figured to abide indefinitely. Justice isn't that perfect.

On the other hand, in his next tournament two weeks later, Tiger shot 43 on the back nine at Quail Hollow, including consecutive double-bogeys and a four-putt, to miss the cut by eight strokes. And in his third tournament back, the Players Championship, he withdrew on the 7th hole Sunday, 2-over-par for the day, twelve strokes and two-and-a-half hours behind the leaders in forty-fifth place. Two days earlier, he had been asked first about his knee ("Knee's good") and then whether he had any other physical issues. "No," he said, "zero, absolutely a hundred percent."

But, after walking off Sunday with a pain in his neck and "tingling" down his fingers, he acknowledged having felt the pain since a couple of weeks before the Masters. "I've been playing through it," he said. "I can't play through it anymore." Following an MRI, therapy—not surgery—was indicated. "I've been playing with a bad neck for quite a while," he said.

No, zero, absolutely a hundred percent. Tiger's word wasn't exactly the coin of the realm.

The next night, swing coach Hank Haney resigned. "I sent him a text," Haney said. "I wished him the best and told him I hope he finds someone else to help him. He first responded, 'Thanks.' Then, two seconds later, he said, 'We're just taking a break, right?' I answered, 'No, we're done.'"

Back in the U.S. Open at Pebble Beach ten years after the master-piece, both Tiger and his gallery seemed their old selves on Satur-day. Stirring the crowd with magical shots, he came home in 31 for a 5-under-par 66 that got him to third place. But Sunday was the Mas-ters all over again: six bogeys in twelve holes and another piece of fourth. Maybe Tiger's Sundays would be like this from now on. Of course, that wasn't the way to bet.

CHAPTER TWENTY-NINE

Putting to the picture seemed a bit simpleminded to Butch Harmon, but Hank Haney's word for it was "genius." "Especially for Tiger," he said, "who likes to figure things out for himself. I always found that, from the fewest directions, Tiger got the most benefit. That's the way he learns best. Don't tell him everything to do. Just guide him along. It didn't surprise me that he liked to be taught this way because he was always taught that way by his father. Earl would lead him in a certain direction and then let him alone to figure out how to travel the rest of the way on his own. Putting to the picture, taking a photograph in your head, is pretty cool stuff. It's Harvey Penick–like, you know? 'Take dead aim.' I think Tiger's father was the greatest coach who ever lived."

In the spring of 2010, Haney didn't believe Woods's travails on the course had very much to do with golf. "I don't know how anybody can look at him," Hank said, "and say the problem is his swing or his swing thoughts or his mechanics. What's changed? Same teacher, same daddy, same golf clubs. Last year he played nineteen tournaments, had seven wins and seventeen top tens. Over the past two and a half years, he won forty-five percent of his tournaments and was in the top ten eighty-five percent of the time. I'll tell you what's changed. Tiger."

At least for the moment, Hank reckoned, Woods had lost himself, not his game.

"Maybe he'll never be the same," he said. "Who knows? But what he's done already puts him on everybody's short list of the greatest athletes in history, doesn't it? The phase of the game in which Tiger really excelled was the mental part, and I give his dad just a ton of credit for that."

When Michael Jordan's father pulled over to the side of a highway to sleep and was murdered for his car, Michael turned momentarily to baseball, James Jordan's favorite sport. Michael was mourning.

"That's a very real phenomenon," Haney said, "and I don't think there's any doubt at all that Tiger had a notion to do something along the same lines. Ken Hitchcock's a friend of mine [the hockey coach who led the Dallas Stars to a Stanley Cup in the '90s]. Ken said they see it in hockey all the time. Guys are making three million a year, their father dies and they want to go to work in a coal mine. When Earl died, I thought there was a strong possibility Tiger was going to give it all up to go in the service."

As early as 2004, a sleepy year when the World Golf Championships Accenture Match Play was Tiger's sole victory on tour, he started jumping out of airplanes at Fort Bragg. Earl told Doug Ferguson of the Associated Press, "He probably wants in the recesses of his mind to walk the steps I walked."

That year, the day after finishing in a tie for twenty-second at the Masters, Tiger flew his private jet to North Carolina for four days of special operations training on his father's old base. In a four-hundred-man formation, he ran four miles, singing cadence, as he said, "at the top of my lungs." Tiger participated in close-quarters combat drills and trained in a vertical wind tunnel with paratroopers. Then he made two tandem jumps with the Golden Knights. Two because, after the first one, he asked jubilantly, "Can I go again?"

To Ferguson, Earl said, "Tiger is an independent individual who plays an independent sport, and he's quite frankly not in the business of people telling him what to do. This will be a new experience for him. Somebody is going to be telling him when to eat, when to sleep, when to go to the bathroom. He'll learn about dedication, service, being a member of an organization and a team. Teamwork. Self hardships. Individual hardships. He'll learn an awful lot about himself. And he better watch out. Because it's going to change him."

"Not all the time, just from time to time, Tiger kept up this training," Haney said. "People don't realize how seriously he took it. He wasn't going to some recreational skydiving schools. He was hanging out with Navy SEALs. He took martial arts training, self-defense, firearms training, the whole deal. I don't think he could ever quite work it out in his mind how to make it all come together. How he was still going to be Tiger Woods, how he was still going to be a father, how he was still going to be a husband, and yet go out and be a soldier like his dad. But I know that's what Tiger wanted deep down. He wanted to be a Navy SEAL. For sure that was on his list. I don't know how close he came. How close is close? But I thought at the time there was a good chance it was going to happen."

In a press gathering at the 2010 Players, I waited for the 9-iron-or-pitching-wedge queries to peter out before I asked Tiger a question that was way off point:

"Do you think Earl would be surprised we have a black president?"

"No, not at all," he said.

"Really?"

(I think he would be flabbergasted.)

"He was hoping that he would see that day," Tiger said. "There's no doubt he was hoping he'd see that day."

"What do you think he'd make of this guy?"

"He'd be very proud."

Surprisingly, considering how Tiger usually avoided all things political, he was the only athlete who participated in the Obama Inaugural Celebration at the Lincoln Memorial in January of 2009. Wearing a dark suit and a dark shirt with a silver tie, looking like a Damon Runyon character, Woods gave a speech that made no reference to Obama, who was sitting directly in front of him. Tiger talked instead about his father and the military.

"I grew up in a military family," he said, "and my role models in life were my mom and dad, Lieutenant Colonel Earl Woods. My dad was a Special Forces operator and many nights friends would visit our home. They represented every branch of the service, and every rank. In my dad and in those guests, I saw firsthand the dedication and commitment of those who serve. They come from every walk of life, from every part of our country. Time and again, across generations, they have defended our safety in the dark of night and far from home.

"Each day, and particularly on this historic day, we honor the men and women in uniform who serve our country and protect our freedom. They travel to the dangerous corners of the world, and we must remember that, for every person who is in uniform, there are families who wait for them to come home safely. I am honored that the military is such an important part, not just of my personal life, but of my professional one as well. The golf tournament we do each year here in Washington is a testament to those unsung heroes. I am the son of a man who dedicated his life to his country, family and the military, and I am a better person for it.

"In the summer of eighteen-sixty-four, Abraham Lincoln, the man at whose memorial we stand, spoke to the hundred and sixty-fourth Ohio Regiment and said, 'I am greatly obliged to you, and to all who have come forward at the call of their country.' Just as they have stood tall for our country, we must always stand by and support the men and women in uniform and their families."

Deciding not to ask my last question in a crowd, I e-mailed him instead:

"Tiger, you looked a little startled today. Here's a question from even deeper in left field:

"How close did you come to joining the military?"

Two days later, he responded. He didn't exactly answer the question, but maybe he didn't know the answer.

"For nearly my entire life," he wrote, "I've wondered what it would be like to be in the military. One of the questions I hear most at my Foundation is what would you be if you weren't a pro golfer? I answer the same way every time. I'd be in Special Ops. Maybe Green Beret like Pop. I know some people that are Army Special Forces, and I'm amazed at what they do. I'm proud to call them my friends."

CHAPTER THIRTY

"One of those old Shell's [*Wonderful World of Golf*] shows is on tonight," Jack Nicklaus mentioned casually in his office. "Me against Crenshaw."

"Let me guess," I said. "You won."

Laughing, he said, "I suppose we're all a little like that." Per accomplishment, he was less like that than almost anyone who ever lived.

We were in North Palm Beach, Florida. It was a workday, but Jack was dressed in shorts. He had one shoe off, showing me his hammertoe, proving that even he had feet of clay. Furthermore, he was shrinking.

"I don't know if I'm even five-nine anymore," he said, "and I was almost six feet as a junior in high school. I was measured at six and a quarter for my basketball physical, but I don't think that was accurate. I think five eleven and three quarters was about the tallest I ever was. If I'm not quite five nine now, that means I'm almost exactly three inches shorter."

Bringing the ball up the floor in high school, Jack was a basketball stalwart. Like Earl, he was the catcher on the baseball team. "The catcher was always the best player," Earl told his sister Mae. Woody Hayes said he would have found a place for Nicklaus on Ohio State's football team if Jack wasn't so obviously meant for golf.

Woody and Charlie Nicklaus were cronies. Football had been Charlie's sport; he played on the line for Ohio State and, after graduating, cashed a few checks with the Portsmouth Spartans, precursors of the Detroit Lions. The cantankerous Hayes claimed to have invented marshaling at Denver's Cherry Hills Country Club in 1960, in the days before gallery ropes, when Ben Hogan's fans were crowding Woody's boy at the U.S. Open. As a twenty-year-old amateur, Jack finished second to Arnold Palmer in that highly charged tournament, when to kick off the final round Palmer drove the par-4 1st green and basically became Palmer. Hayes, the voluntary stringer, called in play-by-play reports every night to both Columbus newspapers.

"I just don't have any disks anymore," Jack said. "If you X-rayed my back, every one of my disks is right on top of the other one. Bone on bone all the way down. That's what happens to people." To golfers, especially.

Of course, standing next to his records, he always looked small. In Asia once, en route to different corporate shows, Nicklaus and the tennis star Bjorn Borg bumped into each other on a department store roof. "Almost simultaneously," Jack said, "we both said, 'I thought you were bigger.'" Nicklaus was a respectable tennis player, too.

It sounds funny, considering how fit Tiger was and how closely the young Nicklaus resembled a sportswriter or an unmade bed. But the truth is, Jack was much the better all-around athlete. Some other truths could be uttered now, too. No matter how their majors contest played out, Woods was the superior golfer. Ernie Els said, "I'd still like to see Tiger at his best against Jack at his best, with today's equipment. That, I'd pay to see." But on his splendid resume, Nicklaus had nothing to compare with shooting 12-under-par at Pebble Beach and winning the U.S. Open by fifteen strokes, not to mention taking the British Open a month later by eight. "He's the best, isn't he, Bear?" Tom Watson gently put it to Jack, who nodded.

At the same time, nobody ever looked into a television camera to say Jack Nicklaus disgraced the game. Johnny Miller said it about Tiger. In that sense, Nicklaus won their race going away. Whenever the obituaries are written, Jack's will be less complicated than Tiger's.

Nicklaus did his best to stay out of Woods's red light district. "It's none of my business," he said steadfastly. Except to state with surety, when no one else had any surety, "I don't think he'll miss the Masters in a million years. He's a golfer. That's what he is." Up to that point, both Tiger and Jack had won exactly half of their majors (seven and nine) at Augusta, Pebble and St. Andrews, three of 2010's four stops. So it was reasonable of Nicklaus to describe 2010 as a critical time in the chase. "If he's going to get his game back on track," Jack said, "he better do it pretty quickly. If he doesn't win one or two of them now, time will start moving on." Those who took this for gamesmanship didn't know Nicklaus very well.

"It's hard for anyone to understand what Tiger's private life is like now," he said. "I feel for him, and for his wife. I've always liked Tiger." Of course, like the rest of us, he never really knew him. In terms of golf alone, the only question was whether Tiger would come back as himself. "If he does," Jack said, "he'll be fine."

In 2002, I told Nicklaus, "Tiger thinks he knows you. Do you know him?"

After a moment's thought, he said, "I think I know what he does and what his motives are. He's a champion, and champions are, well, not born exactly. Obviously they're developed. But they're part born. He has an attitude about what he is doing that I like a lot. It's very similar to what mine was. He doesn't seem to be influenced by outside pressures. He knows the things he has to do to prepare himself. Money isn't an issue with him. He's interested in winning.

"The financial part was never an issue with me, either. You might think, 'Easy for you to say,' and I guess that's right. I was winning all the time. But the point is, after you've done everything or won everything, what keeps you wanting to compete? I mean, what keeps you doing all of the really draining things you have to do in order to stay competitive? People say, with all of today's money, Tiger's going to lose his desire. I say, 'I don't think so.'"

Nicklaus did things on the golf course Woods won't. (Perhaps better to say, probably won't.) In 1998, when he was fifty-eight years old, Jack finished sixth at the Masters. Quietly that may have been his best performance of all, though, as Els would tell you, "quietly" is the wrong word. They were paired together on Sunday. "That's the loudest I've ever heard it on a golf course," Ernie said. "I shot seventy-two. Jack shot sixty-eight. You should have seen the birdie he made at three. My ears were ringing all the way around." Before they teed off, Nicklaus told him something he didn't understand at the time, but did now. "Ernie," Jack whispered, "let's pretend we're the last group."

"Tiger set a goal," Nicklaus said, "to break my record. And that's going to stay his goal until he does it." Jack used to say, "I'll be very surprised if he doesn't break my record. Very surprised." But now he said, "He'll probably break my record, but he still has to do it."

"Even if he does win eighteen majors," I said, "he's not going to finish second in nineteen others."

"Maybe not."

"Or third in nine more."

Or post 72 top tens in major championships.

Seventy-two.

Softly Jack said, "If someone told me I'd finish first or second in thirty-seven majors, I just don't know. What would you have said to me? 'You got to be dreaming, kid.'"

Back when Woody Hayes was directing traffic at Cherry Hills, Nicklaus was studying Ben Hogan. Those were the days of thirty-six-hole Saturday finales. "My dad walked into my room and said, 'Guess who you're playing the last two rounds with. Hogan.' *That* was exciting. I almost won the tournament, except I wasn't watching what I was doing. I was too busy watching Hogan."

Players today probably can't understand what players yesterday thought of Hogan. Byron Nelson, Sam Snead and Hogan were all born in a six-month spread of 1912, and as great as each of them was, two of them kept score by the third. Nelson never detailed the eleven straight tournaments he won in 1945 without mentioning which ones Hogan played. "I was alive when the *Titanic* went down," Byron said triumphantly. "Hogan wasn't."

In 2001, four years after Ben died, Snead was watching television in Hot Springs, Virginia, when an old clip came on the screen that he had seen a hundred times. It was from the presentation ceremony following the 1953 U.S. Open at Oakmont, the fourth and last time Snead finished second in the only major tournament he never won. In the clip he wistfully reached over and rubbed the silverware in Hogan's arms. Ben took the entire trophy and rubbed it up and down Sam. For the first time, it dawned on Snead what Hogan was doing. *You want to touch the trophy? The trophy wants to touch you.* Sam started to cry.

"I learned a ton that day," Nicklaus said, "watching Hogan play golf. The next time I saw him, in a locker room on a practice morning, he said, 'Hey, fella, you got a game?' That's the best compliment I ever received. OK, if I'd have had a brain, maybe I'd have won at Cherry Hills [and Tiger's target would be 19]. But I hadn't learned how to win yet. I only knew how to learn."

Nicklaus didn't expect anyone to believe what he was about to say.

"I know this sounds silly, but I've been rooting for someone to come along and break my records. Whether it's Tiger or somebody else, I'm pulling for them. Bobby Jones was great. My coming along didn't diminish him in the least. I'll be happy for whoever it is. I'll be even happier for golf."

CHAPTER THIRTY-ONE

Basketball star Kobe Bryant came back from an uglier scrape to hear cheers again. In 2010, football quarterback Ben Roethlisberger was hoping to do the same. But neither Bryant nor Roethlisberger had been thought of as extraordinary people, just extraordinary athletes. In that sense, they were never in Tiger's class.

Editorialists tried to rope Woods in with baseball's Barry Bonds and Mark McGwire, too, though the difference was obvious. There's a test for the presence of drugs. There's none for an absence of character.

Some said Tiger was just a casualty of the modern media age, no different from Babe Ruth or Muhammad Ali, if truth were told then as it was now.

I don't go back to Ruth, but Red Smith did, and I go back to Red. Sitting at his kitchen table in New Canaan, Connecticut, holding on to a shaking coffee cup with both hands, the great old sportswriter spoke of the Babe with more than just affection. Of course Ruth was a man of Herculean appetites, sexual and otherwise. He got on so well with children because he was a child himself. But his teammates loved him, even though, when the temperature in the shower changed subtly, they might turn around to find Ruth urinating on their backs, laughing.

His clothes were streaked with ink from all the autographs he signed. "I like to make everyone happy," he said. The Babe was melting from cancer ("The termites got me") when the pitcher Waite Hoyt and his wife were leaving Ruth's apartment for the final time. He called after them, "Wait a minute." Painstakingly lifting himself out of his chair, Ruth went into the kitchen, to the refrigerator. He came back carrying a small vase that had an orchid in it. "Here," he said to Mrs. Hoyt, "I never gave you anything."

Does any of that sound like Tiger Woods?

I also go back to Ali, the cruelest of boxers, good at sticking his thumb in Ernie Terrell's eye and his knife into Joe Frazier's back. Muhammad called Joe an "Uncle Tom" for visiting the White House, Ali's first stop after knocking out George Foreman in Zaire.

He had a mob of wives and demi-wives, and children by nearly all of them, every one of whom he adored. He admitted in Zaire that he had socked Belinda and shipped her home to Chicago. As contemptible as that is, fighters think with their hands. And Veronica Porsche was on deck.

And yet, in spite of all this, it was impossible to be around Ali and not like him. On a starry night, with shadows of hyacinths floating down the Congo River, he tried to tell me the whole fight in a sentence. "Black men scare white men," he said, "more than black men scare black men." That's right. We were afraid of Foreman more than he was.

But, as usual, I didn't listen. When the first round ended, Ali spit out his mouthpiece and shouted over my shoulder to manager Herbert Muhammad, "Leave him to me!" I turned to Vic Ziegel of the *New York Daily News* and said, "Wrong again, Vic." My column that morning was now absurd, and I was thrilled.

You had to be on his trail, I suppose, to understand. Though he was a touchstone for both racism and the Vietnam War, as shootable as anybody in the assassination '60s, Ali walked unguarded through Times Square and life. Leaving the velvet-roped dining rooms, the private blackjack palaces and the VIP "hostesses" to the coming generations of celebrity athletes (Michael Jordan, Charles Barkley, Tiger Woods), he went out into the light.

Ali had a unique greeting for everyone in the caravan. Mine was, "How's Angie? I like her better than you." (Except for one long conversation on the telephone, he never even met her.) In his Las Vegas hotel room the day before the Larry Holmes fight, Ali looked sensational. He had blackened his hair, but he hadn't really trained, just reduced. He couldn't run from here to there.

"Who you pickin'?" he asked.

"I'm picking the other guy, champ."

"You always wrong," he said.

"I hope so."

The morning after that beating at the fists of Holmes, a smaller headline appeared on page one of the Las Vegas newspaper. It read: "CASSIUS CLAY SR. TRICK-ROLLED." Robbed by a prostitute. What a word, trick-rolled. Imagine having a son like that, watching him take a whipping like that, and then going out and getting a prostitute. That's another contrast with Tiger, apparently so fond of a certain kind of woman. Tiger had parents who lived for him. Ruth's parents didn't want him.

Late after the Holmes fight, Ali got a phone call from Joe Bugner in London. Bugner twice went the distance with Ali, a twelve-rounder and a fifteen-rounder, both of them no-hitters. Having killed a man in the ring early in his career, Joe turned into a patty-caker. But he was a pro. He signed for the twelve; he did the twelve.

"Joe, Joe," Ali came on the line to say, "why are you calling me, Joe?"

"Because I wanted to make sure you were OK," Bugner said. "Because I'm worried about you. Because I love you."

Will any of Tiger Woods's opponents call him after he's knocked out? When Tiger Woods loses, will anyone cry?

Tiger doesn't compare to Muhammad Ali or Babe Ruth as an athlete or a man. Hell of a golfer, though.

A few weeks after the Thanksgiving crash, Earl's sister Mae called from Banning, California. "Do you have a home address for Elin at Isleworth?" she asked.

"Mae," I said, "that address has been in every newspaper in the country. Yes, I have it. But I don't think she's there. Why do you want it?"

"I want to write the children," she said. "I just want them to know they have an aunt Mae somewhere who loves them."

EPILOGUE

"I met Earl Woods," Arnold Palmer said, "but I can't say I knew him. You knew him. What was he like?"

"Like me," I said, "full of shit." The great man, just turning eighty, leaned back and laughed. "He was complicated," I said, "like his son. Good-hearted at his best, though, once you got inside the shell. It wasn't easy getting inside the shell."

"Well, you know," Palmer said, "you can see that and feel it in Tiger, too. My father was like that."

The second-to-last time I saw Earl was at Sherwood Country Club in Thousand Oaks, California, where Tiger's own season-ending tournament was under way. The scene was a cocktail party at a clubhouse ballroom in the late afternoon. Both Tida and Tiger were present, in different corners, holding separate courts. Earl was a lost island in the center of the room.

He was wearing a black turtleneck pullover and a diamond and gold medallion. He looked like a lounge lizard at Caesars Palace. The garish disk brought to mind a boardwalk claw machine, but Earl said it cost $35,000. On his arm was an obvious rental. Well, it's possible she wasn't a pro, but she wasn't a nun. She wasn't a rookie, either. She was a veteran of at least a couple of wars.

I gave him a look that said, *Christ, Earl,* and he responded with a wink, "My niece."

The last time I saw him, he was sitting in his easy chair at Cypress, uneasy.

"What's this for again?" he asked.

"Nothing in particular," I said. "I was just in the neighborhood." It was for the obituary.

Not fooled, he said softly, "Don't worry about it, Stud. I'm glad you're here. I'm afraid to go to sleep. Oh my God, I've been petrified. And, you know, that's not me. I sit up and watch movies all night long. If I lie down, it's like I can't breathe. Look at this: I've got a twitch in my finger, too. It's those damned steroids. And my legs, they're like balloons, full of water. I'm developing claustrophobic feelings, too. God-damned steroids."

His prior position, that he had no fear of death, was now inoperative. In Earl's repertoire of monologues, what he called his "actual-death-not-just-near-death experience" may have been his personal favorite.

"After that last heart thing," he'd begin, "I was lying in bed in the recovery room. Tiger and my wife were sitting there talking, and I decided I was going to sit up. So I did, and I began to feel pretty good. I felt better and better and better. I was in a tunnel. I saw this light down at the end. I got closer and closer, and the light got brighter and brighter. I was drifting along. I never felt this good my whole life. I couldn't tell I was moving. I just saw the light was getting brighter. All of a sudden, I heard this female voice—it was the nurse—saying, 'Are you all right?' And I replied, 'I don't think so.' And she looked at a gauge and said, 'Oh, my God!' The blood pressure was down nearly to zero. I felt kind of woozy. She ran and got something, gave me a shot—adrenaline, I presume. It scared the hell out of Tiger. Me, all I felt was a momentary pang of regret that I was back in the hospital. That tunnel was so peaceful, just like people describe. Five minutes later, I'm up walking to the bathroom by myself. I've never feared death since."

Right.

"I promised Tiger I'd be around until I was eighty-four," he said, a target he would miss by a decade. The catcher called for a pitchout. "That was years ago," he said. "I reiterated it recently. Eighty-four just sounded like the number. I don't want to be a liability. I've had so many illnesses. Nine surgeries. Open-heart, cancer, prostate, drainage under my arm and eye, sinuses, both eyes, cataracts, glaucoma, every damn thing. I've got sleep apnea now, too. Don't write that down, Stud. That's why I'm afraid to go to sleep. I'm afraid I won't wake up."

Next to the easy chair stood a rack of Tiger's putters, ones he used at momentous occasions.

"You should lock those up," I told Earl.

"I like looking at them," he said.

Earl believed in both heaven and hell, reasoning, "There has to be a positive and a negative to everything, for balance. Final judgment. No paroles. I imagine heaven is a very pleasant place—no need for sleep, I'd envision—where people aren't just blissfully happy but totally fulfilled. No bickering, no arguments. They're kind to one another. They get along. In heaven, the worst part of growing old is alleviated."

What was the worst part of growing old?

"The realization that if you knew then what you know now you could have made life better for everybody you ever met, and for yourself, too."

What were the best parts?

"Quiet. Peace. Tranquility. The resources to enjoy oneself. The knowledge to make a few last-minute corrections."

Not that Earl doubted he was going to heaven. He hadn't fallen out of love with himself, and said so in just those words. "I love my-self," he said. "I love who I am." Obviously, Earl's est training took. "Man keeps looking for a truth that fits his reality," Warner Erhard preached. "Given our reality, truth doesn't fit."

"Right after est," Earl said, "I took a seminar on money. How money affects you, controls you, corrupts your life or doesn't, etcet-era. One of the exercises was to take a page and write down what you wanted next week, next month, next year and five years from now. Ten years or so later, I was looking through my dresser and found that paper. I started laughing. I laughed like hell. Because I had attained everything on my list. Sports car. I had two, including a 300ZX. Ten thousand dollars in the bank, free and clear. Well, I had a lot more than that. This. Check. That. Check. Check, check, check. I had it all, everything I thought I wanted. But nowhere on my list were the things I really wanted, the things that really mattered. No solutions. No cures. Isn't it a bitch? By the time you get what you thought you wanted, it isn't what you really wanted at all."

He asked oddly, "What would you say is the great healer?"

"Time?" I guessed.

"I wish. Oh well, maybe in heaven."

He said, "You want to hear something crazy? I miss golf [not Ti-ger's, his own]. I'm sure there'll be golf in heaven—why not?—but you'll still hit bad shots. Because golf's a game. It's only a game. It isn't life. There's a difference. Damn, that's a revelation right there!"

He was learning really fast now.

The minor moments with Tiger, not the major successes, were washing back over him. "Once," he said, "when Tiger was about four-teen or fifteen, he blew his tee time at a tournament in San Diego. You know how some people cross their sevens? Well, the way it was writ-ten on the sheet, he misread his starting time. 'OK, you screwed up,' I said. 'Let's go home.' During the drive, after he finally came out of his funk, we got to talking about grinding for a score. Just then we passed a public golf course. 'Dad,' he said, 'can we stop here and practice grinding?' We played seven holes. He birdied five of them. When I see Tiger grinding now, that's what I think of, so long ago."

If I'd have thought of it, I'd have told Earl he made his mark. He was the one who gave Tiger the dream. He was the one who taught him how to achieve it. Of course, he was also the one who showed him, three years hence, how to spoil it. Were the women what made Earl and Tiger tick, or were they just what made them human? You tell me.

In a way, Tiger handed down his own sentence when, during the Fuzzy Zoeller fried chicken and collard greens affair, he said, "I forgive but I don't forget." No one will ever forget his hypocrisies. No one will ever look at him the same way. Of course, redemption is as available to Tiger Woods as it is to anyone. That would be a great story.

From the rack of putters, I plucked the one engraved MASTERS, 1997, and swished it back and forth, asking Earl, "How do you like my stroke?" I expected him to say, "I don't."

But, when I looked up, his eyes were closed. He started to snore. On the night of the Escalade, that's how one of the neighbors described Tiger on the ground. ("Actually, he was snoring.") He was his father's son.

I liked Earl. I'm just as glad he wasn't around for the Christmas season of 2009, even if there might have been some justice in that.

Squaring the club, I looked at the target, looked at the ball, looked at the target, looked at the ball, forward-pressed slightly and putted to the picture.

ACKNOWLEDGMENTS

Many helped, but particular thanks are due Pat Patton and the other archivists at Kansas State University; Cliff Schrock, Christian Iooss and the picture department at *Golf Digest* magazine; John Huggan, Bill Nack, Dave Kindred, Dom Furore, Mike O'Malley, Guy Yocom, Jaime Diaz, Doug Ferguson and Kathy Stachura; Mabel Woods Moore, Barbara Ann Gary, Earl Dennison Woods Jr., Royce Woods, Kevin Woods (though we spoke, Kevin didn't want to be quoted, and he wasn't), Cheyenne Woods, Don Slater, Gerry Walton, Pete McDaniel, Ernie and Ben Els, Jack Nicklaus, Arnold Palmer, Steve Ethun, John Boyette, Hank Haney, Mark O'Meara, Scott Tolley, Doc Giffin, Larry Harris, Ben Van Hook, Jim Mandeville, Howdy Giles, Christian Golon, Ken Bennett, Bev Norwood, Kathy Battaglia, Mark Steinberg, Glenn Greenspan, Vuong Phuoc, Lan Luu, Nancy Weber, Steve Szurlej, J. D. Cuban, Bill Fields, John Strege, Matt Rudy, Gary Petit, Larry Mondi, John Currie, Kenny Lannou, Ryan Lackey, John Hewig, Lou Sleater, Jerry Tarde, Rebecca Ann Callahan, Thomas Matthew Callahan, Angela Callahan, David Black, Cara Bedick, Travers Johnson, Patrick Mulligan (the perfectly named golf editor), Bill Shinker and the unfailingly kind people at *Golf Digest* and Condé Nast, the David Black Literary Agency, Gotham Books and the Penguin Group.

TIGER WOODS'S
RECORD OF WINNING

1990 *(age 14)*

- Won Optimist International Junior World (fifth time)
- Won Insurance Youth Golf Classic

1991

- Won U.S. Junior Amateur Championship (Bay Hill, Orlando, FL)
  - Defeated Brad Zwetschke in the finals, 19 holes
- Won Optimist International Junior World (sixth time)
- Won CIF-SCGA High School Invitational Championship
- Won Southern California Junior Championship
- Won PING Phoenix Junior (AJGA)
- Won Edgewood Tahoe Junior Classic (AJGA)
- Won Los Angeles City Junior Championship
- Won Orange Bowl Junior International

1992

- Won U.S. Junior Amateur Championship (Wollaston GC, Milton, MA)
  - Defeated Mark Wilson in the finals, 1 up
- Won PING Phoenix Junior (AJGA)
- Won Nabisco Mission Hills Desert Junior (AJGA)
- Won Pro Gear San Antonio Shootout (AJGA)
- Won Insurance Youth Golf Classic

1993

- Won U.S. Junior Amateur Championship (Waverly CC, Portland, OR)
  - Defeated Ryan Armour in the finals, 19 holes
- Won Southern California Junior Best Ball Championship

1994

- Won U.S. Amateur Championship (Sawgrass, Ponte Vedra Beach, FL)
  - Defeated Vaughn Moise, 2 & 1
  - Defeated Michael Flynn, 6 & 5
  - Defeated Buddy Alexander, 1 up
  - Defeated Tim Jackson, 1 up
  - Defeated Eric Frishette, 5 & 3
  - Defeated Trip Kuehne, 2 up
- Won Western Amateur Championship
- Won Southern California Golf Association Amateur Championship
- Won Pacific Northwest Amateur Championship
- Won William Tucker Invitational
- Won Jerry Pate Invitational

1995

- Won U.S. Amateur Championship (Newport CC, Newport, RI)
  - Defeated Patrick Lee, 3 & 2
  - Defeated Chad Campbell, 4 & 2
  - Defeated Sean Knapp, 2 & 1
  - Defeated Scott Kammann, 2 & 1
  - Defeated Mark Plummer, 2 & 1
  - Defeated George E. Marucci Jr., 2 up
- Won Stanford Invitational

1996

- Won U.S. Amateur Championship (Pumpkin Ridge GC, Cornelius, OR)
  - Defeated J. D. Manning, 3 & 2
  - Defeated Jerry Courville Jr., 4 & 2
  - Defeated Charles Howell III, 3 & 1
  - Defeated D. A. Points, 3 & 2
  - Defeated Joel Kribel, 2 & 1
  - Defeated Steve Scott, 38 holes
- Won NCAA Championship (The Honors Course, Chattanooga, TN)
- Won John A. Burns Invitational
- Won Cleveland Golf Championship
- Won Tri-Match (Stanford, Arizona, Arizona State)
- Won Cougar Classic
- Won Pac-10 Championship
- Won NCAA West Regional
- Won Las Vegas Invitational
- Won Disney World/Oldsmobile Classic

1997

- Won Masters Tournament
  - **Tiger Woods, 70-66-65-69—270**
  - Tom Kite, 77-69-66-70—282
  - Tommy Tolles, 72-72-72-67—283
  - Tom Watson, 75-68-69-72—284
  - Costantino Rocca, 71-69-70-75—285
  - Paul Stankowski, 68-74-69-74—285
- Won Mercedes Championships
- Won Asian Honda Classic (Thailand)
- Won GTE Byron Nelson Classic
- Won Motorola Western Open

1998

- Won Johnnie Walker Classic (Thailand)
- Won BellSouth Classic
- Won PGA Grand Slam

1999

- Won Buick Invitational
- Won Deutsche Bank—SAP Open (Germany)
- Won Memorial Tournament
- Won Motorola Western Open
- Won PGA Championship (Medinah CC, Medinah, IL)
  - **Tiger Woods, 70-67-68-72—277**
  - Sergio Garcia, 66-73-68-71—278
  - Stewart Cink, 69-70-68-73—280
  - Jay Haas, 68-67-75-70—280
  - Nick Price, 70-71-69-71—281

- Won WGC NEC Invitational
- Won National Car Rental Classic
- Won Tour Championship
- Won WGC American Express Championship
- Won World Cup individual and team titles (with Mark O'Meara)
- Won PGA Grand Slam

2000

- Won Mercedes Championships
- Won AT&T Pebble Beach National Pro-Am
- Won Bay Hill Invitational
- Won Memorial Tournament
- Won U.S. Open (Pebble Beach GL, Pebble Beach, CA)
  - **Tiger Woods, 65-69-71-67—272**
  - Ernie Els, 74-73-68-72—287
  - Miguel A. Jimenez, 66-74-76-71—287
  - John Huston, 67-75-76-70—288
  - Padraig Harrington, 73-71-72-73—289
  - Lee Westwood, 71-71-76-71—289
- Won British Open (St. Andrews, Scotland)
  - **Tiger Woods, 67-66-67-69—269**
  - Ernie Els, 66-72-70-69—277
  - Thomas Bjorn, 69-69-68-71—277
  - Tom Lehman, 68-70-70-70—278
  - David Toms, 69-67-71-71—278
- Won PGA Championship (Valhalla GC, Louisville, KY)
  - **Tiger Woods, 66-67-70-67—270**
  - Bob May, 72-66-66-66—270
  - Thomas Bjorn, 72-68-67-68—275
  - Greg Chalmers, 71-69-66-70—276
  - Jose Maria Olazabal, 76-68-63-69—276

- Stuart Appleby, 70-69-68-69—276
- Playoff
  - **Woods birdie-par-par**
  - May par-par-par
- Won WGC NEC Invitational
- Won Bell Canadian Open
- Won Johnnie Walker Classic
- Won PGA Grand Slam
- Won WGC EMC World Cup (team title with David Duval)

2001

- Won Bay Hill Invitational
- Won The Players Championship
- Won Masters Tournament
  - **Tiger Woods, 70-66-68-68—272**
  - David Duval, 71-66-70-67—274
  - Phil Mickelson, 67-69-69-70—275
  - Mark Calcavecchia, 72-66-68-72—278
  - Toshi Izawa, 71-66-74-67—278
  - Ernie Els, 71-68-68-72—279
- Won Deutsche Bank—SAP Open
- Won Memorial Tournament
- Won WGC NEC Invitational
- Won PGA Grand Slam
- Won Williams World Challenge

2002

- Won Bay Hill Invitational
- Won Masters Tournament
  - **Tiger Woods, 70-69-66-71—276**

- Retief Goosen, 69-67-69-74—279
- Phil Mickelson, 69-72-68-71—280
- Jose Maria Olazabal, 70-69-71-71—281
- Ernie Els, 70-67-72-73—282
- Padraig Harrington, 69-70-72-71—282
- Won Deutsche Bank—SAP Open
- Won U.S. Open (Bethpage Black, Farmingdale, NY)
  - **Tiger Woods, 67-68-70-72—277**
  - Phil Mickelson, 70-73-67-70—280
  - Jeff Maggert, 69-73-68-72—282
  - Sergio Garcia, 68-74-67-74—283
  - Scott Hoch, 71-75-70-69—285
  - Billy Mayfair, 69-74-68-74—285
  - Nick Faldo, 70-76-66-73—285
- Won Buick Open
- Won WGC American Express Championship
- Won PGA Grand Slam

2003

- Won Buick Invitational
- Won WGC Accenture Match Play
- Won Bay Hill Invitational
- Won Western Open
- Won WGC American Express Championship

2004

- Won WGC Accenture Match Play
- Won Dunlop Phoenix
- Won Target World Challenge

2005

- Won Buick Invitational
- Won Ford Championship
- Won Masters Tournament
  - **Tiger Woods, 74-66-65-71—276**
  - Chris DiMarco, 67-67-74-68—276
  - Luke Donald, 68-77-69-69—283
  - Retief Goosen, 71-75-70-67—283
  - Playoff
    - **Woods** birdie
    - DiMarco par
- Won British Open (St. Andrews, Scotland)
  - **Tiger Woods, 66-67-71-70—274**
  - Colin Montgomerie, 71-66-70-72—279
  - Fred Couples, 68-71-73-68—280
  - Jose Maria Olazabal, 68-70-68-74—280
- Won WGC NEC Invitational
- Won WGC American Express
- Won Dunlop Phoenix
- Won PGA Grand Slam

2006

- Won Buick Invitational
- Won Dubai Desert Classic
- Won Ford Championship
- Won British Open (Royal Liverpool, England)
  - **Tiger Woods, 67-65-71-67—270**
  - Chris DiMarco, 70-65-69-68—272
  - Ernie Els, 68-65-71-71—275

- Jim Furyk, 68-71-66-71—276
- Sergio Garcia, 68-71-65-73—277
- Hideto Tanihara, 72-68-66-71—277
- Won Buick Open
- Won PGA Championship (Medinah CC, Medinah, IL)
  - **Tiger Woods, 69-68-65-68—270**
  - Shaun Micheel, 69-70-67-69—275
  - Adam Scott, 71-69-69-67—276
  - Sergio Garcia, 69-70-67-70—276
  - Luke Donald, 68-68-66-74—276
- Won WGC Bridgestone
- Won Deutsche Bank Championship
- Won WGC American Express

2007

- Won Buick Invitational
- Won WGC CA Championship
- Won Wachovia Championship
- Won WGC Bridgestone Invitational
- Won PGA Championship (Southern Hills CC, Tulsa, OK)
  - **Tiger Woods, 71-63-69-69—272**
  - Woody Austin, 68-70-69-67—274
  - Ernie Els, 72-68-69-66—275
  - Aaron Oberholser, 68-72-70-69—279
  - John Senden, 69-70-69-71—279
- Won BMW Championship
- Won The Tour Championship
- Won Target World Challenge

2008

- Won Buick Invitational
- Won Dubai Desert Classic
- Won WGC Accenture Match Play
- Won Arnold Palmer Invitational
- Won U.S. Open (Torrey Pines, San Diego, CA)
  - **Tiger Woods, 72-68-70-73—283**
  - Rocco Mediate, 69-71-72-71—283
  - Lee Westwood, 70-71-70-73—284
  - Robert Karlsson, 70-70-75-71—286
  - D. J. Trahan, 72-69-73-72—286
  - Playoff
    - **Woods, 444-443-345(35)445-444-344(36)—71**
    - Mediate, 542-454-436(37)534-433-345(34)—71
  - Sudden Death
    - Woods par
    - Mediate bogey

2009 *(age 33)*

- Won Arnold Palmer Invitational
- Won Memorial Tournament
- Won AT&T National Hosted by Tiger Woods
- Won the Buick Open
- Won the WGC Bridgestone Invitational
- Won the BMW Championship
- Won the JBWere Masters (Kingston Heath GC, Melbourne, Australia)

Most Professional Major Championships

Jack Nicklaus 18
Tiger Woods 14
Walter Hagen 11
Ben Hogan 9
Gary Player 9
Tom Watson 8
Harry Vardon 7
Bobby Jones 7
Gene Sarazen 7
Sam Snead 7
Arnold Palmer 7

Most PGA Tour Victories

Sam Snead 82
Jack Nicklaus 73
Tiger Woods 71
Ben Hogan 64
Arnold Palmer 62
Byron Nelson 52
Billy Casper 51
Walter Hagen 44
Cary Middlecoff 40
Gene Sarazen 39
Tom Watson 39

Most PGA Tour Victories in One Year

Byron Nelson (1945) 18
Ben Hogan (1946) 13

Sam Snead (1950) 11

Ben Hogan (1948) 10

Paul Runyan (1933) 9

Tiger Woods (2000) 9

Vijay Singh (2004) 9

Career World Money List (*Through 2009*)

Tiger Woods $111,356,267

Vijay Singh $75,381,713

Ernie Els $70,925,441

Phil Mickelson $61,880,755

Jim Furyk $53,346,574

Davis Love III $48,024,986

Padraig Harrington $42,720,916

Retief Goosen $42,256,042

Sergio Garcia $40,945,608

Colin Montgomerie $40,733,741

Woods's Prize Money by Year

PGA Tournaments Other Victories Entered and Won Around the World PGA Winnings Total Winnings

Year	PGA Tournaments	Other Victories	Tournaments Entered and Won Around the World	PGA Winnings	Total Winnings	Rank
1996	8	2	0	$790,594	$940,420	24
1997	21	4	1	$2,066,833	$2,440,831	1
1998	20	1	2	$1,841,117	$2,927,006	4
1999	21	8	3	$6,616,585	$7,681,625	1
2000	20	9	2	$9,188,321	$11,034,530	1
2001	19	5	3	$5,687,777	$7,771,562	1
2002	18	5	2	$6,912,625	$8,417,188	1
2003	18	5	0	$6,673,413	$7,400,288	2
2004	19	1	2	$5,365,472	$7,379,407	4
2005	21	6	2	$10,628,024	$12,158,439	1
2006	15	8	3	$9,941,563	$13,025,558	1
2007	15	7	1	$10,867,052	$12,352,706	1
2008	6	4	1	$5,775,000	$6,196,717	2
2009	18	6	2	$10,508,163	$11,055,805	1
Totals	240	71	24	$92,862,539	$111,356,267*	

* Counting prize money, commercial endorsements, golf course design and appearance fees, *Forbes* magazine estimated Woods went past $1 billion in 2009, becoming the first billionaire athlete.

INDEX

Aaron, Henry, 107
Accenture Match Play, 177
advertising campaigns, 66–67. *See also*
    sponsorships
Alexander, Buddy, 260
Ali, Muhammad, 203, 247, 248–50
Amen Corner, 104, 140
American Nike Tour, 103
Amos 'N Andy, 109
Anderson, Jamie, 125
Anderson, Ken, 188
Anderson, Willie, 115
Anselmo, John, 58, 59, 121
Appleby, Stuart, 194, 264
Argentina Open, 103
The Arizona Republic, 151–52
Armour, Ryan, 57, 260
Armour, Tommy, 125
Army of the Republic of Vietnam
    (ARVN), 76
Arnie's Army, 145
AT&T Pro-Am, 99
Augusta National. *See also* The Masters
    Tournament
  Amen Corner, 104, 140
  and Arnie's Army, 145
  course modifications, 143

  and the Crow's Nest, 85–86
  Garcia on, 103–4
  and Ike's Pond, 144
  Nicklaus on, 144, 148
  and race issues, 90, 109, 144, 226
  Tiger's practice round, 82
  Tiger's return to golf, 226
Austin, Woody, 191, 267
Axley, Eric, 193
Azinger, Paul, 91, 228

Ballesteros, Severiano, 87–88, 125, 126, 141
Barkley, Charles, 152, 153
Barnes, Long Jim, 115
baseball, 1–2, 4, 7–9, 11, 15, 111
basketball, 241–42
Bay Hill Invitational, 208, 211, 222
B.C. Open, 135
Bean, Andy, 67
Beck, Martin, 56
Begay, Notah, 204
Bel-Air Country Club, 128
Bellsouth Classic, 100
Bergstol, Brian, 194
Bethpage State Park, 154–59
Big 12, 14
Big Seven Conference, 11

Bjorn, Thomas
  and the British Open, 122, 123, 124, 163
  and the PGA Championship, 263
  and Tiger's major victories, 185
Blair, Paul, 36
Bob Hope Chrysler Classic, 122
Bonallack, Michael, 121
Bonds, Barry, 247
bookmakers, 121, 168
Borg, Bjorn, 242
Boston Celtics, 12
Bradley, Ed, 173–74
Braid, James, 125
Brewer, Gay, 145
British Amateur Championship, 104, 201
British Open Championship
  and Els, 122, 124, 163, 214, 266
  and May, 132
  and Nicklaus, 122, 157–58, 168
  and O'Meara, 100
  scoring records, 93
  Tiger's victories, 121–25, 134, 135,
    157–58, 166–70, 176–81, 243, 263,
    266–67
  Woods's family rented home, 97
Brown, Paul, 188
Bryant, Kobe, 247
Buchholz, Tom, 231
Buckle, Andrew, 179
Buddhism, 31, 71, 120, 221
Bugner, Joe, 249–50
Burke, Jackie, 86
Byers, Walter, 12
Byron Nelson Championship, 134

Cabrera, Angel
  and the British Open, 179
  and the Masters, 146
  at Oakmont, 182
Calcavecchia, Mark, 264
Caldwell, Allen F., III, 93
Campanella, Roy, 8
Campbell, Chad, 261
Carnoustie, 155
Casper, Billy, 145, 269
Catalonia Open, 103
Cepelak, Brenna, 207

Chalmers, Greg, 263
Champions Dinner, 94, 145, 162–63
Champions Golf Club, 58
Champions' Locker Room, 86
Chang, Jerry, xi
Cherry Hills Country Club, 242
Cink, Stewart, 262
Clarke, Darren, 129, 177
Clarke, Heather, 177
Clinton, Bill, 94
Cook, Chuck, 98
Cook, Greg, 188
Cook, John, 98
Cookie League baseball, 1, 4
Cooper, Chuck, 12
Correll, Charles, 109
Cotton, Henry, 125, 170, 216
Couples, Freddie, 104, 217, 266
course design, 143, 148
Courville, Jerry, Jr., 261
Cousy, Bob, 12
Cowan, Mike (Fluff), 102, 103
Crane, Ben, 179
Crenshaw, Ben, 163, 200
Crenshaw, Polly, 200
Crosby, Cathy Lee, 42
Crow's Nest, 85–86

Daly, John, 148, 190–91, 212–13
Davis, Miles, 23
Dent, Jim, 144
Dial Award, 56
Diaz, Jaime, 53–54, 119
Dien Bien Phu (battle), 32
Dillard, Harrison, 189
DiMarco, Chris
  and the British Open, 180, 266
  and the Masters, 139, 162, 163–65, 266
  mother's death, 177
  and Tiger's major victories, 185
DiMarco, Norma, 177
Dinwiddie, Robert, 194
Disney World/Oldsmobile Classic, 70–71
Donald, Luke, 184, 266, 267
Donald, Mike, 67
Douglas, Mike, 42
drug-use, 220

Duncan, Tim, 152
Dunlap, Scott, 129, 130
Duran, Rudy, 58
Duval, David
  and the British Open, 122–25
  and the Masters, 139, 140–42, 264
  number one ranking, 100
  and Tiger's majors, 185

Eisenhower, Dwight, 109
Elder, Lee, 91, 144
Elizabeth II, Queen of England, 207
Elliott, Easter Ray, 14
Elliott, John, 68
Els, Ben, 214, 215
Els, Ernie
  and the British Open, 122, 124, 163,
    214, 266
  career earnings, 270
  competitive nature, 211–12
  errant tee shots, 232
  and the Johnny Walker Classic, 100
  majors record, 177, 182, 214
  and the Masters, 114, 139, 143, 146–47,
    148–49, 214, 244, 264, 265
  and Nicklaus, 168
  and the PGA Championship, 191, 267
  and son's autism, 215
  Tiger on, 211–12
  and Tiger's major victories, 185
  on Tiger's skill, 210–11, 242–43
  on Tiger's troubles, 212–16
  and the U.S. Open, 114–15, 263
  on young Tiger, x, 208–10, 212
Els, Liezl, 168, 212, 215
Els, Samantha, 215
endorsement deals, 57–58, 65–67, 94,
    203–4, 227, 271
Erhard, Warner, 254
ESPN, 206
est training, 47–48, 253
European Order of Merit, 92

Faldo, Gill, 207
Faldo, Melanie, 207
Faldo, Nick
  and the British Open, 125

and the Masters, 91, 92
  pairing with Woods, 179
  relationship troubles, 207
  and the U.S. Open, 265
Faldo, Valerie, 207
Fathauer, Derek, 194
Father's Day, 115
Fazio, Tom, 143
Feller, "Rapid Robert," 8
Ferguson, Doug, 237–38
Ferguson, Robert, 125
Fernandez-Castano, Gonzalo, 179
Finchem, Tim, 203
Five Lessons: The Modern Fundamentals of
    Golf (Hogan), 38
Fleischer, Ari, 201
Fleisher, Bruce, 67
Floyd, Raymond, 88, 102, 121, 140
fly fishing, 99, 162
Flynn, Michael, 260
football, ix, 14, 15, 187–89, 242
Ford, Doug, 145
Foreman, George, 248
Fort Bragg, 26, 28, 237
Fort Gordon, 145
Fort Hamilton, 38
Fort Totten, 28
Foster, Billy, 232
The Fountainhead (Rand), 122
Fouts, Dan, ix, 188
Franklin, Aretha, 33
Frazier, Joe, 248
Freedom of Information Act, 72
Friends of Golf (FOG) tournament, 128
Frishette, Eric, 260
Furyk, Jim
  and the British Open, 180, 267
  career earnings, 270
  and Tiger's return to golf, 217

Galea, Anthony, 219, 220
Garcia, Sergio
  and the British Open, 180, 267
  career earnings, 270
  and the Masters, 146–48
  and the PGA Championship, 103–6,
    262, 267

Garcia, Sergio (*cont.*)
  and Tiger's major victories, 185
  and the U.S. Open, 155–57, 265
Garcia, Victor, 103
Gentle Path clinic, 203
Giancana, Sam, 183
Gibson, Josh, 9
Gilder, Bob, 67
Golden Knights, 238
Golf Channel, 204–5
Golf Digest, 43, 53, 72–73, 86, 118
Golf My Way (Nicklaus), 38
Goodwin, Wally, 48
Goosen, Retief
  and the British Open, 179
  career earnings, 270
  and the Masters, 146–47, 147–48,
    265, 266
  and Tiger's major victories, 185
  and the U.S. Open, 214
Gosden, Freeman, 109
Graham, Lou, 182–83
Graham, "Rammin' Ralph," 14
grand slams, 87, 125, 138, 148, 170
Granny Clark's Wynd, 124
Greater Hartford Open, 67, 90
Greater Milwaukee Open, 65, 67–69
Griffith Park, 7
Grout, Jack, 38–39
Guinness, Alec, x

Haas, Jay, 262
Hagen, Walter
  British Open victory, 125
  majors record, 269
  and PGA Championship, 192
  tour victory record, 269
Hallberg, Gary, 67
Hamilton, Todd, 214
Haney, Hank
  and the British Open, 179
  on London terrorist bombings, 166
  on "putting to the picture," 151
  resignation, 235
  and Tiger's return to golf, 221–22,
    236–37

Harmon, Butch
  fired, 103
  and the Masters, 233
  as swing coach, 58–61, 99–100
  on Tiger's strategy, 148
  and the U.S. Open, 111–12
Harmon, Claude, Sr., 60–61
Harrington, Padraig
  career earnings, 270
  and the Masters, 148, 265
  and the U.S. Open, 115, 156, 263
Hart, Barbara Ann
  and Earl's death, 175
  in Germany, 22–23
  marriage to Earl, 16–21
  in New York, 23
  separation from Earl, 28–30
Hart, Dale, 17
Hart, Jeff, 68
Hart, Joe, 30
Hartsfield, Zeke, 90
Hayes, Woody, 242, 245
Heartwell Golf Park, 58
Hickman, Rosa, 5–7, 14
Hicks, Mike, 112
Hill, Jim, 42, 45
Hillman, Dennis, 54
Hitchcock, Ken, 237
Hoch, Scott, 265
Ho Chi Minh City, Vietnam, 73, 76–77
Hogan, Ben
  and Earl's introduction to golf, 38
  and Hayes, 242
  majors record, 121, 125, 164, 269
  as role model, 245
  single-year victory record, 269, 270
  tournament win record, 102
  tour victory record, 269, 270
Holmberg, Barbro, 201
Holmes, Larry, 249
Hope, Bob, 42
Horne, Lena, 6
Howell, Charles, III, 261
Hoylake (Royal Liverpool Golf Club),
  177–79
Hoyt, Waite, 248

HP Byron Nelson Championship, 134
Hunt, Kelly, 231
Huston, John, 91, 263
Hutchinson, Jock, 125

Ike's Pond, 144
integration, 28
International Management Group (IMG),
    43, 65, 97, 209, 227–28
Iraq War, 166
Isleworth Golf & Country Club, 87
Issel, Dan, 188
Izawa, Toshi, 264

Jackson, Bo, 66
Jackson, Stonewall, 189
Jackson, Tim, 260
James, LeBron, 151
jazz, 23–24
Jimenez, Miguel Angel
    and Tiger's major victories, 185
    and the U.S. Open, 115, 193, 263
Johnny Walker Classic, 100
Johnson, Hootie, 143
Joiner, Charlie, ix, 188
Jones, Bobby
    and the British Open, 125
    majors record, 138, 148, 158, 170, 269
    and Nicklaus, 93, 169, 246
    on the Old Course, 167
    as role model, 227
    and the U.S. Open, x
Jordan, Michael, 237

Kammann, Scott, 261
Kansas City Monarchs, 7–8, 15
Kansas State University, 2, 10–14, 16
Karlsson, Robert, 179, 193–94, 268
Katayama, Shingo, 179
Kert, Larry, 23
King, Larry, 48
Kite, Tom
    and the Masters, 93, 262
    and Stewart, 98
    and Tiger's major victories, 185
Kmart, 94

Knapp, Sean, 261
Knight, Phil, 57, 66, 204
Kostis, Peter, 232–33
Kratzert, Bill, 67
Kribel, Joel, 261
Kuehne, Trip, 260

L.A. Open, 85, 90, 131
Ladbrokes (bookmaker), 121
Las Vegas Invitational, 70–71
Lawrence, Carol, 23
Lee, Patrick, 261
Leggatt, Ian, 194
Lehman, Tom, 163, 208
Leonard, James, 12
Leonard, Justin, 211
links courses, 177–79
"Little Saigon" radio, 76
Locke, Bobby, 125
Los Alamitos Country Club, 131
Los Angeles Times, ix
Louis, Joe, 6, 127, 131
Love, Davis, III
    career earnings, 270
    and Els, 211
    and the Las Vegas Invitational, 70
    and the Masters, 146
    and the PGA Championship, 129
    Tida Woods on, 120
    and the U.S. Open, 155
Luu, Lan, 75

Mackay, Bones, 231
Maggert, Jeff, 265
Mahaffey, John, 182
major victories of Woods
    British Open (2000), 121–25, 263
    British Open (2005), 166–70, 266
    British Open (2006), 176–81, 266–67
    Masters (1997), 85–94, 262
    Masters (2001), 138–42, 264
    Masters (2002), 143–44, 145–46, 146–49,
        264–65
    Masters (2005), 161–65, 266
    PGA Championship (1999),
        104–6, 263

major victories of Woods (*cont.*)
  PGA Championship (2000), 129–31, 131–35, 263
  PGA Championship (2006), 183–86, 267
  PGA Championship (2007), 187–90, 190–92, 267
  U.S. Open (2000), 110–16, 263
  U.S. Open (2002), 154–59, 265
  U.S. Open (2008), 193–98, 268
Mandela, Nelson, 101
Manhattan, Kansas, 46
Manhattan High School, 14
The Manhattan Mercury, 2
Manning, J. D., 261
Marucci, George E., Jr., 261
Massengale, Rik, 67
The Masters Tournament
  and Ballesteros, 88
  Champions Dinner, 94, 145, 162–63
  and Earl's recovery from surgery, 116
  and Els, 114, 214
  and Nicklaus, 93, 126–27, 140–41, 162
  O'Meara victory, 100
  and swing coaching, 99
  Tiger's practice round, 82
  Tiger's return to golf, 208, 228–30, 230–31, 231–35
  Tiger's victories, 85–94, 138–42, 143–44, 145–46, 146–49, 161–65, 262, 264–65, 266
May, Bob
  back injury, 134
  and the PGA Championship, 129, 131–34, 263–64
  as role model, 128
  and Tiger's major victories, 185
May, Jerry, 131
May, Muriel, 131
Mayfair, Billy, 265
McCormack, Mark, 228
McDaniel, Pete, 15
McGleno, Phillip (Mac O'Grady), 67–68
McGwire, Mark, 247
Mediate, Rocco, 193–98, 268
Medinah Country Club, 102, 183–86
Men's Fitness, 205
Merrick, John, 193

Merrins, Eddie, 128
Micheel, Shaun, 185, 267
Mickelson, Amanda, 231
Mickelson, Amy, 230, 233–324
Mickelson, Mary, 230–31, 233
Mickelson, Phil
  and the British Open, 179
  career earnings, 270
  competitive nature, 210, 211
  family life, 230–31
  introduction to golf, 42
  majors record, 214
  and the Masters, 139–41, 143–44, 146–48, 231–34, 264, 265
  and the PGA Championship, 170, 184
  Tida Woods on, 118
  and Tiger's major victories, 185
  and the U.S. Open, 157, 196, 265
Middlecoff, Cary, 269
The Mike Douglas Show, 42, 131
Miller, Johnny
  and the British Open, 125
  low score records, 190
  major victories, 182
  on Steve Scott, 64
  on Tiger's troubles, 243
  tournament win records, 102
Moise, Vaughn, 260
Montana, Joe, 188–89
Montgomerie, Colin
  Bjorn on, 122
  and the British Open, 169, 266
  career earnings, 270
  and the Masters, 92
  and Tiger's major victories, 185
  and the Victor Chandler British Masters, 131
Morris, Tom, Jr. (Young Tom), 93, 115, 125
Morris, Tom, Sr. (Old Tom), 93, 125
Muhammad, Herbert, 248
Mui Ne, Vietnam, 75

Nantz, Jim, 135
National Collegiate Athletic Association (NCAA), 12
National Personnel Records Center, 72

Nationwide Tour, 135
Navy Seals, 238
Nedbank Million Dollar Challenge, 101
Negro Leagues, 7–9, 15
Nelson, Byron
  and Champions Dinner, 162–63
  cuts-made record, 162
  death, 163
  as role model, 245
  single-year victory record, 269
  Tida Woods on, 120
  tour victory record, 269
Nelson, Larry, 182
Newport Country Club, 193
New York Daily News, 248
New York Post, 202
New York Times, The 102
Nguyen Phong. *See* Phong, "Tiger"
Nicklaus, Charlie, x, 130, 138, 242
Nicklaus, Jack
  and Augusta National, 144, 148
  and Ballesteros, 88
  and the British Open, 122, 157–58, 168
  career milestones, ix–x
  competitive nature, 241
  and the Eagle's Nest, 85
  and Earl Woods, 38–39, 125–27
  education, 210
  and high school sports, 241–42
  low score records, 190
  on luck, 123
  majors record, 121, 125, 157–58,
    161–62, 164, 170, 192, 243–46, 269
  and the Masters, 93, 126–27,
    140–41, 162
  and PGA Championship, 129–31, 192
  practice round with Tiger, 82
  as role model, 227
  strategy, 148
  Tiger compared to, 69, 242–44
  and Tiger's goals for golf, 42
  tour victory record, 269
  and U.S. Open Championship, 111
  Woods's first meeting with, 128–29
Nicklaus, Jackie (Jack's son), 140
Nicklaus, Jake Walter, 162
Nicklaus, Steve (Jack's son), 168

Nicklaus, Stevie (Jack's grandson), 162
Nike, 57–58, 65–66, 203–4
Nike Tour, 103, 131
Nordegren, Elin, 153, 158–59, 192, 202–4,
    206–7, 215, 222
Norman, Greg
  and the British Open, 125
  caddie, 102, 140
  Els on, 211
  low score records, 190
  and the Masters, 91, 104, 147
  and Nicklaus, 127
  rankings record, 162
  swing coach, 58
  and Tiger's amateur tournaments, 62
  and the U.S. Open, 226
North, Oliver, 72, 73
Norton, Hughes, 43, 65
Norwood, Bev, 65, 97
The Now Principle, 136

Obama, Barack, 238–39
Oberholser, Aaron, 267
Ocean Dunes, 73, 75
Ochoa, Lorena, 152
O'Grady, Mac, 67–68
Olazabal, Jose Maria
  and the British Open, 166, 169, 266
  and the Masters, 148, 265
  and the PGA Championship, 132, 263
  practice rounds with Tiger, 87
Old Course at St. Andrews
  and the 1970 British Open, 200–201
  and the 2000 British Open, 121–25
  and the 2005 British Open, 167–70
  Jones on, 167
  Thomson on, 178
  Tiger on, 142
  and Tiger's major record, 243
O'Meara, Alicia, 201
O'Meara, Mark
  divorce, 201
  friendship with Tiger, 97, 98–99, 184
  and Garcia, 104
  and the Masters, 100
  and Nicklaus, 162
  practice rounds with Tiger, 87, 217–18

Oprah, 64
Orange Bowl Junior Classic, 52–53
Orange County Register, The, 131
Orlando Sentinel, The, 202
Outside the Lines (ESPN), 206
Owens, James, 189

Paige, Satchel, 8
Palmer, Arnold
  Bay Hill Invitational, 208
  and the British Open, 125
  and Earl Woods, 251
  majors record, 121, 148, 269
  marriage, 200
  and the Masters, 100, 145–46
  and Nicklaus, 128
  practice round with Tiger, 82
  as role model, 227
  tour victory record, 269
  and the U.S. Open, 242
Palmer, Winifred, 200
Park, Willie, 125
Parnevik, Jesper, 154, 158, 206
Parnevik, Mia, 158
Parr-Gravell, Dina, 160
Payne, Billy, 226–27
Pebble Beach
  crowd capacity, 156
  and Duval, 122
  and Nicklaus's retirement, 168
  Tiger on, 142
  and Tiger's childhood, 109–10
  and Tiger's return to golf, 235
  and the U.S. Open, 115, 243
Penick, Harvey, 236
performance-enhancing drugs, 219
Pettersson, Carl, 193
PGA Tour Championship
  and Stewart, 98
  and Tiger's return to golf, 213
  Tiger's victories, 103–6, 129–31,
    131–35, 183–86, 187–90, 190–92, 262,
    263–64, 267
  and Valhalla, 142
PGA Tour Qualifying School, 67, 70, 135
Phan Thiet, Vietnam, 74, 76

Phong, "Tiger," 32–37, 71–75, 75–77,
  77–80
Player, Gary
  black clothing, 180
  majors record, 121, 125, 164, 269
Players Championship, 161
Playing Through (Woods), 10, 11, 95
Plummer, Mark, 261
Points, D. A., 261
police report on car accident, 199–200
Pollom, Jim, 12
Porsche, Veronica, 248
press conferences, 217–25
Price, Nick, 62, 101, 112–13, 211, 262
Punsawad, Kultida. *See* Woods, Kultida
  "Tida"
putting
  and course management, 86–87, 111,
    155, 157
  and Earl's coaching, 53, 88–90, 93, 176,
    185, 236
  and Mediate, 195
  "putting to the picture," 89–90, 151,
    236, 255
  and Tiger's childhood, 41–42, 43
  and Tiger's coaches, 60
  and Tiger's return to golf, 231–32, 234

qualifying school, 67, 70, 135

race issues
  and Augusta National, 90, 109,
    144, 226
  and Earl's car accident, 20–21
  and Earl's college years, 12–13
  and Earl's first wife, 20–21, 28
  and media coverage, 54–55
  and the military, 18–20, 28
  and professional golf, 90–91
  and Tiger's childhood, 107–9
  Tiger's media statement on, 63–64
Ray, Ted, 125, 170
Reitemeier, Perk, 11
Renner, Jack, 67
Rhodes, Teddy, 90
Rinaldi, Tom, 204

Road Hole bunker, 124
Robards, Jason, 23
Roberts, Clifford, 109, 144
Roberts, Ricci, 147
Robinson, Eddie, ix
Robinson, Harold, 14
Robinson, Jackie, 6, 94
Rocca, Costantino, 92, 262
Rock, Robert, 179
Rodgers, Phil, 85
Roethlisberger, Ben, 247
role models, 127–28, 136–37, 227, 239
Romero, Andres, 179
Romero, Eduardo, 131
Rostenkowski, Dan, 182–83
Royal Birkdale, 100–101
Royal Liverpool Golf Club, 177–79
Royal Lytham & St. Annes, 97
Runyan, Paul, 270
Ruth, Babe, 247–48

Sadler, Barry, 25
Salas, Lauro, 189
Sanders, Doug, 200–201
Sanders, Scotty, 200
San Francisco Examiner, 54
Sarazen, Gene
    and the British Open, 125
    and Champions Dinner, 162–63
    majors record, 121, 125, 148, 170, 269
    tour victory record, 269
Sargent, Tom, 48
Scheu's Café, 14
Scott, Adam, 179, 196, 267
Scott, Steve, 64–65, 133–34, 261
Seaver, Tom, 100–101
Senden, John, 267
Shinnecock Hills, 63, 156
Shute, Denny, 135
Sifford, Charlie, 89–90, 90–91, 94
Singh, Vijay
    career earnings, 270
    low score records, 190
    and the Masters, 146–48, 226
    single-year victory record, 270
    and sportsmanship, 210

tour victory record, 270
    and the U.S. Open, 114
60 Minutes, 120, 173–74
Slater, Don, 5–6, 10–11
Slocum, Heath, 193
Smith, Red, 247
Smith, Willie, 115
Snead, Sam
    and the British Open, 125
    majors record, 121, 148, 269
    as role model, 245
    single-year victory record, 270
    tour victory record, 269, 270
Snedeker, Brandt, 193
Soltau, Mark, 54
Spearman, Jesse, 16, 20
special operations training, 237–38
Spiller, Bill, 90
sponsorships, 131, 204, 224. *See also*
    endorsement deals
St. Andrews, Scotland, 216. *See also* Old
    Course at St. Andrews
Stanford University, 48–50, 85, 88, 187,
    204, 210
Stankowski, Paul, 91, 262
Stapleton, Maureen, 23
Stauffer, Gene, 13
Steinberg, Mark, 222
Stewart, James, 42–43
Stewart, Payne
    and Daly, 213
    death, 112
    and sportsmanship, 98
    and Tiger's first pro season, 70–71
Strange, Curtis, 68, 210, 211
Strayhorn, Billy, 36
Strege, John, 56
Sun City, 101–2
Sunshine Tour, 213
Sutton, Hal, 200
Swilcan Bridge, 168
swing coaching, 58–60. *See also* Haney,
    Hank; Harmon, Butch

Tanihara, Hideto, 267
Tarkenton, Fran, x, 42

Taylor, John H., 125
temper of Woods, 112–14, 232–33
tennis, 32–33, 36, 104, 212, 242
Terrell, Ernie, 248
Tet Offensive, 71–72, 73
Thailand, 28, 119–20
That's Incredible!, 42
Thomas, Debi, 48
Thompson, Leonard, 67
Thomson, Peter, 125, 177
Tiger Woods Foundation, 117
Tilghman, Kelly, 204–5
Titleist, 67
Tolles, Tommy, 262
Toms, David, 163
Tournament of Champions, 67
Trahan, D. J., 193, 268
Trevino, Lee, 121, 125, 209
Triple-A Nike Tour, 131
Trung (Tiger Phong's son), 33

U.S. Amateur Championship
  and Nicklaus, x
  and O'Meara, 87
  Tiger's consecutive victories, 55
  Tiger's final loss at, 58
  and Tiger's mental toughness, 51
U.S. Junior Amateur Championship,
  54–57, 66
U.S. Open Championship
  and Claude Harmon, 60
  and Daly, 213
  and Els, 214
  low score records, 190
  and Montgomerie, 92
  and Tiger's media statement, 63
  Tiger's missed cut, 175
  Tiger's return to golf, 235
  Tiger's victories, 110–16, 243, 263,
    265, 268
  Walsh on, 189

Valhalla Golf Club, 129, 142
Valley of Sin, 124, 168
Van, Ly Thi Bich, 77, 78–79
Vardon, Harry, 125, 148, 269

Venturi, Ken, 135, 189
Verplank, Scott, 190
Victor Chandler British Masters, 131
Vietnam War, 25, 31, 32–35, 71–72, 73
Vietnam War Memorial, 72
Village Vanguard, 23
Vinh Phu, Vietnam, 75
Vuong Dang Phong. *See* Phong, "Tiger"

Wadkins, Lanny, 210
Wake Forest University, 150–51, 153
Wall, Art, 100
Walsh, Bill, 187–90
Walsh, Steve, 187
Watson, Denis, 200
Watson, Hilary, 200
Watson, Linda, 200
Watson, Tom
  and the British Open, 125, 168
  divorce, 200
  majors record, 121, 164, 269
  and the Masters, 228, 262
  and Nicklaus, 128, 243
  and Tiger's childhood, 42
  tour victory record, 269
  and the U.S. Open, 110, 226
Watts, Brian, 100
Wauthier, Ray, 11–12, 13
Wayne, John, 26
Weiskopf, Tom, 170, 190
Westmoreland, William, 28
Westwood, Lee, 193, 196, 232, 263, 268
William Hill (bookmaker), 121, 168
Williams, Steve
  and the British Open, 180
  hired as Tiger's caddie, 102
  and the Masters, 140
  and the PGA Championship, 105–6,
    184–85
  and Tiger's return to golf, 222, 223
  and Tiger's temper, 232
  and the U.S. Open, 114, 197
Wilson, Mark, 260
Wilson, Nancy, 24, 33
Winged Foot, 60, 175
Winslow, Kellen, ix

Woods, Cheyenne, 151–54
Woods, Earl Dennison
  automobile accident, 20–21
  and baseball, 7–9, 11–15, 27–28, 36
  childhood of, 1–6, 10–11, 14
  competitive nature, 38–40, 50–51
  death, 175
  education, 6
  on Els, 100
  and exaggeration, 70–72, 251
  health problems, 88, 96, 99, 113–14,
    115–16, 137–38, 171–75, 252–55
  introduction to golf, 38–40
  love of music, 23–25, 33, 36
  on marriage, 102
  marriage to Barbara Ann Hart, 11,
    16–21, 22–25, 28–30, 31, 109
  marriage to Tida Punsawad, 30–31, 71,
    95–96
  and Masters tournaments, 91–92, 143,
    148, 149
  military service, 18–20, 22, 25–28, 30,
    31–35, 71–73, 237–38
  and the Now Principle, 136
  and Palmer, 251
  and putting, 53, 88–90, 93, 176, 185, 236
  and race issues, 12–13, 20–21, 28,
    63–64, 107–9
  on role models, 136–37
  and ROTC, 16
  television appearances, 42–43
  and Tiger Phong, 32–37, 71–75, 75–77,
    77–80
  on Tiger's best shots, 164–65
  and Tiger's childhood, 45–47
  and Tiger's golf training, 93
  on Tiger's natural talent, 70
  on Tiger's superstition, 85–86
  on Tiger's temper, 113
  on U.S. Open strategy, 111
  womanizing, 96–98, 102, 160–61
Woods, Earl Dennison, Jr. "Den"
  and baseball, 27–28
  birth, 22
  daughter, 153–54
  and Earl's love of music, 23

  and Earl's military service, 25–27
  relationship with Tiger, 43, 44–45
  and Woods family dynamics, 96
Woods, Eldrick Tont "Tiger"
  auto accident, 199–200, 201–2
  birth, 41
  career earnings, 270–71
  career wins records, 259–69
  childhood, 41–43, 43–45, 46–47, 107–9,
    118–20
  college choice, 48–50
  comparisons to Nicklaus, 242–44
  competitive nature, 50–51
  early golf lessons, 45–48
  given name, 41
  grand slams, 125, 138, 148
  introduction to golf, 41–42
  lying, 108, 137, 221, 223, 225
  majors record, 243, 269 (see also major
    victories of Woods)
  marriage, 158, 173, 204–7, 215–16
  and military training, 237–39
  net worth estimate, 271
  prize money by year, 270–71
  and putting, 41–42, 43, 53, 60, 88–90,
    93, 176, 185, 236
  and race issues, 63–64, 107–9
  and role models, 127–28, 136–37
  siblings, 43–45
  single-year victory record, 270
  temper, 112–14, 232–33
  and Tiger Phong's family, 79
  tour victory record, 269, 270
Woods, Freda, 1
Woods, Hattie Belle
  and Earl's childhood, 1–3, 5–6,
    10–11, 14
  and Earl's first marriage, 18
  education, 6
  marriage, 16, 20
  and Tiger's childhood, 46
Woods, James Leonard, 1
Woods, Kevin, 22, 25, 27, 43
Woods, Kultida "Tida"
  and Buddhism, 31, 71, 120, 221
  competitive nature, 120–21

Woods, Kultida "Tida" (*cont.*)
  and Earl's death, 175
  and family tensions, 161
  first meeting with Earl, 30–31
  home purchased by Tiger, 96
  and London terrorist attacks, 166–67
  and media coverage, 54
  on Mickelson, 118
  on race issues, 64
  separation, 95
  and Tiger Phong's family, 79
  and Tiger's accident, 201
  and Tiger's birth, 41
  and Tiger's childhood, 42, 44, 46–47,
    118–20
  and Tiger's press conference, 203, 206
  and Woods family dynamics, xi, 96, 117
Woods, Lillian, 1, 6
Woods, Mabel Lee "Mae" (Earl's sister),
  1–2, 6, 96, 250
Woods, Maude, 1–3, 6–7
Woods, Miles, Jr., 1

Woods, Miles ("Froggy"), 1, 6–7
Woods, Royce
  and Earl's health, 171–73
  and Earl's love of music, 25
  and Earl's military service, 22, 25–27, 33
  on race issues, 107
  relationship with Tiger, 43–45
  and Tiger's mugging, 50
  on Tiger's troubles, 213
  and Woods family dynamics, 96
Woods, Sam Alexis, 51, 192, 194–95
Woods, Viola Etta, 2, 5
World Golf Championship, 177
Wrenn, Robert, 67

Yang, Y. E., 213
Yates, Charlie, 103–4
Young, Steve, 188, 189

Ziegel, Vic, 248
Zoeller, Fuzzy, 94, 255
Zwetschke, Brad, 259